Anatomies of Egotism

Anatomies of Egotism

A Reading of the Last Novels of H. G. Wells

Robert Bloom

UNIVERSITY OF NEBRASKA
LINCOLN AND LONDON

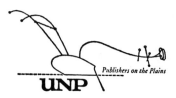

Publishers on the Plains
UNP

Library of Congress Cataloging in Publication Data

Bloom, Robert, 1930–
  Anatomies of egotism.

  Includes bibliographical references and index.
  1. Wells, Herbert George, 1866–1946—Criticism and
interpretation. I. Title.
PR5777.B56   823'.9'12   76–47559
ISBN 0–8032–0907–X

For Claudia, Madeline, and Jonathan

Contents

Acknowledgments

I WISH TO THANK the Executors of the H. G. Wells Estate for their kind permission to quote from all the works of Wells under discussion except *Experiment in Autobiography*, permission for which was graciously granted by Professor G. P. Wells, Victor Gollancz Ltd., and J. B. Lippincott and Company. For quotations from Wells's *Brynhild* I am, in addition, grateful to Methuen & Co. Ltd.

I want also especially to thank the University of California, Berkeley for providing me with time and support during the planning and writing of this study; my parents for endless encouragement and endless trust; my wife for prodigious faith and patience; and my children, to whom the book is dedicated, for helping me when they know it not by the heartening example of their lives.

R.B.

Anatomies of Egotism

Introduction

H. G. WELLS has had a great fall. During the period from *The Time Machine (1895)* to *The History of Mr. Polly* (1910) he established himself as the most gifted imaginative writer of his generation, first as a scientific romancer, then as a post-Dickensian comic realist. *Tono-Bungay* (1909) remains alive and fairly well among us still as a monument to his powers in those years. But as early as *Anticipations* (1901), *Mankind in the Making* (1903), and *A Modern Utopia* (1905), Wells launched a simultaneous career as a seer, scientific thinker, educator, socialist, sociologist, and political theorist that grew, by means of forays into military science, religion, philosophy, history, economics, and, climactically, the gospel of world government, into a major activity of his life. By the time he published *The Outline of History* in 1920 he had transcended journalism, prophecy, and encyclopedism alike and emerged as a guardian of civilization itself. From this point on, it became altogether fitting for him to confer with Franklin Roosevelt, Lenin, and Stalin on the fate of the world and to expend major energy working to eliminate war and to ensure the future of the human race.

Wells's fiction reflected these concerns. They were so intense and heartfelt that any other course would have been impossible for him, constituting a kind of imaginative duplicity. Critics had always complained somewhat about the presence of ideas, of what they took to be extraliterary ends, in his fiction, but the objections began to gather new force with the appearance of *Ann Veronica* (1909) and its insistence on the sexual liberation of women. *The New Machiavelli* (1911), with its complex exploration of English political life, compounded the problem by introducing large elements of unpalatable autobiographical experience so that, looking back, critics could complain of Wells's enslavement not only to ideas but to his own personality with its unsettling sexual demands and general truculence. Henry James had been taking Wells to task privately for several years for his inability to work in a more objective mode and his general disregard of the artistic and formal possibilities of the novel. This exchange erupted into print and by 1915 brought the friendship between the two men to a close. The effect of the quarrel has been disastrous for Wells's reputation as a novelist, since the subsequent triumph of Jamesian aesthetics has tended to rob Wells of a serious hearing from those most interested in the novel. With the public, at least, Wells was able to recover much of the artistic esteem that he lost with *Marriage* (1912), *The Passionate Friends* (1913), and *The Wife of Sir Isaac Harmon* (1914) by bringing out *Mr. Britling Sees It Through* (1916) in the middle of World War I. Here the extraliterary consideration—the total absorption of England in the agony of the war—worked in his behalf and enabled him to move his countrymen and give memorable expression to their pain and their hope not by surrendering either ideas or autobiography but by managing to validate them. It is here too that religion enters Wells's already endless area of concern as he allows God to become a part of the human dilemma.

His success, however, was only temporary. As a novelist Wells was less and less heeded in the years following 1916 by both public and literary people alike. Two subsequent religious novels, *The Soul of a Bishop* (1917) and *The Undying Fire* (1919) never really made their way, despite Wells's fondness for them, and his ambitious novel on education, *Joan and Peter* (1918), which sought to revolutionize teaching methods, failed to make much of an impression. The astounding success of *The Outline of History* in 1920 brought him the largest audience he had ever had, but it also helped to fix his identity as a sage rather than a novelist. *The Secret Places of the Heart* (1922) went largely unnoticed, *Christina Alberta's Father* (1925) seemed to be a rehash of *Ann Veronica*, and *The World of William Clissold* (1926), in which Wells tried to give a fictional account of what he knew about the quality of modern life, persuaded everyone, instead, that he was no longer a novelist at all. From this point, though he continued to stride the world as thinker, conscience, and commentator, he had essentially no audience for his fiction.

Before long his influence on the thought of his time began to dwindle as well. The younger generation, which had always formed his most enthusiastic audience, began, in the general disillusionment of the post-World War I years, to fall away from him. His companion volumes to *The Outline of History*—*The Science of Life* (1930) on biology and *The Work,*

Wealth and Happiness of Mankind (1931) on sociology and economics—had nothing like the audience for the first of the series. His subsequent wrestlings with international problems—*Democracy Under Revision* (1927), *The Open Conspiracy* (1928), *The Anatomy of Frustration: A Modern Synthesis* (1936), *World Brain* (1938), and *The Fate of Homo Sapiens* (1939)—seemed irrelevant after the failure of the League of Nations and during the depression years as fascism took hold in Europe and the world moved helplessly and grimly toward the next war. Only the *Experiment in Autobiography* (1934) attracted genuine interest, but this was more a tribute to what Wells had been and had meant earlier in the century than a sign of continuing favor. As if in recognition of his situation, Wells devoted three-quarters of the autobiography to the first thirty-four years of his life, bringing his account up to 1900, and then gave the remainder over to his efforts on behalf of "The Idea of a Planned World."[1]

So much is known. What is not usually realized is that despite the neglect and isolation and illness that Wells lived in until his death in 1946, he continued to write novels, publishing his last one in 1941. His persistence is surprising but may perhaps be understood in several ways. Stubbornness is one—an ill-tempered refusal to accept the world's estimate of his imaginative powers. Habit another—an inability to surrender a form that he had utilized throughout his career in order to vindicate his intellectual and emotional life. Art yet another—perhaps he was, after all, a novelist and found it quite impossible to stop being one, to stop scrutinizing life through the lens of imagined individual experience, even in the face of fairly well-organized discouragement. In any case, whatever the reason for its existence, I found myself curious about this last, virtually unknown, segment of Wells's imaginative career, especially since I have always admired such "impure" novels from the problematic period as *The New Machiavelli* and *The World of William Clissold* more than his critics and have done so for reasons that I take to be legitimately novelistic. Another consideration drew me on as well. It began to become clear in the period following the Second World War that the main lines of Wells's thinking about human society, the need for social justice, the difficulty of organizing a genuinely rewarding personal life, the outmodedness of a purely nationalistic outlook, the dangers of a scientific-technological future, and the imperative need for a truly cooperative world order, were essentially sound; that he was far less beside the point as a thinker than he was almost universally held to be toward the end of his life; and that even

his much debated pessimism about the human future was newly understandable.[2] Since he had been prematurely cast aside as a thinker, I
wondered if perhaps he had not been inexcusably neglected at the end as a
novelist as well, for reasons, both extraliterary and literary, that might
themselves be open to question. It was difficult to believe that so great a
gift could come to nothing, or even to nothing interesting. Perhaps the
novels of this last phase might make it possible, great fall or no, to start
putting Wells together again on a new basis.[3]

What I found constitutes the substance of this study and has meaning, I
think, for Wells and for the novel at large. The titles of the novels of this
last period are not likely to be familiar to readers or even students of modern letters: *The Bulpington of Blup* (1932), *Brynhild: or The Show of
Things* (1937), *Apropos of Dolores* (1938), *The Holy Terror* (1939), *Babes
in the Darkling Wood* (1940), and *You Can't Be Too Careful* (1941). My
hope is that my examination of them will go some way toward making
them more familiar, although I do not want my pleasure in these books to
lead me into exaggerated claims for them. Some are considerably better
than others, and most are more beset by ideas and speculation than our sensibilities will ordinarily allow, unless we are reading Tolstoy, or Dos-
toevsky, or Mann. But the intelligence, grace, feeling, wit, and truth that
is in them deserves a hearing. Their style—Wells's extraordinary natural-
ness and ease of sentence-making, his acute observation, his deployment
of complex comic ironies, and his superb dramatic instinct—is note-
worthy, despite the legend of his general haste and carelessness. These
novels render and enact life in narrative form—the complexities, impasses,
delusions, anxieties, aspirations—with unmistakable Wellsian richness,
vitality, and immediacy; and they help us to gauge as well as experience
these things with unmistakable Wellsian urgency. He never ceased to be a
compelling writer or, as I hope to show, a compelling novelist, even when
he no longer compelled, or even won, any serious attention. Decidedly, it
is an occasion for redress and amends. My conviction is that Wells the
novelist, not merely Wells the scientific romancer, or Wells the prophet, or
Wells the educator, or Wells the anti-utopian utopian, or Wells the thinker,
or Wells the savior, will have his day. If it be not now, yet it will come.[4]

Before discussing the novels themselves, I have devoted the first chapter
to an examination of Wells's views on the novel, a matter that he thought
about through most of his life. The first part of the chapter, dealing with
material up through the publication of *Boon* in 1915, may be familiar to

some readers. However, that material is here focused, interpreted, and evaluated freshly, and a clear grasp of it from this special point of view is quite indispensable to the understanding of Wells's later achievement that I propose to trace in the main body of this study. Some of his pronouncements have a beleaguered, defensive ring, made as they are in the heat of battle or in behalf of his own practice; but this is true of any writer's statement of principles and often, even in its exaggeration, helps to illuminate his work. Some of Wells's views, on the other hand, have a more comprehensive value and serve to enlarge, or at least test, our very notion of the novel itself. This larger value is particularly important now, since Wells is almost always responding, literally or retrospectively, to the theory and practice of Henry James, and it is James, more than any other figure, who has influenced our idea, in America and England at least, of what the novel is.[5] Wells's quarrel is thus, in some sense, ours, since it still proceeds among us. His voice is clearly discernible, for instance, behind that of C. P. Snow or Kingsley Amis as they have been arguing in recent years against the limitations of the art novel. Looking back it is possible to see that Wells made a heroic effort, in an age disposed to retreat into personal mysteries, visions, symbols, and intuitions, to keep literature open for the mind, to allow the rational intelligence at its best to participate, as it did with Voltaire, or Swift, or George Eliot, in the imaginative life, and always to keep the imagination in touch, as it was in Tolstoy, with as much of life as the understanding could command. Like most heroic efforts, however, it was not notable for discretion and proportion.

My treatment of the novels themselves in Chapters 1 through 5 may best be called a reading. Because all these books are currently out of print and accessible only in unusually well-stocked libraries, I have made a point of offering a very full account of them, especially of the three most important ones, *The Bulpington of Blup, Brynhild,* and *Apropos of Dolores*, which together constitute Wells's most penetrating study of the guises of egotism, his major novelistic theme of this period. I am less interested in placing these novels in the context of Wells's work or life than I am in revealing as faithfully as possible what they are like and what their value is. I have tried to do so by tracing and reenacting in my pages a sympathetic, yet critical, reader's encounter with these books—the experience of reading them and of reflecting on them as they unfold. Toward this end of full presentation—of a near reproduction of the reading experience, so far as this is feasible and desirable—I have also quoted extensively from the texts. The quotations serve both to verify my reading and to convey the actuality of Wells's mind and style as, on a number of occasions, only his own words can.

My thesis is that Wells, in three novels at least, remained a remarkable novelist to the end. In order to advance and demonstrate it I have avoided the customary critical procedure of selecting some single strand of interest—either thematic, psychological, stylistic, social, philosophical, structural, or moral—and establishing its presence in the fabric of all the works under discussion. Instead, I have endeavored to present these works as wholes, as novels in fact that a reader might wish richly to come to know, for this totality is the basis on which I wish to argue their merit. Thus although I discuss the preoccupation with egotism, the role of ideas in a fictional structure, style, sexual relations, narrative method, and a number of other matters, I look at each of these things not as a sufficient justification of interest in itself but as parts of the total justification, which is the novels themselves. Indeed, I think of this study as a hearing as well as a reading, for it uses the customary critical merging of elucidation and comment to enter a plea, before the courts of attention and concern, for Wells the novelist to be heard once again as he completes the great imaginative work of a lifetime. He has earned, I hope to show, nothing less.

CHAPTER I

Art and Life:
Once More Unto the Breach

WHAT WE MOST REMEMBER NOW of the lively quarrel between Henry James and H. G. Wells in 1915 is the passionate, almost unanswerable declaration of faith with which James brought his last letter to Wells to a close: "It is art that *makes* life, makes interest, makes importance, for our consideration and application of these things, and I know of no substitute whatever for the force and beauty of its process."[1] What we forget is that Wells, who shared neither Jamesian, nor post-Jamesian, aesthetic priorities, did answer immediately and managed, at once firmly and sorrowfully, to cling to his own orders of concern:

> I don't clearly understand your concluding phrases—which shews no doubt how completely they define our difference. When you say "it is art that *makes* life, makes interest, makes importance," I can only read sense into it by assuming that you are using "art" for every conscious human activity. I use the word for a research and attainment that is technical and special.[2]

This final exchange between the two antagonists epitomizes their essential differences over the seventeen years of their friendship. For James life would be literally as well as figuratively unthinkable without art, while for Wells it would be thinkable but impoverished. Yet Wells's subordination of art, or his willingness, at least, to have it merely take its place among a host of other human concerns and activities—science, history, philosophy, religion, sociology, psychology, politics—is often exaggerated, by himself as well as his critics, and consequently misunderstood. His habit of calling himself a journalist rather than an artist is more a weary and gracious concession to the tireless aesthetic admonitions of James and his other nagging friends, Arnold Bennett, George Gissing, and Conrad, than a fair statement of his position. As early as 1911, with *Kipps, Tono-Bungay, The History of Mr. Polly,* and *The New Machiavelli* behind him, he was prepared in a talk given before the Times Book Club to make extraordinary claims for the importance of the novel.[3] The terms in which Wells develops that importance would not satisfy James, but they enable Wells to bring art and life seminally together—for him too there is a sense in which art makes life—and they help to explain why despite his passion to redeem the world he could never leave the novel alone.

There are numerous indications in his talk, later serialized as "The Contemporary Novel," of Wells's struggle with Jamesian principles, though he does not mention the master by name. Later on in life he was ready to make a number of admissions about the validity of some of James's views, but now the keynote is defiance. He speaks here in 1911 of the fallacy of assuming "that the novel, like the [short] story, aims at a single concentrated impression" (pp. 139–40). While irrelevance is fatal in the short story, Wells maintains that nothing can be irrelevant in the inclusive, responsive mode of the novel if it sorts with the novelist's mood—certainly not the novelist's personality or "any comment that seems to admit that, after all, fiction is fiction, a change in manner between part and part, burlesque, parody, invective . . . ." He proceeds to defend first-person interventions on the part of novelists as a feature of some of our greatest novels, Thackeray—James's horrible example of this practice—being objectionable when he intervenes only because he does so dishonestly, vulgarly, and affectedly, not because intervention itself is inadmissible. He cites *Lord Jim*, identifying Marlow with Conrad "for all practical purposes," as an instance of the depth and "subjective reality" that such a procedure can bring to the novel.

He also dissents from James in the large matter of traditions, precedents, and models for fiction. Where James had made a point of repudiating the loose, critically unconscious, formally haphazard English Novel as early as "The Art of Fiction" (1884), Wells heartily endorses the "lax freedom of form, the rambling discursiveness, the right to roam" of the English tradition in preference to "more exacting and cramping conceptions of artistic perfection" (pp. 137–38). When he turns to continental models, it is to the "exhaustiveness" of Roman Rolland's *Jean Christophe* and to the Flaubert not of *Madame Bovary*, but of *Bouvard et Pécuchet*. "Flaubert," says Wells, "the bulk of whose life was spent upon the most austere and restrained fiction—Turgenev was not more austere and restrained—broke out at last into this gay, sad miracle of intellectual abundance" (p. 139).

Although James's feelings about Flaubert were ambivalent enough, Wells's ingenious conversion of Flaubert, the high priest of the art of the novel, into "the Continental emancipator of the novel from the restrictions of form" testifies to his critical resourcefulness. But not content with such a provocation, he adds, quite unerringly as a further exorcism of the James influence, "the master to whom we of the English persuasion, we of the discursive school, must for ever recur is he, whom I will maintain against all comers to be the subtlest and greatest *artist*—I lay great stress upon that word artist—that Great Britain has ever produced in all that is essentially the novel, Laurence Sterne . . . ."

These rejections of Jamesian strictness are not, however, signs of Wells's refusal to take the novel seriously. As he proceeds in the remainder of his talk to define the function of the novel, it becomes clear that his fundamental quarrel with James and all formalists in fiction is that they do not take the novel, as a heuristic and civilizing force, seriously enough. The ideal of objectivity in fiction—another Jamesian keystone—is for Wells a fallacy. "The novel," he says, "has inseparable moral conse-quences. It leaves impressions, not simply of things seen, but of acts judged and made attractive or unattractive." The novelist may attempt to be utterly impartial, but he nonetheless cannot prevent himself from mak-ing moral suggestions to his reader at every turn, or from betraying his own approval or disapproval of conduct and characters. "And I think it is just in this, that the novel is not simply a fictitious record of conduct, but also a study and judgment of conduct, and through that of the ideas that lead to conduct, that the real and increasing value—or perhaps to avoid contro-versy I had better say the real and increasing importance—of the novel and of the novelist in modern life comes in" (p. 144). Wells's distinction here between "value" and "importance" is instructive, allowing him to back away from the question of the whole nature, meaning, use, and sig-nificance of fiction and address himself instead to the one function that he wishes to urge upon his readers.

That function is an august one. Wells develops the idea, not unfamiliar to us today, that although the novel had from the outset, in Fielding and Richardson and their followers, been viewed as "a powerful instrument of moral suggestion," there was far more certitude about moral values and standards of conduct in the past than in the present. Men might disagree in the eighteenth or nineteenth centuries, but they were "emphatic, cocksure, and unteachable about whatever they did happen to believe to a degree that no longer obtains." The novel reflected this certitude and assurance and

utilized it to make its characteristic revelations of the profound goodness of
apparent villains or the hypocrisy of apparent saints. But this has all
changed, changed utterly. "Today," says Wells,

> while we live in a period of tightening and extending social organiza-
> tion, we live also in a period of adventurous and insurgent thought,
> in an intellectual spring unprecedented in the world's history. There
> is an enormous criticism going on of the faiths upon which men's
> lives and associations are based, and of every standard and rule of
> conduct. And it is inevitable that the novel, just in the measure of its
> sincerity and ability, should reflect and co-operate in the atmosphere
> and uncertainties and changing variety of this seething and creative
> time.
>   And I do not mean merely that the novel is unavoidably charged
> with the representation of this wide and wonderful conflict. It is a
> necessary part of the conflict. [P. 147]

Beginning to sound more and more like a theorist of our own period,
Wells goes on to speak of this intellectual revolution as philosophically a
revival of nominalism rechristened as pragmatism, and to characterize it as
essentially "the reassertion of the importance of the individual instance as
against the generalization."[4] He maintains that recent inquiries into social,
political, and moral problems have been marked by a new, inquiring,
experimental spirit which has no patience with abstract principles. Only the
novel, with its characteristically rich attention to the particular and
concrete complexities of existence, can provide this order of enlightenment: "And this is where the value and opportunity of the modern novel
comes in. So far as I can see it is the only medium through which we can
discuss the great majority of the problems that are being raised in such
bristling multitude by our contemporary social development" (p. 148).
After examining the problem of obtaining civil servants and officials in
England who are equipped to deal with the complexities of modern
experience and the role that fiction might play in bringing sweetness and
health to official life, Wells rises to his penultimate claim for the
importance of the novel in the modern world:

> We must have not only the fullest treatment of the temptations,
> vanities, abuses, and absurdities of office, but all its dreams, its
> sense of constructive order, its consolations, its sense of service, and
> its nobler satisfactions. You may say that is demanding more insight
> and power in our novels and novelists than we can possibly hope to
> find in them. So much the worse for us. I stick to my thesis that the
> complicated social organisation of to-day cannot get along without

the amount of mutual understanding and mutual explanation such a range of characterisation in our novels implies. The success of civilisation amounts ultimately to a success of sympathy and understanding. If people cannot be brought to an interest in one another greater than they feel to-day, to curiosities and criticisms far keener, and co-operations far subtler than we have now; if class cannot be brought to measure itself against, and interchange experience and sympathy with class, and temperament with temperament, then we shall never struggle very far beyond the confused discomforts and uneasiness of to-day, and the changes and complications of human life will remain as they are now, very like the crumplings and separations and complications of an immense avalanche that is sliding down a hill. And in this tremendous work of human reconciliation and elucidation, it seems to me it is the novel that must attempt most and achieve most. [Pp. 151–52]

The nearest competing forms will not serve these ends nearly so well. Drama—and Shaw's plays merely confirm Wells's opinion—"excites our sympathies intensely, but it seems to me it is far too objective a medium to widen them appreciably." This rejection puts us obliquely in mind of the Wells-James difference again, for it is the very heart of James's conception of the novel that it approach the condition of dramatic objectivity. Biography and autobiography, Wells continues, would seem serious contenders against the novel, for their very substance is concrete, personal actuality. But the biographer can never be totally frank, must always out of consideration for "continuing interests and sensitive survivors" engage in that worst of falsehoods, "the falsehood of omission." Autobiography would seem to present the greatest opportunity of all, but "to turn upon oneself and explain oneself is given to no one." Summing up these latter eliminations, Wells says, "The novel has neither the intense self-consciousness of autobiography nor the paralysing responsibilities of the biographer. It is by comparison irresponsible and free. Because its characters are figments and phantoms, they can be made entirely transparent. Because they are fictions, and you know they are fictions, so that they cannot hold you for an instant as soon as they cease to be true, they have a power of veracity quite beyond that of actual records" (p. 154).

Having thus sketched the role of the novel in the transformation of society, Wells now enunciates his prodigious climactic claims:

You see now the scope of the claim I am making for the novel; it is to be the social mediator, the vehicle of understanding, the instrument of self-examination, the parade of morals and the exchange of manners, the factory of customs, the criticism of laws and institutions and of social dogmas and ideas. It is to be the home confessional, the initiator of knowledge, the seed of fruitful self-questioning . . . . The novelist is going to be the most potent of artists, because he is going to present conduct, devise beautiful conduct, discuss conduct, analyse conduct, suggest conduct, illuminate it through and through . . . . We are going to write, subject only to our limitations, about the whole of human life. We are going to deal with political questions and religious questions and social questions. We cannot present people unless we have this free hand, this unrestricted field. What is the good of telling stories about people's lives if one may not deal freely with the religious beliefs and organisations that have controlled or failed to control them? What is the good of pretending to write about love, and the loyalties and treacheries and quarrels of men and women, if one must not glance at those varieties of physical temperament and organic quality, those deeply passionate needs and distresses from which half the storms of human life are brewed? . . . We are going to write about it all. We are going to write about business and finance and politics and precedence and pretentiousness and decorum and indecorum, until a thousand pretences and ten thousand impostures shrivel in the cold, clear air of our elucidations. We are going to write of wasted opportunities and latent beauties until a thousand new ways of living open to men and women. We are going to appeal to the young and the hopeful and the curious, against the established, the dignified, and defensive. Before we have done, we will have all life within the scope of the novel. [Pp. 154–56]

It is not, certainly, a case for the autonomy of art or its special province, but it is more exalted and grandiose than almost all such cases dare to be. If Wells conceives the novel at the last as only an instrument for salvaging civilization and humanizing its members, it is to his mind an instrument almost omnipotent and transcendent in its operations. Art in "The Contemporary Novel" still does not make life in James's terms—help us to construe it, to imagine and create it for ourselves in the forms that most afford interest and importance, to contemplate enduring essences and shed what does not sort with them—but if it does not make life, it is thought to have the power to make life better. Wells's confidence that the novel can do so is breathtaking. If he errs, if his ascription of such dazzling morally and socially ameliorative powers to fiction suggests a questionable understanding of the real nature and quality of imaginative literature—a matter at least debatable, at most inconclusive—then he is guilty, at this stage of his career, of exaggerating rather than underestimating the importance of fiction. Indeed, his hopes for it in 1911 seem unbounded. A part of our concern in tracing his later views will be to try to determine, when it became clearer and clearer to Wells that the world would more or less remain the world no matter how devotedly and urgently he might devise schemes for its improvement, what he made of this high early faith in the novel.

Not content with resisting Wells's conception and practice of the novel in conversation and letters, James resorted to print in 1914 with "The Younger Generation," a survey of the younger novelists in which only a few of them—notably Edith Wharton—escaped whipping.[5] The common malady that James diagnoses in the group is what he calls "saturation"— "a closer notation, a sharper specification of the signs of life and consciousness" than the novel had customarily employed. Although he had himself argued eloquently for "solidity of specification" as "the supreme virtue of a novel" in "The Art of Fiction," he makes it clear in his survey that no vivid account of the details and workings of experience can ever be an end in itself but must always serve a structure of meaning, a center of interest. This interest, however, is what he cannot find in the fiction of his juniors, who parade their knowledge of life, or better, of a particular scene, state of mind, or transaction as though the mere verisimilitude and their mastery of it were itself enough. "They squeeze out to the utmost," he says in a frequently reiterated figure, "the plump and more or less juicy orange of a particular acquainted state and let this affirmation of energy, however directed or undirected, constitute for them the 'treatment' of the theme" (pp. 182–83). In contemporary critical circles, James says, it is enough for a writer to show that he knows all about something for him to stir interest. The great villain here is Tolstoy, serving "execrably, pestilentially" as a model of the failure to put the material of life to proper novelistic use: "from no other great projector of the human image and the human idea is so much truth to be extracted under an equal leakage of its value, that is an equal failure to exhibit, to present the value" (pp. 185–86).

James's language in dealing with Tolstoy, like his disciple Percy Lub-bock's in *The Craft of Fiction*, is shrill, as though only something excessive could begin to discredit so transcendently gifted a practitioner of the form, whose achievements, "loose baggy monsters" notwithstanding, flatly contradict all of one's faith. James's attack is really more appropriate for slice-of-life naturalism than for Tolstoy, who had very large purposes to which he addressed his material. Wells, too, is not an altogether appropriate sinner here, but with some shifting of ground James takes him on under the terms of the general indictment.

Wells's intellect, his eagerness to take all knowledge for his province, affords James his initial target. "It is literally Mr. Wells's own mind, and the experience of his own mind, incessant and extraordinarily various, extraordinarily reflective, even with all sorts of conditions made, of whatever he may expose it to, that forms the reservoir tapped by him, that suffices for his exhibition of grounds of interest. The more he knows and knows, or at any rate learns and learns—the more, in other words, he establishes his saturation—the greater is our impression of his holding it good enough for us, such as we are, that he shall but turn out his mind and its contents upon us by any free familiar gesture and as from a high window forever open . . ." (pp. 189–90). It is a measure of James's ambivalence in regard to Wells that he assigns Wells a window in his hallowed "house of fiction," yet has him turning out the contents of his mind upon us from it as though he were dumping garbage.

And no wonder, for there is a very deepseated ambivalence about intellect in James. His own was—and we have Wells's testimony for this—very considerable, yet he made a point of totally aestheticizing it, reserving it for special purposes and sensitivities and fending off as much as possible the contamination of general ideas. It is this circumspection that T. S. Eliot celebrates in his famous remark about James's mind being so fine that it had never been violated by an idea. Yet James's respect for Wells's intellectual powers is manifested again and again in their correspondence. And as a critic James, both early and late, did not hesitate to use the mind as an ultimate criterion for the novel. Early, we have this from "The Art of Fiction": "the deepest quality of a work of art will always be the quality of the mind of the producer. In proportion as that intelligence is fine will the novel, the picture, the statue partake of the substance of beauty and truth. To be constituted of such elements is, to my vision, to have purpose enough." Even if James is construing mind here more as what we now call sensibility, the passage celebrates that quality as a sufficient end in itself—precisely the recognition that James refuses Wells in 1914 by relegating knowledge to the purposelessness of "saturation." This is reminiscent of James's reversal on "solidity of specification." Indeed, in the very same year that he made the remarks on Wells, James was prepared in *Notes on Novelists* (1914) quite systematically and repeatedly to use insufficiency of mind and intellect, here construed in unmistakably intellectual terms, as his ultimate reservation about the work of George Sand, Flaubert, and even Balzac, whom he took to be at this time, all in all, the greatest of novelists. James is doubtless concerned with matters of proportion and balance within any given writer, but the concern lends itself handily to strategic emphases in any given case which inevitably issue in the desired reservation.

James proceeds to attribute "leakage" to Wells, as he had to Tolstoy, calling his recent novels "very much more attestations of the presence of material than of an interest in the use of it," but the example that he cites from *Marriage* (1912) is a curious contradiction of the case that he wishes to make. He charges Wells with having failed to specify the growing relationship between the hero and heroine by means of a love scene that Wells chooses not to present, so that when they achieve intimacy "the participants have *not* been shown us as on the way to it," and we are "mystified" by it. In the general context of "saturation" this objection has very little logical basis, nor does it sort well with some of James's own major omissions, such as the climactic scene between Merton Densher and Milly Theale in *The Wings of the Dove*; but it is a fair specimen of the mingling of admiration and consternation that always marks James's contemplation of Wells's fiction. It is quite in keeping with this ambivalence that James should close his consideration of Wells in "The Younger Generation" by returning briefly to the group indictment—our imperfect understanding of what a book like *The Passionate Friends* (1913) is, as a composition, "specifically about and where, for treatment of this interest, it undertakes to find its centre"—but then go on to say that such a consideration "falls away before the large assurance and incorrigible levity with which this adventurer [Wells] carries his lapses, for more of an adventurer as he is than any other of the company." And then relenting still more, though not really in essentials, James returns to the autobiographical heresy: "The composition, as we have called it, heaven save the mark! is simply at any and every moment 'about' Mr. Wells's own most general adventure; which is quite enough while it preserves, as we trust it will long continue to do, its present robust pitch."

But ambivalence and charitable, condescending indulgence were not enough for Wells. He responded to "The Younger Generation" with the publication of *Boon* in 1915, which in its unbridled cruelty to a friend gives some measure of Wells's need to liberate himself from Jamesian aesthetics and think of the novel in his own way. For all of its personal indecorum, and inhumanity, it remains one of the most pointed and devastating general repudiations of James's assumptions and practice that we have, and like many that came after, a curious blend of bitterness and principle.

Throughout the whole chapter that he devoted to James in *Boon*, Wells makes use of his impressive ability to ape and parody the late James style.[6] But it is through Wells's spokesman, George Boon, that he makes his most important observations on James's influence. " 'You see,' Boon said, 'you can't now talk of literature without going through James. James is unavoidable. James is to criticism what Immanuel Kant is to philosophy— a partially comprehensible, essential, an inevitable introduction.' " Boon maintains, with numerous allusions to the argument of "The Younger Generation," that James's great error is his confusion of literature with painting, his importation of an aesthetic for the visual arts into the novel. "He wants a novel to be simply and completely *done*. He wants it to have a unity, he demands a homogeneity. . . . Why *should* a book have that? For a picture it's reasonable, because you have to see it all at once. But there's no need to see a book all at once. It's like wanting to have a whole county done in one style and period of architecture. It's like insisting that a walking tour must stick to one valley . . ." (p. 104). This leads directly to a reflection on James's mind, prompted, no doubt, by James's earlier reflections on Wells's. "James *begins* by taking it for granted that a novel is a work of art that must be judged by its oneness. Judged first by its one-ness. Some one gave him that idea in the beginning of things and he has never found it out. He doesn't find things out. He doesn't even seem to want to find things out. You can see that in him; he is eager to accept things—elaborately. You can see from his books that he accepts etiquettes, precedences, associations, claims. That is his peculiarity. He accepts very readily and then—elaborates. He has, I am convinced, one of the strongest, most abundant minds alive in the whole world, and he has the smallest penetration. Indeed, he has no penetration. He is the culmination of the Superficial type. Or else he would have gone into philosophy and been greater even than his wonderful brother . . ." (pp. 104–5). The gratuitous injection of William, Henry's natural, inescapable rival for intellectual distinction, suggests Wells's eagerness to avenge the somewhat fulsome tributes to intellect that James was forever paying him in the course of analyzing Wells's artistic shortcomings.

But it is the aspiration to unity, what James had called "theme," "interest," or "center," that draws Wells's heaviest fire as he attempts to vindicate its opposite, the "saturation" with life that James had excoriated in "The Younger Generation." Wells's tactic is to have Boon charge

Jamesian unity with belying and impoverishing "the sweet complexity of life" and leaving us instead with sterilities and omissions, with inconsequential aesthetic symmetries. It is a reformulation of the affirmations of "The Contemporary Novel," fashioned this time directly from the rubble of the Jamesian monument:

> But if the novel is to follow life it must be various and discursive. Life is diversity and entertainment, not completeness and satisfaction. All actions are half-hearted, shot delightfully with wandering thoughts—about something else. All true stories are a felt of irrelevances. But James sets out to make his novels with the presupposition that they can be made continuously relevant. And perceiving the discordant things he tries to get rid of them. He sets himself to pick the straws out of the hair of Life before he paints her. But without the straws she is no longer the mad woman we love. He talks of "selection," and of making all of a novel definitely *about* a theme. He objects to a "saturation" that isn't oriented. And he objects, if you go into it, for no clear reason at all. Following up his conception of selection, see what in his own practice he omits. In practice James's selection becomes just omission and nothing more. [Pp. 106–7]

This becomes the classical, timeless, endless debate about the proper relations between art and life, with the defect of Jamesian virtue being lifelessness and that of Wellsian, chaos. As such, it is an important enough matter, but more important for our purposes is the extent to which Wells actually practiced the celebration of life that he has Boon commend so fetchingly in the "mad woman we love" figure without regard to "theme," "interest," "unity," or form.

It is not difficult to persuade anyone interested in the novel these days that the brilliant ridicule of James's omissions that Boon now proceeds to offer, along with his unforgettable treatment of misguided reverence for trivialities, is an exaggeration of nothing more than a tendency in James's art, and that in fact there is more vitality, complexity, and centrality in James's novels than Boon can find it in himself to admit. It is, though, considerably more difficult to find a similar willingness among commentators to relent from all extremes of satirical and argumentative and critical formulation in Wells's case and to consent to a more temperate and just estimate of his performance. The fact is, though, that the author of *Kipps, Tono-Bungay, The History of Mr. Polly,* and *The New Machiavelli* was far more interested in aesthetically selecting and ordering his material than he himself appears to be or to sanction in *Boon*; moreover, he proceeds to

become more interested in such matters in the last novels. The encomium
on life's intractability, like the affectation of journalistic carelessness,
while very much a part of Wells's bargain with himself, of his understanding of how he wrote and could write, and of what writing was all
about, are by no means a sufficient guide to what he actually achieved as a
writer.

The gathering cruelty of what follows from Boon is perhaps an
indication that Wells, for his part, sought in obvious exaggeration an
escape from accountability. What was said in jest could serve to relieve
one's own resentments, liberate one's own art, and yet be dismissed as
satirical hyperbole. If so, Wells miscalculated, for James, rightly enough,
was deeply wounded, and the attack itself has survived all the dramatic
reversals of James's posthumous reputation. It eventually makes its way to
the lips or pen of anyone impatient with James, late or, in extreme cases,
middle or early. Perhaps, on the other hand, it was necessary for the writer
who hoped to bring "all life within the scope of the novel" and who had
been rewarded by the metaphor of the squeezed orange to retaliate in some
such terms as these. Echoing James's echo in *Hawthorne* of Hawthorne's
list in the Preface to *The Marble Faun* of the omissions in American life,
Boon proceeds to enumerate what is absent from James's novels as a result
of James's distortion of life by means of "selection":

> He omits everything that demands digressive treatment or collateral
> statement. For example, he omits opinions. In all his novels you will
> find no people with defined political opinions, no people with
> religious opinions, none with clear partisanships or with lusts or
> whims, none definitely up to any specific impersonal thing. There
> are no poor people dominated by the imperatives of Saturday night
> and Monday morning, no dreaming types—and don't we all more or
> less live dreaming? And none are ever decently forgetful. All that
> much of humanity he clears out before he begins a story. It's like
> cleaning rabbits for the table.
>
> But you see how relentlessly it follows from the supposition that
> the novel is a work of art aiming at pictorial unities!
>
> All art too acutely self-centered comes to this sort of thing.
> James's denatured people are only the equivalent in fiction of those
> egg-faced, black-haired ladies, who sit and sit, in the Japanese
> colour-prints, the unresisting stuff for an arrangement of blacks
> . . . . [Pp. 107–8]

Boon goes on to speak of the trivial nature of the stories that James
fashions for these "eviscerated people," who "never make lusty love,
never go to angry war, never shout at an election or perspire at poker."

We recognize it as a classic indictment of what James, with some allowance for exaggeration, does not characteristically do; but more, it is a compendium of what Wells feels is worth doing in the novel and, in fact, had already set about doing. Boon points to a similar discrepancy in his last reflection on the issue of theme and selection as unifying devices: "The thing his novel is *about* is always there. It is like a church lit but without a congregation to distract you, with every light and line focused on the high altar. And on the altar, very reverently placed, intensely there, is a dead kitten, an egg-shell, a bit of string . . . ." The burden of this is not that James's practice of fiction is insignificant, but that by never relenting from his center of thematic interest, and by bringing all the mighty engines of his art to bear on it, he seeks a virtual inversion of significance; the realm of his art is not merely removed from life but somewhat perversely dedicated to refusing to recognize the most urgent issues and values of his time, first by eliminating them from consideration and then by invoking intense reverential consideration for other things utterly negligible in actual experience. Art here does not so much make life as remake it by simply denying its real lineaments. Again, Wells always purports, by contrast, to utilize the significances and impositions of reality as ordering principles of his own fiction.

Summing up this immense misappropriation of genius and concern in James, Boon says:

> Having first made sure that he has scarcely anything left to express, he then sets to work to express it, with an industry, a wealth of intellectual stuff that dwarfs Newton. He spares no resource in telling of his dead inventions. He brings up every device of language to state and define. Bare verbs he rarely tolerates. He splits his infinitives and fills them up with adverbial stuffing. He presses the passing colloquialism into his service. His vast paragraphs sweat and struggle; they could not sweat and elbow and struggle more if God Himself was the processional meaning to which they sought to come. And all for tales of nothingness. . . . It is leviathan retrieving pebbles. It is a magnificent but painful hippopotamus resolved at any cost, even at the cost of its dignity, upon picking up a pea which has got into a corner of its den. Most things, it insists, are beyond it, but it can, at any rate, modestly, and with an artistic singleness of mind, pick up that pea. . . ." [Pp. 109–10]

This recurring insistence on the disproportion of means to end in James is then illustrated with considerable sensitivity to James's style in an extended parody called "The Spoils of Mr. Blandish." Unlike Max Beerbohm's spoof, "The Mote in the Middle Distance," it expresses no

affection for what it ridicules and, together with the commentary preceding
it, made any continuation of the friendship impossible. Among the several
reversals of value that we have been noting in the course of the
Wells-James exchange, perhaps not the least is that of the very disproportion that forms Boon's climactic indictment. If James could be twitted
about a massive, hypersensitive concern with trivial ends, it was Wells on
the other hand who more and more after this notable encounter came to be
criticized for casualness in the fictional treatment of his most urgent and
exalted aims.

Despite *Boon*, the end of the friendship, and James's death in 1916,
Wells was far from having exorcised the ghost. Almost ten years after
Boon he presided over a collected edition of his own work in twenty-eight
volumes bearing a curious resemblance to the New York Edition of
James's novels.[7] The format of Wells's Atlantic Edition, with its aesthetic
bindings, expensive paper, large type, and sepia-tinted frontispieces,
comes very close to the James model. There are even prefaces furnished by
Wells for almost all of the volumes; but they are decidedly un-Jamesian,
deliberately cultivating instead brevity and directness and offering very
little in the way of detailed comment on the works themselves. The whole
production makes a bid physically for some such importance as Wells's
great antagonist had won for himself, but the voice is still very much the
voice of Wells.

In his General Introduction to the entire set (Vol. 1), Wells disclaims all
finish and artistry for the collected edition, which, he says, has none of the
"processional dignity" of the works of Henry James, those "triumphs of
conception and treatment." Devoted as they are to commenting on and
enhancing "the interest of life itself," Wells says, in the now familiar
gesture, that his own books are Journalism rather than Art. And he
expresses his characteristic pride in carelessness as well, in more reckless
terms than ever: "There are things reprinted here that were done almost as
casually as the faces one sketches on one's blotting pad."

For art, too, Wells continues, despite its finish and pretensions, has its
limits. It cannot claim the order of importance that belongs to any writing
devoted to the urgent task of reordering life. Gaining assurance, Wells lays
on with a will: "For to be a little franker than he was in his opening
paragraphs, the writer confesses his profound disbelief in any perfect or
permanent work of art. All art, all science, and still more certainly all

writing are experiments in statement. There will come a time for every work of art when it will have served its purpose and be bereft of its last rag of significance.''

This sense of a rapidly and profoundly altering reality, of the unprecedented rate and depth of change, forms the real center of the General Introduction and of Wells's conception at this time of his performance and role as a writer. For him all art, Jamesian as well, is based on a stasis, social, intellectual, spiritual. Art's business is the meticulous exploration of the present—arrangements and relations of almost endless complexity. But his own commitment as man, thinker, and writer is to the future. Speaking of the influence of his early experience on this commitment, the connections between what shaped him, what shapes the modern world, and what shapes his books, Wells says:

> Himself a child of change, born in a home that was broken up by failure in retail trade, and escaping only by very desperate exertions from a life of servitude and frustration, he has been made aware of, and is still enormously aware of and eager to understand and express, the process of adaptation, destruction, and reconstruction of old moral and intellectual and political and economic formulae that is going on all about us. Indeed these volumes are all about unrest and change. Even in his novels his characters, like Kipps and Mr. Polly, are either change-driven and unable to understand, or like Benham of ''The Research Magnificent'' or Stratton in ''The Passionate Friends,'' they are attempting desperately to understand, and still more desperately attempting to thrust at or interfere with change. [1:xvii]

Looking back over his work Wells maintains that as a writer one of his central preoccupations has always been the emergence of a Collective Mind accompanying the changes abroad in the modern world, ''arising out of and using and passing on beyond our individual minds.'' And as a novelist he has been interested in the frictions generated by those people who refuse to participate in this evolution of extrapersonal consciousness: ''The theme of several of the novels is the reaction of the passionate ego-centered individual to the growing consciousness and the gathering imperatives of such a collective mind.''

We recognize the accuracy of Wells's account of his own major theme as a writer as it figures both in the work he had already produced in the first quarter of the twentieth century and in the work yet to come. The delineation of the imperatives of change and the resistances to it is his great subject first and last. But the new note sounded here is the emphasis on the "passionate ego-centered individual" as the heart of the resistance. For the last novels, as we shall have occasion to see, are widely and deeply concerned with egotism as a bar to amelioration and renewal. Through this concern they become more entrammeled in the blood and the mire of life in the present than Wells is often thought to be, yet they escape the mode of autobiographical incontinence or personal vindication that often drew critical fire in the earlier work when it did treat the present.

Wells's increasing ability to extend his command over the intractabilities of character and to refine his sense of the problematic relationship between the life that he knew and the life that he dreamed is glimpsed in a rare and fleeting confession that appears in the Preface to *The Food of the Gods* volume of the Atlantic Edition. Speaking of himself, Wells writes, "Temperamentally he is egotistic and romantic, intellectually he is clearly aware that the egotistic and romantic must go" (5: ix). The confession is arresting because it makes Wells himself liable to foibles that he was now busy studying and anatomizing in others and suggests that the novels written from here on derive from an access of self-knowledge. It also intimates that these foibles are not simply foibles but formidable forces, capable of ruling even the leader of the opposition himself. The intensity of any struggle to purge humanity at large, as well as oneself, of petty self-absorption and delusion and to imagine a future without them may be observed in Wells's ferocious rejoinder to critics who persisted in finding his utopian visions thin and impoverished in relation to the rich imperfection of life in the present: "Of course the present life is richer in interest for such people; that is undeniable; just as a rat infested drain is richer in interest for a dog than a library or a laboratory" (28: xi).[8]

At a few points in the Prefaces Wells offers similarly revealing estimates of his own work and the critical reception of it. When he wrote *Love and Mr. Lewisham* (1900) with great care and sought to make it "consciously a work of art" his efforts, he says, were in vain: "It was not a very successful book, no critic discovered any sort of beauty or technical ability in it . . ." (7: ix). So too with *Tono-Bungay* (1909) which he is "disposed to regard as the finest and most finished novel upon the accepted lines that he has written or is ever likely to write." But "its reception disappointed him. He realized that the fully developed novel, like the fully developed Gothic cathedral, is a fabric too elaborate for contemporary needs and uses" (12: ix). With *Mr. Polly* there is a reverse disagreement. "A small but influential group of critics maintain that 'The History of Mr. Polly' is the writer's best book. He does not agree with them in that, but certainly it is his happiest book and the one he cares for most'' (17, n.p.). Nor does he agree with Virginia Woolf, who in her essay "Modern Fiction" speaks of the "crudity and coarseness of his human beings," especially the protagonists of *Joan and Peter* (1918), as they serve to illustrate the transition from present imperfection to future rectification: "what more damaging criticism can there be both of [Wells's] earth and of his Heaven than that they are to be inhabited here and hereafter by his Joans and his Peters?''[9] Looking back, Wells has it quite otherwise: "Joan the author fell in love with himself as she grew; and she is still his favorite and, he thinks, in many ways his best done heroine'' (23:ix). There is weariness and defeat in his account of *The Secret Places of the Heart* (1922), and the demurral in this case is rather disheartened: "It had a mixed reception; a number of reviewers hissed the characters in a manner that has now become traditional with the author's novels, and it was generally felt that Sir Richmond was not nearly such a dear as Kipps. The author clings to the persuasion that it is quite a good piece of work'' (25:ix).

Thus the prefaces to the Atlantic Edition indicate that by the mid-1920s Wells understood the major preoccupations of his own fiction, but was resigned to being misunderstood, or at least disagreed with, by a new generation of critics. The disagreement, as before, is aesthetic, involving an inability to come together with the more purely literary writers—the heirs of James—on the nature and function of literature.

Almost a decade later Wells devoted a section of his autobiography to the novel, attempting to set his mature views in order.[10] They turn out this time to be curiously mixed, defensive yet yielding, not so much an accurate account of his practice as a revelation of principles, ambitions, and defeats. As an account this "Digression about Novels" stands suggestively between what he had already accomplished in fiction and what he was yet, almost unbeknownst to himself, to do. Characteristically he tells us he is working from material gathered in a folder labeled "Whether I am a Novelist." The question is not quite resolved.

Perhaps more significant than anything else is his modesty and self-disparagement, which, while not unmixed with sporadic expressions of tentative, pleading satisfaction with his work, have been responsible for still further critical deprecation of his novels. Inevitably a writer's published criticism of himself, no matter how false, will be seized upon,

amplified, and invoked against him, its authority appearing so unimpeach-
able. Here, however, as with others, the self-reproach is self-conscious and
unfair.

Once again, Henry James comes immediately to the fore. Wells begins
by reiterating his own view of the novel as an "ethical inquiry" into
human relations, especially those between men and women, governed by
the questions "How did they treat each other? How might they have treated
each other? How should they treat each other?" Opposed to this view, he
says, is James's idea of the novel as "the rendering of a system of impressions" and as an Art Form, quite useless as a help to conduct. The issue is
thus formulated by Wells as one of the fundamental divergences between
classical and modern aesthetics. It serves once again to remind us that the
older, freer English novel that James was at pains to repudiate in "The Art
of Fiction" is in many respects the form that Wells sought to perpetuate,
with modifications, in the twentieth century. In reply to the aesthetic claim,
Wells offers urgency, utility, involvement in the world's great affairs. In
one of those disarming melodramatic rejections that surrender much
without necessarily gaining anything, Wells maintains that throughout his
career he was "disposed to regard a novel as about as much an art form as a
market place or a boulevard. It had not even necessarily to get anywhere.
You went by it on your various occasions" (p. 411). Yet we may reflect, as
we do often with Wells, that the novel is a curious route for a man of affairs
on his various occasions to take.

Following this Wells reverts to the attack that James had made on the
omitted love scene in *Marriage* (1912) both in conversation and in
correspondence—curiously enough Wells does not refer to the public
airing of the same point in James's "The Younger Generation." After
allowing James to make his case fully and persuasively in his own words
by quoting from a letter of 1912, Wells makes a startling admission of
guilt, but really only in order that he may make his own major point, once
again, about the varieties of fictional experience. It is the place where he
and James can after all agree about this most prodigious of literary forms:

> Tried by Henry James's standards I doubt if any of my novels can
> be taken in any other fashion. There are flashes and veins of
> character duly "treated" and living individuals in many of them, but
> none that satisfy his requirements fully. A lot of *Kipps* may pass,
> some of *Tono Bungay, Mr. Britling Sees It Through* and *Joan and
> Peter* and let me add, I have a weakness for Lady Harmon [*The Wife
> of Sir Isaac Harmon* (1914)] and for Theodore Bulpington [*The
> Bulpington of Blup* (1932)] and—But I will not run on. These are

pleas in extenuation. The main indictment is sound, that I sketch out scenes and individuals, often quite crudely, and resort even to conventional types and symbols, in order to get on to a discussion of relationships. The important point which I tried to argue with Henry James was that the novel of completely consistent characterization arranged beautifully in a story and painted deep and round and solid, no more exhausts the possibilities of the novel than the art of Velasquez exhausts the possibilities of the painted picture. [P. 414]

Wells is arguing here in theory for critical liberality, for an openness and freedom which would allow novelists to discover their own predilections, methods, and forms, much as James, in theory, had always done. When it came to cases, however, each lapsed into approving that particular form of the novel which he himself practiced. James's advice to other novelists in his letters, no matter what the range and variety of the presentation copies that he was responding to, always comes round obsessively to James's own absorption in impersonality, dramatization, point of view, etc., as though his own particular conception could somehow comprehend all the others that are theoretically, at least, admissible. Wells, too, is inclined to universalize his own example, but he is more receptively conscious than James of the existence of alternatives which may, in the long run, prove to have been valid. There is magnanimity too in "Digression about Novels" —"I had a queer feeling," says Wells, "that we [James and he] were both incompatibly right"—and a historical view of the evolution of the novel which enables him to justify his own work not only by looking back to the pre-Jamesian English tradition, but also by pointing suggestively to modern developments. He had done both in "The Contemporary Novel," but here in 1934 the delineation of the modern situation is less diagrammatically prescriptive and more instructive in connection with contemporary fiction generally.

Wells maintains that the nineteenth- and early twentieth-century novel, with its strong interest in individuation and characterization—the novel as Scott practiced it and handed it down to posterity—is a consequence of a "prevalent sense of social stability." Intensely conservative, Scott "saw events . . . as a play of individualities in a rigid frame of values never more to be questioned or permanently changed." But as fixities and values came to be questioned in the twentieth century, "the splintering frame began to get into the picture." Wells is talking here not about the evolution of techniques, but about the novel as an instrument for exploring and challenging social, moral, and political values which had hitherto been assumed. "I suppose for a time," he says with some pride, "I was the outstanding instance among writers of fiction in English of the frame getting into the picture.'' He then quotes his brave words from ''The Contemporary Novel'' (1911; 1914), ending with ''Before we have done we will have all life within the scope of the novel,'' as evidence of his subconscious desire even then to free the novel from its obsession with character and from its refusal to discuss values.

His point is that the novel of social, cultural, political, and intellectual discovery is necessarily intensely and directly concerned with the life of its time, with the urgent public problems and personal experience that are for the most part alien to James's interests on the one hand and to Dickens's on the other. The Novel with a Purpose of the earlier nineteenth century, Wells maintains, ''examined no essential ideas; its values were established values, it merely assailed some particular evil, exposed some little known abuse. It kept well within the frame. The majority of the Dickens novels were novels with a purpose, but they never deal with any inner confusion, any conflicts of opinion within the individual characters, any subjective essential change.'' The propaganda novel, says Wells, comes closer to the extensive novel that he was advocating in 1911, but it is unlike his own novels in its advocacy of the doctrine of a particular group or party, whereas he sought only to express and explore his own views.

It was some time, Wells says, before he understood that he was working toward ''something outside any established formula for the novel altogether.'' His interest was in expressing interior conflict within a character, ''controversial matter stewing and fermenting'' in the mind and issuing in action. ''I could not see how,'' he goes on, ''if we were to grapple with new ideas, a sort of argument with the reader, an explanation of the theory that is being exhibited, could be avoided. I began therefore to make my characters indulge in impossibly explicit monologues and duologues.'' This tendency led him, with the writing of *The Undying Fire* (1919), a modernization of the Job story, to what he calls the Dialogue Novel, which is influenced by the Platonic dialogue and constitutes ''an attempt to revive the Dialogue in narrative form.''

It is in these terms that Wells explains his progress to what is essentially the novel of ideas. It is notable in the ''Digression'' that when he speaks of interior conflict in his novels, he means not an emotional dilemma or even a moral or spiritual one—these are after all standard Jamesian fare—but a sorting, probing formulating and testing of ideas on rather a high conceptual plane. Without saying so, he is describing his practice of what we may call the speculative novel, which is a novel in the sense that its speculations occur within a narrative structure and are accompanied—again, though he does not say so—by appropriate feelings. In rejecting the concern with character that he attributes to both the nineteenth-century novelists and James, what he wishes to convey is that the speculations of his characters are really his own speculations, and that this is why he finds the novel ultimately autobiographical in conception, with all Jamesian notions of invention, creation, and objectivity rather spurious. What interests him as a man is what interests him as a novelist and his impulse is to deal directly with it.

Yet at the last he cannot liberate himself from the question of characterization in the novel or from James, who embodies it for him. After disarmingly admitting that most of his fiction was written "lightly and with a certain haste," Wells says: "Only one or two of my novels deal primarily with personality, and then rather in the spirit of what David Low calls the caricature-portrait, than for the purpose of such exhaustive rendering as Henry James had in mind." But after mentioning a handful of successful "caricature-portraits" in his novels, he feels constrained to say, "I doubt if any of these persons have that sort of vitality which endures into new social phases. In the course of a few decades they may become incomprehensible; the snobbery of Kipps for example or the bookish illiteracy of Mr. Polly may be altogether inexplicable." But out of this sense of failure, or better, of minimal success, comes a recognition and indication of new interest that bears significantly on the last novels:

> Exhaustive character study is an adult occupation, a philosophical occupation. So much of my life has been a prolonged and enlarged adolescence, an encounter with the world in general, that the observation of character began to play a leading part in it only in my later years. It was necessary for me to reconstruct the frame in which individual lives as a whole had to be lived, before I could concentrate upon any of the individual problems of fitting them into this frame. I am taking more interest now in individuality than ever I did before. [P. 422]

This observation points to a discernible development in the novels that we will be examining—a willingness to contemplate and treat personality more fully as a reality meriting interest and not solely as a frame attesting to the reality of a cluster of ideas.

Indeed, so compelling is the new interest in personality that it tempts Wells to speculate on the demise of the novel in the years to come. If the novel is conceived as a means of analyzing and evaluating the character of living people—and Wells fairly consistently argues that novelists draw figures primarily from life, the only source open to them—then there are other literary forms, biography and autobiography, that allow for more searching and faithful treatment. He predicts that these may well supplant the novel. We recognize here a sad retraction of the claims made in "The Contemporary Novel" twenty years earlier. His own pleasure in writing the *Experiment in Autobiography* has been so great, he says, "so much more real and interesting and satisfying that I doubt if I shall ever again turn back toward The Novel. I may write a story or so more—a dialogue, an adventure or an anecdote. But I shall never again come as near to a deliberate attempt upon The Novel again as I did in *Tono Bungay*." The ironic upper case letters becloud the issue somewhat, for Wells is repudiating The Novel as an art form once again and does not necessarily mean that he plans no more lower-case novels. Yet his terms, "a dialogue, an adventure, an anecdote," hardly sound like major exceptions to his rule. In fact, he proceeded to write and publish five full-length, considerable novels in the period between the *Experiment in Autobiography* and his death in 1946.

This is only another instance of the encompassing ambivalence toward the novel that marks all his discussions of it. It is clear that he could neither give himself entirely to it, as he knew that James had, nor leave it alone. On the whole, I hope to be able to suggest in the chapters to come, this is an occasion for interest rather than critical neglect. Wells's mixed mode itself represents a certain kind of opportunity for fiction—an order of importance and urgency that does the novel honor even while appearing not to.

The digression ends with yet more mixed feelings. Wells says that even *Tono Bungay* was not much of a concession to James's "conception of an intensified rendering of feeling and characterization as the proper business of the novelist." Indisputably a Novel, it was yet "extensive" rather than "intensive," which is to say it "presented characters only as part of a *scene*," having been planned as a "social panorama in the vein of Balzac." Once again Wells designates the subordination of character, this time to extensive social treatment, as the quintessential Jamesian sin— actually James wrote some socially rather panoramic novels himself—and sets Balzac up as an opposing model. The matter is complicated by our recalling that James considered Balzac the greatest of all novelists.[11] Wells, for his part, complicates it more by maintaining that the vein of

Balzac has produced many crude and superficial books as well as some great ones, and then yet again by claiming that historical, biographical, and sociological studies, "an industrious treatment of early nineteenth century records . . . would make Balzac's *Comédie Humaine* seem flighty stuff." Here Wells and James have changed places altogether over the example of Balzac. When Wells concludes this section by exempting only Tolstoy from his general preference for historical and biographical studies—"Yet in *War and Peace* one may perhaps find a justification for the enhancement and animation of history by fictitious moods and scenes"—he chooses the one extensive, panoramic novelist that James found most pernicious.

The issue is how much mixture of baser matter we are prepared to accept in the novel. James, placing both the novelist's personal life and general ideas in this category, will accept none at all. But this exclusion, however much we are drawn to it in theory, has never been and is not now widely practiced. Fielding and Sterne were, as Wells knew, mixing discursive and personal elements freely with strictly fictional ones in the eighteenth century, and Dickens, George Eliot, Thackeray, Trollope, Meredith, and Hardy were doing so in the nineteenth. The greatest continental practitioners of that same century—not only Balzac, but Zola, Dostoyevsky, and Tolstoy—were profoundly interested in the ideas and ideologies of their age, the latter two seizing the opportunity as egregiously as ever Wells did to advance their personal views on the problems of their time. Flaubert came to it as well in *A Sentimental Education* and *Bouvard and Pécuchet*. In the next century Joyce is drenched in autobiography, and Lawrence, beginning there with *Sons and Lovers*, goes on to formulate abstract prescription after prescription about abstraction, the great enemy, and about blood knowledge, instinct, and spontaneity, the great redeemers. Proust is more autobiographical than anyone except Joyce, and Thomas Mann felt but little hesitation in novels like *The Magic Mountain* and *Doctor Faustus* about attempting to sum up the mind of Europe. More recently Norman Mailer has been making novelistic transcriptions of social and political reality, presenting them as personal eye-witness accounts; and a major figure like Saul Bellow has utilized in *Herzog* and *Mr. Sammler's Planet* precisely the Wellsian formula of a protagonist very like the author, who is to be known primarily by his anxious, troubled grappling with the major intellectual and cultural stresses of his time, in order to furnish us with deeply personal and deeply comprehensive books. *Mr. Sammler's Planet* is even specifically haunted by the figure of Wells himself, whom

Sammler has known personally and on whom Sammler is pledged to write a memoir. Wells stalks Bellow's novel as an emblem of the predicament that the novel itself treats.

With such a rich tradition to support his conception of fiction and so recent and relatively small a body of work to discountenance it, we owe it to the history of the novel at large to dismiss Wells's case with at least a little less of the customary alacrity. A certain amount of hypocrisy beclouds the issue, or better, makes it misleadingly clear and simple. We have, in fact, always eaten the cake of discursive and personal fiction—James himself heaped up large servings of the public novel formed in the light of a deep personal assessment in *The Bostonians, The Princess Casamassima,* and *The Tragic Muse*—however much, at the same time, we have wanted to have the cake of impersonal and pure fiction. The "extensive" novels, usually political as well, of such writers as Dreiser, Sinclair Lewis, Malraux, Aldous Huxley, Arthur Koestler, J. B. Preistly, Joyce Cary, C. P. Snow, Angus Wilson, Pasternak, and Solzhenitsyn indicate that the form is alive in the world at large.[12]

It is, then, a sprightly critical dance that we find Wells and James engaged in, with Wells continuing it solo years after the quarrel had actually ended and James had died, and even ourselves occasionally rising on our light fantastic toes in the years following Wells's death. What emerges from his discussions of the novel is that Wells could not break free of Jamesian imperatives whenever he thought about fiction. He could be eloquent as in "The Contemporary Novel," sardonic as in *Boon,* or conciliatory and defensive as in his autobiography, but he could not quite persuade himself or his critics that he had devised a significant alternative to The Novel as an Art Form. His substitutes, at least as he formulates them critically, tend to break down into mere constituents of a novel. His dialogue novel utilizes just the intellectual component; his caricature-portrait, his late-blooming observation of character and individuality, and his interest in biography combine to form just the characterological component; and his earlier moral concern focuses on the novel almost exclusively as an instrument of social amelioration. In none of these cases is the novel anything like the one bright book of life dealing with the whole range of human experience.

But Wells did learn a great deal in the process of seeking to vindicate himself and exorcise James's ghost. What he learned, essentially, was to write his own kind of novel in his own way in order to achieve his own purposes, yet at the same time to assimilate other forms of novelistic value and interest. We may see this development not in his criticism but in the novels that he wrote at the end. They are the work of a great writer who decided at last to do something about some of his old, on the whole, rather debilitating habits and in the course of doing so produced books that we should be reading now instead of dismissing sight unseen.

There are two obsessive foci in Wells's novels: his interest in his own ideas and his interest in his own experience, erotic, social, intellectual, political. James was right in perceiving that these obsessions meant that, in a more complete sense than is usual with novelists, Wells's novels were always about himself. Wells's way of seeing this was to say that they were about life—an addendum and aid that afforded relief and ventilation for him, edification and encouragement for others.

It *is* possible to write significant fiction on this basis. Given enough talent, it is possible to write significant fiction on almost any basis—personality or impersonality, meticulous craft or overwhelming passion. James knew this, though Jamesians often do not. James's predilections and strictures, his whole Art of the Novel, expressed a personal preference. He understood that there was and ought to be a non-Jamesian literature as well.

The last novels of Wells continue to reflect his two obsessions and the fundamental devotion to himself that is their source. But these books also reveal a willingness to escape from such limitations, to establish a new balance between these matters and other matters, between himself and other people, between his ideas and conflicting ideas, and sometimes between the novel as an unburdening and the novel as a thing of interest quite apart from the writer's personal connection with it, an artifact that may work its way into the lives and apprehension of others, regardless of what subjective habitation and name it began in.

Wells's means of moving in this more aesthetic direction consist, for one thing, in his readiness to connect the ideas in his novels more intimately with action, character, scene, form, emotion, and total purport; the ideas gain force and interest from the kind of modulation that the narrative imposes on them while reciprocally the narrative is raised to importance by the quality of thought that it must somehow find itself equal to. There are also modifications of the ideas themselves. They tend to be less abstract and detachedly speculative or less programmatically urged and more closely connected with the situations and psyches in which they purportedly arise, which is to say that they belong more to the characters than to Wells himself. Hence the novel, rather than Wells's intellectual career,

becomes the ground of their being. As for the personal element, it is still
very much present, with the people drawn from Wells's life still filling his
pages. But they are there for a new reason—not to participate in Wells's
lifelong activity of vindication and self-justification, but to constitute
sources of interest for readers quite unacquainted with Wells, his companions, and his embroilments. That is, they have the reality of figures in a
novel, to whom the novel gives such life as they have, not the attested
reality of autobiography. It no longer matters whether they have an original
or not. Their importance derives more than ever before from their
participation in, their contribution to, a work of fiction.

There are signs, appropriately enough, of Wells's critical consciousness
of some of these developments in the introductions that he supplied for his
last two novels. The introduction to *Babes in the Darkling Wood* (1940) is
called "The Novel of Ideas" and is marked by a return to the old certitude
about the past and by a new clarity about his recent work.[13] Looking back,
he is as resentful as ever about the delusions and pretensions of his
aesthetic friends: "My early life as a naïve, spontaneous writer was much
afflicted by the vehement advocacy by Henry James II, Joseph Conrad,
Edward Garnett and Ford Madox Hueffer, of something called *The* Novel,
and by George Moore of something called *The* Short Story. There were all
sorts of things forbidden for *The* Novel; there must be no explanation of the
ideas animating the characters, and the author himself had to be as invisible
and unheard-of as God; for no conceivable reason. So far as *The* Short
Story went, it gave George Moore the consolation of calling Kipling's
stories, and in fact any short stories that provoked his ready jealousy,
'anecdotes.' " Against this groundless arbitrariness, Wells says, he long
ago formulated the freedom by which he had always worked: "I declared
that the novel . . . could be any sort of treatment of the realities of human
behavior in narrative form. Conduct was the novel's distinctive theme. It
was and is and must be, if we are to have any definition of a novel. All
writing should be done as well as it can be done, wit and vigour are as God
wills, but pretentious artistry is a minor amateurism on the flank of
literature."

Turning to the present, he proceeds to offer his fullest description of the
dialogue novel, since *Babes in the Darkling Wood* is the "most comprehensive and ambitious" example of the form he has ever attempted. Its
roots are in the Platonic dialogue. Its justification lies in the very nature of
the mind's apprehension of conduct: "Very early, men realised the
impossibility of abstracting any philosophy of human behaviour from

actual observable flesh and blood. As soon can you tear a brain away from its blood and membranes: it dies. Abstract philosophy is the deadest of stuff; one disintegrating *hortus siccus* follows another; I am astounded at the implacable scholarly industry of those who still write Textbooks of Philosophy.'' Hence the crucial importance of character in the imaginative literature of conduct and ideas. ''From opposite directions Shaw and I approach what is to us and, I submit, firmly and immodestly, to all really intelligent people, the most interesting thing in the world, the problems of human life and behaviour as we find them incarnate in persons.''

Wells maintains that critics have misunderstood the function of the talkers in his novels as far back as *Ann Veronica* (1909), mistaking them for his personal spokesmen when they were often actually charged with saying very different things from those that he himself believed. He feels, though, that of late he has been able to come closer to the ''fully developed novel of ideas'' by shaping his fictions successfully as ''discussions carried on through living characters.'' *Babes in the Darkling Wood,* he feels, is his highest achievement in the form because it concerns itself with ideas of the first magnitude, ''a very great burden of fresh philosophical matter,'' examined and debated by characters equipped through experience, training, intelligence, sensibility, and articulateness to deal with them. Because it is a novel, their dialogue is more connected, chastened, edited, and polished than their actual speech would be—a shorthand between people who have been educated similarly, read the same books, and could finish one another's sentences, or sometimes a longhand as they grope their way to meaning over unfamiliar territory. But what Wells seeks to represent, by clarifying, condensing, expanding, or underlining their words, is what they imagined they were saying, and what they actually meant. Here he takes an opportunity to distinguish his intentions and means from those of a yet more recent form of the art novel: ''That magnification and clarification applies in a greater or lesser degree to nearly all the talk in every novel of ideas. It is the exact opposite of that 'flow of consciousness' technique, with which Virginia Woolf, following in the footsteps of Dorothy Richardson, has experimented more or less successfully. Thereby personalities are supposed to be stippled out by dabs of response—which after all have to be verbalised.''

The introduction to *You Can't Be Too Careful* (1941), on the other hand, takes another tack with ideas in fiction.[14] Since the book's hero, Edward Albert Tewler, is decidedly unintellectual and repulsive to his creator, the introduction offers Wells an opportunity to be sardonic toward Tewler and the multitudinous critics of his idea novels at the same time: "So be it. You shall have [Tewler] unadorned; you shall have his plain unvarnished record. Nothing fulsome about it. This is a plain straight story of deeds and character—not character in general but the character you get in characters. What they did, what they said—there must, you know, be a sound track to a picture nowadays—but nothing like thought, no sort of consecutive thought. No dissertations, no arguments, above all no projects nor incitements nor propaganda, shall break the flow of the narrative; no more of these damned 'Ideers' shall there be, than mice in the Small Cats' House. For anything of that sort this tale will leave you unruffled." Beneath the chafing, the downright antagonism, of this intellectual self-denial there is another recognition of the primacy of character, though it is a little ambiguous here, being, by and large, recognized as another man's primacy. But, again sardonically enough, the introduction ends with a diagram that puts the matter of character clearly, if negatively, into what had always been for Wells a heartfelt relation to society. Just as he was frequently attacked for slighting character in favor of ideas, so also was he criticized for slighting individual character in favor of society, for being a social rather than a personal novelist.[15] He always maintained that the two were inexorably joined together. In 1933, for example, he had written, "I have never been able to get away from life in the mass and life in general as distinguished from life in the individual experience, in any book I have ever written. I differ from contemporary criticism in finding them inseparable."[16] And here in 1941, the inseparability is reasserted by means of a captioned optical illusion. Its purport is that while for Wells the life of society and individual experience are inseparable, unfortunately the modern novel has disintegrated into the exclusively personal or the exclusively social varieties:

Here we have a picture of the modern novel. Look at it hard and alternately you see the vase, the social vessel, and nothing else, and then the social vessel vanishes and you see individuals and nothing more.

The chapters ahead will seek to demonstrate that Wells managed to join his individuals and the social vessel inseparably together in his last novels by centering his concern on an exhaustive exploration of the dimensions and consequences of egotism, the inexorable obtrusion of the self, most narrowly conceived, on life in general. He came eventually to see egotism at large as the last, all but irremediable infirmity of man, the ultimate impediment to all noble promise and noble hope; yet this recognition made him more adept than ever at the savage, if heartsore, delineation of egotism and its workings "as we find them incarnate in persons." His climactic subject matter generated his climactic forms. Wells's particular rendering of this great theme, at once private and universal, allowed him to transmute obsession, and interest too, into wider meaning—meaning which the novel could legitimately contain and elaborate. The transmutation takes different forms in each of the novels, and it is more fully achieved in some than in others. But in all cases it will afford us a basis for describing and measuring Wells's imaginative accomplishment at the end of his life, when, if he could not decide whether or not he was a novelist, perhaps we can.

CHAPTER II

The Bulpington of Blup

WITH THE PUBLICATION OF *The Bulpington of Blup* in 1932 Wells delivered himself of his most profound and elaborate indictment of the aestheticism that had been dogging him all his creative life. But because it is a novel, it is more than an indictment. It takes into its purview not only James, the old enemy, but Whistler, Wilde, the nineties, George Moore, post-war reactionary and experimental writing, Ford Madox Ford, and T. S. Eliot, and not merely art but religion, science, and history. Nor is its interest in these things only ideological. The entire book is deeply rooted in the personal life of its hero, Theodore Bulpington, and the emotional, sexual, moral, and spiritual relations that help to shape him. Because Theodore is at once an aesthete and a complex being, Wells is able to explore ideas and values in a legitimately novelistic way.

The idea that he wishes most intensely to explore in *Bulpington*, his own more or less settled belief, irony, and satire notwithstanding, is our relation to reality, which tends, of course, to be the preoccupation of all good novels. The particular form that the idea takes in *Bulpington* is that the novel's hero has very little taste for reality and that this disinclination is actively nourished by his interest in the arts. That sounds like indictment enough, but Wells's novelistic skill in devising Bulpington's peculiar aesthetic self-regard gives the work as much the air of a special case as of a general position. And Wells's incomparable intellectual power as he ranges, with the appearance of utter disinterestedness, among alternative, indeed quite opposed views manages to persuade us that something very like justice is being done. When toward the end of the novel we withdraw almost with loathing from Theodore, we are responding to what a character in a fiction has made of his life, not to an argument of his creator's. So it is that in *Bulpington* Wells is able to make his most comprehensive, variegated, and effective statement against aestheticism, Jamesian and non-Jamesian, with considerable aesthetic success.

One hesitates to put the cart of Theodore Bulpington's upbringing before the horse of his temperament, but certain it is that he is reared during the closing years of the last century in formidably aesthetic circumstances, hermetically removed from the world that is real for others less fortunately placed. His father, Raymond,

> who had come down from Oxford with a brilliant reputation for brilliance, as full of promise as an egg is full of meat, was already something of an invalid in Theodore's childhood. There had been a brief glittering bachelor-time in London, studios and the Café Royal, epigrams before breakfast and the brilliant promise breaking out in the most scathing criticisms of established reputations. He contributed to the *Saturday Review* and the *Yellow Book*, drew women of new and startling shapes in black and white, and played quite a prominent part in the Revival of Wickedness in progress at that time. Then Clorinda got him.[1]

Clorinda is Theodore's mother, "one of the ten Spink girls who had partaken, all of them, of the earlier crude vintages of the higher education for women" and married Raymond "rather inattentively" because "she wanted someone 'uncommon' and she wanted to cut a dash intellectually" (p. 4). Advanced, liberated, and vaguely artistic, between them they manage to rear, by neglect and example, the little boy who when offered a penny for his thoughts by a visitor replies, "I was wondering why it is that Berlioz so often falls just short of greatness" (p. 9).

Wells extends a certain amount of sympathy to the young Theodore as a victim of his posturing *fin de siècle* parents and their world, but before very long it becomes clear that for Wells Theodore is decidedly an antihero, not in the sense that he is unheroic but in the sense that his creator detests him. One of the triumphs of *Bulpington* is that it succeeds on these terms, that with the relish and penetration of his aversion Wells is able to fashion a figure who is unfailingly interesting and, in a curious way, deserving of the reader's sympathy, even if he has been cut off from his author's.

The book's title is an epitome of these matters. It represents at once Theodore's most cherished daydream and Wells's sense of its absurdity and repulsiveness. After Raymond's health breaks down about the time of Theodore's birth in the nineties, the Bulpingtons leave London for the sea air of Blayport, a resort town on the English Channel. Encouraged as a youngster to sketch, play the piano, read voraciously, and write verse, the fanciful Theodore one day at the beach concludes that the ancient name of Blayport must have been Blup, much as he had learned from his history mistress that Brighton had been Brighthelmstone and London Londinium. Having conjured it up, he is quite taken with it. "*Blup*. It sounded like a great cliff, a 'bluff'; it sounded like the smack of waves; it made him think of a horde of pirates, desperate fellows, harbouring there, Bulpingtons all. And among them a leader, one, head of the clan, spite of his tender years, the best of the breed, *The* Bulpington—himself" (p. 8). So the myth of himself as leader, adventurer, warrior, lover is born, the dream into which he falls from out of the life which Wells would prefer him to face; and as he explores and modulates this fantasy throughout the novel, Theodore is pursued by the phonetic snigger of the name Blup.

A short time later Theodore fashions an ancillary symbolic personage and completes his dream world. Having discovered his mother, Clorinda, making love to a young visitor in that freest of households, Theodore becomes persuaded that he and The Bulpington of Blup had been changed at birth and that "the true mother of The Bulpington of Blup was as different from Clorinda as could be" (p. 14). For a while she is like Leonardo's Virgin of the Rocks, then like Prud'hon's Sleeping Psyche, very "calm and loving," and finally, but only very briefly, she is the Delphic Sibyl from Michelangelo's great ceiling. But with this possibility comes another, more exciting and more lasting. The Delphic Sibyl is much too young to be his mother. This "lovely being, with her sweet wide eyes, her awakening youth," becomes "the Bulpington of Blup's own true love" (p. 14). Thus while still but a boy, Theodore evolves the phantasm of an ideal self and the phantasm of an ideal beloved which, between them, govern his adult life. They comprise the axes of the little world of romance, perfection, and refuge in which he chiefly lives.

Just as Michelangelo's art supplies Theodore with the image of an ideal woman, so art in general nourishes his inwardness and dreaming, authorizing and even implementing his impulse to fend off reality. The house at Blayport is full of music, and it too becomes part of the dream. "Deep in his heart and unconfessed he most loved Berlioz because when he played him—and especially the *Symphonie Fantasque* [sic]—the Bulpington of Blup, moody and magnificent, enlarged to colossal dimensions, stalked through his imagination unrestrained. Theodore vanished" (p. 12). The very medium in which the boy lives is aesthetic and he is encouraged to find it sufficient:

. . . Art was a powerful reality in that little Blayport home—Art and, still more, talking about Art.

You exalted, you defended, you attacked and you denounced. You waylaid and stabbed with sneers. . . . There were fellows who tried to pass off Anecdotes as true Short Stories and give you sentiments for feeling [an echo of the Introduction to *Babes in the Darkling Wood*, p. ix]. There was George Moore who was certainly all right and Hardy who perhaps wasn't. George Moore said he wasn't. . . . Theodore was already a rather confused partisan by fourteen. He was a Socialist Medievalist. He thought machinery the devil, and Manchester and Birmingham the devil's own dominions. He hoped one day to see Florence. And Siena. . . . He was smilingly severe upon the architecture of Blayport and the fashions in Blayport shops. He begged for two Japanese prints to put up in his bedroom to replace a Madonna of Raphael's that he found "tedious." He objected to collars on aesthetic grounds and went to school in an orange neckwrap. He drew decorative borders in the style of Walter Crane on the paper they gave out for mathematics. For his present on his fourteenth birthday he asked for a really good book about the Troubadours.

Even Raymond admitted, "The boy has taste." [Pp. 23–24]

As the Socialist Medievalism, the abhorrence of industrialism, and the interest in the Troubadours suggest, in Theodore the romanticism of art goes hand in hand with a romanticism of history. His father, upon coming to Blayport, has quite Casaubon-like "flung himself into a History of the Varangians that was to outshine Doughty, a task from which he never emerged, from which indeed nothing emerged" (p. 5). For both father and son history is a refuge from the present as art and dream—at least daydream—are a refuge from reality. Wells is delineating the predilections of the aesthetic-literary-cultural reactionary against whom C. P. Snow was to rail on pretty much the same terms twenty-five years later in *The Two Cultures and the Scientific Revolution*. Like Snow, Wells turns to the scientific mentality for opposition to this backward-looking escapism, this refusal to deal with the world that lies before the eye and under the hand. But in *Bulpington*, which has real claims to being considered a serious novel of ideas, the debate is richer and more complex; and Theodore's romantic, reactionary aestheticism, even at its most distasteful, especially at its most distasteful, is rendered with a fullness, a strange compulsive antagonistic scrupulousness that is impressive. It is as though having determined to exorcise a set of attitudes that he finds monstrous and dangerous to life itself, Wells is bent on setting them down as accurately as he can. Without portraying them fully, without allowing them such power and seductiveness as they have for Theodore, Wells cannot be sure of a meaningful victory, satirically, intellectually, novelistically, over them. One of his enduring attractions as a writer is his ability to realize his detestations vividly in their essence, to destroy them, as it were, by knowing them. His parody of James's late style in *Boon*, for example, remains the best of the many that we have had because his mastery of what he disliked in James was so complete.

The treatment of young Theodore's solipsistic inner life gains immensely from this ulterior sympathetic insight. Wells's high good will on one notable occasion even reaches out to embrace a mystical experience of Theodore's. As Wells introduces the episode, we look expectantly for signs that he is preparing to make a mockery of it but find instead only intimations of serious consideration:

> And then one summer evening when he was a little past sixteen, something inexplicable happened to Theodore, something that may have had in it other elements beyond a dazzling spasm of the imagination. It is something that has happened to many people, and to this day none of these to whom it has come is quite able to explain it and put it into relation with other experiences. Some dismiss it, some forget it, some live by it. It was an experience of immense importance to Wordsworth. It is the Wordsworthian ecstasy. It is something almost indescribable—but we must do our best with it. [P. 67]

It is true that Wells's reiteration of the elusiveness of the experience—its inexplicableness and indescribability—hints at skepticism, but if so, it is the skepticism of one who has doubts about something that has been real for others. Moreover the phrase "some live by it" and the invocation of "Wordsworthian ecstasy" tend to allay those doubts, or to make them decidedly indecorous.

Theodore's ecstasy occurs while he is watching a sunset and one additional sign of Wells's sympathy on this occasion, or at least of his patience with it, is the magnificent physical description of sun and heavens and landscape that he proceeds to offer. If this is somewhat undermined by its being the only aspect of the scene and experience that a thoroughgoing skeptic *would* find real, the account of Theodore's mystical response to the shifting light that follows reinstates Wells's good offices:

> And as he watched these changes the miracle happened.
> The sunset was there still, but suddenly it was transfigured. The weedy rocks below him, the flaming pools and runlets, the wide bay of the estuary shining responsive to the sky, were transfigured. The

universe was transfigured—as though it smiled, as though it opened
itself out to him, as though it took him into complete communion
with itself. The scene was no longer a scene. It was a Being. It was
as if it had become alive, quite still, but altogether living, an
immense living thing englobing himself. He was at the very centre of
the sphere of Being. He was one with it. . . . The sunset and the sky
and the visible world and Theodore and Theodore's mind, were
One . . . .[P. 68]

It is a classical account of the mystical experience, couched in the classical
terms, possessed of as much authority and legitimacy as any such
accounts. Its function is to force us to take Theodore's inner life more
seriously, to reckon with it as a larger deeper impulse than exclusive
attention to the Bulpington of Blup and the Delphic Sibyl would suggest.
And yet, having provided this taste of authenticity, Wells moves us back
into the shadows along with it. When he concludes the sequence it is not
that Blup and Sibyl are lit with the radiance of Wordsworthian ecstasy so
much as that the "very centre of the sphere of Being" becomes located, or
at least locatable, in their fantasized domain. We are left with the feeling
that Theodore's interior, visionary world is passing rich, and strange, and
perhaps exalted, but still quite beside the point. The point, of course, as
always in Wells, is this world:

> If time was still passing, it passed unperceived, until Theodore
> found himself thinking like a faint rivulet on the melting edge of
> Heaven. This he realized quite clearly was the world when the veil of
> events and purposes was drawn aside, this was the timeless world in
> which everything is different and lovely and right. This was Reality.
> [P. 69]

The reader, on the other hand, realizes that Theodore's Reality is not his
and not Wells's. Theodore's is different, lovely, and right, the very fairy-
land where the Bulpington of Blup and his Sibyl dwell, the very heaven
where they sport timelessly with Theodore's mystical presences, Theodore's God.

In Theodore, Wells achieves a portrait of the modern romantic sensibility that ranks with Conrad's Jim and Fitzgerald's Gatsby; but where
Conrad and Fitzgerald, despite their reservations, admire, Wells, despite
his understanding, demurs.

Wells's plan in *Bulpington* is to spawn his romantic-aesthetic shirker of
a hero in a suitably turn of the century romantic-aesthetic environment,
expose him subsequently to a range of inimical ideas and experience to

which he remains impervious, or which drives him deeper into fantasy, and
then to bring him, with all his evasions and yearnings upon his head, into
and through the First World War. Wells thus obligates himself in some
measure to present the reality that Theodore shrinks from, along with
alternative ways of construing it. His solution is to push *Bulpington* in the
direction of what he came to call the dialogue novel, that is to say, to use it
not only as he had always used fiction, to examine "the problems of human
life and behaviour as we find them incarnate in persons," but to approach
that purer form where novels become "primarily discussions carried on
through living characters"—discussions of considerable intellectual depth
and suppleness, taking for their model the Platonic dialogue.[2] Wells is
quite aware that in order for the speakers in such a fictional dialogue to
become "persons" or "living characters" they need to do more than
entertain ideas, and in *Bulpington* he takes more care to establish the
dramatic force of their experience, feeling, and interaction than he was
disposed to take in such rigorously conceived dialogue novels as *The Holy
Terror* or *Babes in the Darkling Wood*. Thus in *Bulpington*, Wells provides
a number of convincingly incarnate voices and outlooks that conflict with
Theodore's, together with an action, a range of experience, for Theodore
that Theodore's own outlook cannot quite accommodate.

The first of these alternative possibilities is religion, which threads its
way ambiguously in and out of Theodore's romanticism. It comes to him
first incarnate in the person of Mr. Enoch Wimperdick, a friend of his
parents during the early Blayport days. Wimperdick, the "eminent convert
and Catholic apologist," who "had a lot of fat that did not fit him . . . as
if he was wearing the fat of a much bigger man," is modeled on G. K.
Chesterton and like Chesterton speaks in behalf of a Catholicism that has
far-reaching cultural and social implications. These are not lost on young
Theodore, even if they are not entirely assimilated either. Overhearing
Wimperdick's conversation he learns of a classification of the universe into
things which are "jolly" ("Jahly" in Wimperdick's mouth) and things
which fail to be so. "The Catholic Church it was evident was quintessentially Jahly. And so also were the Middle Ages, craftsmen, armies with
banners, sailing ships and the brass on carthorses. Those were Jahly too.
Tapestries again" (p. 20). Against these stand the Adversaries: Progress,
Protestantism, Factory Chimneys, Pitiless Machinery, Jews, Puritans,
Liberals, Darwin, and Huxley. Clearly this division of things is compatible
with Theodore's impulse to look back to a golden age, but his first
encounters with Wimperdick leave him confused about such essential

considerations as sin, the crucifixion, and the nature of God, none of which strike him as Jahly. It is a confusion from which he never wholly emerges, although he does have subsequent brushes with religion in which he presumably seeks to augment his understanding of life and his own experience.

Wells uses one of these subsequent occasions to suggest the limits of young Theodore's interest in the realities of religion. Returning home one day to Wimperdick, Raymond, and Clorinda after a visit to their famous neighbor Professor Broxted's biological laboratory, Theodore offers a defense of the doctrine of evolution. The grownups immediately take the bait—Wimperdick especially—and initiate rather an intelligent dialogue on the controversy between science and religion, which remains a dramatic conversation, with each participant speaking in character, even as it explores the intricacies, emotional as well as intellectual, of the problem. Wimperdick begins by calling Huxley the "Boanerges of Biology" and denouncing the biologists who have summoned us to look facts in the face through a microscope. "But facts vanish under a microscope," says Wimperdick. "They become little confusing crowds of innumerable particulars" (p. 45). He goes on to maintain that the Church has always known about evolution and rejects only natural selection because this is the scientists' way of getting rid of God; but modern science is only one of many heresies and it too will pass. Raymond replies that modern science is really something new, more formidable than any heresy—an "unbelief, not a wrong belief," which seeks to destroy the very foundations of all traditional belief. "It is dissolving our world," he says, "and leaving us nothing divine or human in its place." He mentions *The Inheritors* by Conrad and Ford Madox Hueffer, which he is currently reviewing, and its description of a new race without pity or scruples "destroying the time-honoured life of man"—just the kind of people science was producing. "Beauty disappears before them, moral values vanish, faith, honour, purity, loyalty, love; tradition becomes a legacy of old errors that had better be got rid of. All the fine, enduring tested things on which we live, by which we live—were threatened and going" (p. 46). As Raymond, the devoted chronicler of the Varangians, sounds this note, Wimperdick, the Jahly Catholic apologist, confidently disparages the same tendency as a "flash in the pan."

Here Clorinda, whose higher education has been throbbing within her and who has long wished to take on Wimperdick, lunges. She salutes the new attitude not as a flash in the pan but "a dawn." Science, she says, is "nothing more and nothing less than an escape from words and phrases—to fact—verifiable fact." It is a "recovery after a long invalidism . . . daylight breaking through those fogs of verbalism—in which the human mind lived—for such ages." She charges Wimperdick with being a Scholastic Realist whose devil is science and explains that science only became possible when the Neo-Nominalists triumphed over the Realists. That is when the "end of deduction" occurred, the "dethronement of words." Wimperdick takes her to task on the results of science, which she has cited as justification enough for its existence. Rejecting her notion of an intellectual liberation from the oppression of the past, he points to nasty, noisy, smelly machines, millions of cheap and ugly things in place of a few beautiful ones, insane rushing about. Meanwhile, he continues, "Nothing is left of the normal wholesome life of man. Nothing is left of morality. The soul has gone out of things" (p. 47). Her reply is that only the "bird-cage of belief is broken. . . . Nothing worthwhile is lost. There is only an opening up. I envy the new generation . . . growing up in the daylight."

Here her eye falls on Theodore, the putative beneficiary of this new intellectual freedom. "I pity the new generation," says Raymond, "growing up in the windy void." "I pray for it," says Wimperdick. Clorinda replies, "They will be in more direct contact with reality than any generation before them." "No. No. No," says Wimperdick. "You do not know what reality is. The only reality is . . . God. And He is Incomprehensible. That is why we are wrapped about in history and teaching—the teaching of the Church, which mediates between us and the blinding light of the One Reality." Clorinda instantly transforms the image: "Hangs like a tattered old curtain between us and the clear light of day." Then Raymond has the last aesthetic word. "But why shouldn't we have curtains? Even if we know they are curtains. You may be right so far as fact goes, Clorinda, you and your atheists and materialists. . . . But who wants to live in a bare and naked world: Who wants to be right in fact? If you strip the world, you can't leave it shivering. You'll have to wrap it up again in something . . ." (p. 48).

But Theodore's attention has wandered. The young representative of the generation in question, the living embodiment, cannot quite absorb all the vivacious talk about religion, science, and reality. Wells has presented it to remind us of the concerns that were in the air, convey the blur that they represent to Theodore, and to suggest that although any resolution of the conflict among the adults is improbable, their various ways of confronting it, or evading it, are a part of Theodore's childhood experience and will leave their mark on his development. We know enough about him even at this early stage to guess that his attitude toward the problem will resemble Raymond's more than either of the others', that he will always require that a curtain, often a rather elaborate curtain, be interposed between him and any number of realities. Indeed, the fashioning of that curtain comes to be the chief business of his life. But it is no easy matter, and in the process of fashioning it Theodore has a good deal more confused grappling to do with the positions of Wimperdick and Clorinda as they have been set forth in this scene.

A similar pattern governs the next encounter between the religious and scientific understanding. This time the combatants are the Chestertonian Wimperdick and the Huxleian Professor Broxted—Wells as a young man had studied elementary biology and zoology under Thomas Henry Huxley at the London Normal School of Science and later collaborated with Thomas Henry's grandson, Julian Huxley, on *The Science of Life* (1930). Wimperdick attacks the philosophical foundations of Broxted's empiricism and Broxted waves the objection irritably aside: "He not only would not discuss his philosophical foundations. He had an air of exasperation at the mere suggestion that he required philosophical foundations" (p. 61). Once again Theodore can make little sense of the quarrel. "The two men seemed to the young listener to be each right from his own point of departure as he spoke, and yet neither was confuting the other. Which was very perplexing." Afterwards, in his perplexity, he broods over the conflict, still at this stage of his life interested in getting to the Real Truth of Things:

> When at last someone got to this Real Truth that science was struggling towards, would everything change? Were all the faiths and doctrines of Wimperdick wrong and would they vanish in the new light? Would there be a strange change in things when at last one saw through them and the Real Truth appeared? Would one find God sitting there? Or would they find those Inheritors? [P. 61]

But in a moment the Delphic Sibyl enters Theodore's mind, enigmatic as ever, with the great secret, the Real Truth, perhaps contained in the parchment roll she holds in her hand; and in another moment, trying to banish her and concentrate on the problem, he is asleep.

Even the aftermath has the same outcome. On the following evening Clorinda analyzes the discrepancy between Wimperdick and Broxted with considerable cogency. "You and Professor Broxted will never arrive at any plain issue because you are arguing in different universes of discourse.

. . . You are in different dimensions of thought. You are thinking in different fashion. . . . It is like a fish in an aquarium trying to follow the movements of a man on the other side of the glass'' (p. 63). She then offers the details:

> But see how impossible it is for you ever to get together until one or other of your minds is absolutely born again! *You* think for instance that God is a Reality, beyond argument. And an old-fashioned Atheist of your scholastic realist type would say he did not exist—just as positively. But there is no such yes or no for the Professor. He thinks God is simply a working hypothesis—and, he is inclined to think, an unnecessary hypothesis. Whether God is or is not doesn't seem a reasonable question to him. Names are just counters to him. That name particularly. He can use a word provisionally and you can't. He thinks all logical terms connote rough assemblies with a marginal error. You think that classes of things all centre on an ideal type which endures for ever. Every scientific generalization is provisional, but you are always talking and thinking as though scientific theories were meant to last for ever, just as religious dogmas were meant to last. [P. 63]

But once again, Theodore cannot follow the argument. On this occasion the failure appears to be particularly regrettable to Wells because as narrator he allows himself, in remarking Theodore's confusion, to endorse Clorinda's assessment: ''[Theodore] did not realize, in spite of Clorinda's explicitness, that the essence of the matter they debated was the opposition of the two different fashions in which our minds make us for ourselves, out of disposition and suggestion and experience.'' This antagonism between Realist Religion and Nominalist Science is lost on Theodore. Instead, the episode closes by tracing a somewhat different split—a more schizophrenic one—in Theodore himself. For him the spectacle of two contradictory mentalities is only a dispute about the existence of God. We learn, surprisingly enough, that his own feeling about this dispute is that there is no God, or at least no God ''at all like the God of contemporary faith and imprecations.'' But the Bulpington of Blup, that other self—that sublimation of the fundamental Theodore—believed in God, and in fair return God believed in the Bulpington of Blup. They were mutually dependent. If one was the sublimation of an unsatisfactory personality, the other was the sublimation of a difficult world'' (p. 65). Wells here sets the course of Theodore's remaining experience, or better, use, of religion. In various hours of need, unsatisfactoriness, and difficulty, it is the sublimating Bulpington of Blup who presides over Theodore's religious life.

Religion drops from view at this point until Raymond's death years later on the eve of World War I. Summoned to Blayport from London where he has been studying art, Theodore searches in vain among his father's effects for the manuscript of the book on the Varangians that had supposedly occupied the closing decades of Raymond's life, for in an access of filial devotion Theodore entertains the idea of finishing the great work. But there is no manuscript. "Raymond had never finished that book, he realized; had never with any sincerity begun it. It had been his topic of conversation; his imaginative refuge. All this became plain now to his son, with the swift understanding of a kindred mind" (p. 157). In addition to the kinship of an empty, dilettantish life there is that of death. Theodore spends a fearful night envisioning his own death, but soon in a seizure of absolute conviction "all the passion to live which saturates us in adolescence suffused his mind and swamped his reason" (p. 166). Wanting desperately never "to be as dead as Raymond was," he is soon persuaded by the guardian angels of his childhood and their "attendant world of escape" that he need never be. But seeking confirmation of this summarily willed immortality, he calls once again on Wimperdick. The fear of death, the most overpowering and unsettling reality that Theodore has been called upon to face, impels him.

Wimperdick proves to be all that Theodore could ask. He intones the Church's absolute assurance of immortal life, even if the form of that life is "essentially incommunicable" (p. 171). Theodore finds the combination of certitude and vagueness irresistible: "Wimperdick talked on, and as he talked the Church as an undying witness became more and more solid and dominating and the particulars of the Faith it sustained more elusive. Theodore found something subtly congenial in that elusiveness." Drawing a distinction between the Protestant notion of Eternity as unlimited time and the Catholic view of Eternity as the antithesis of time, Wimperdick proceeds to a formulation that Theodore finds congenial in the extreme, for it affords him an ascendancy over reality—the reality of death, the reality of pain, the reality of others: "The Incarnation, the Sacrifice of the Mass, the Redemption, are not *events in time* like the Coronation or a Bank Holiday; they are everlasting realities. They did not occur and pass. They constantly and permanently *are*. Beyond any beginning. Beyond any end. Before the beginning was the Crucified. These are realities beyond fact. Just as our immortality is a reality beyond fact. Don't you see the point?" Indeed, Theodore does, and he clings gratefully to this "fundamental antithesis of absolute and factual values" and to the "great and difficult idea of eternal realities such as his immortal soul being in contrast with the stream of events it mirrored'' (p. 174).

Later that evening Theodore listens to a theological conversation between Wimperdick and some of his cronies which releases him from Wimperdick's Catholicism yet leaves him in possession of what he most wants; he concludes that as an Anglican he may enjoy the difference between ''eternal and factual values and the essential freedom of Faith from space and time'' without undergoing the rigors of Roman discipline. And later still, in bed that night, he takes characteristic possession of the idea as a refuge for the self: ''He could thrust aside the space-and-time garment quite easily, he found. He floated as an immortal soul then, an eternal being, in the bosom of the absolute. He found it not only easy but extremely comfortable to do so. His space-time existence, with its birth, its string of events and its death, its death above all, became of comparative insignificance, a picture that he, aloof and protected, regarded from an enduring standpoint. A profound contentment descended upon him'' (p. 175). It remains only for Theodore to aestheticize the feeling, and this he does easily and naturally. If every church is now for Theodore a portal through which one ''escaped to the Absolute—from death,'' music too takes on a new significance: ''He realized how Bach, Handel and Beethoven in particular, with their effect of vast reasoned revelation, their mighty vistas and their ever broadening and ascending magnificence, subserved the great escape.'' It is the ''Majestic refinement'' of St. Paul's that helps to decide him between Anglicanism and Romanism, and it is ''in the ordered ceremony and the decoration of religion that he found his comfort, the chanting, the moving responses, the high roofs and arches and the organ music; and whenever he could escape the sermon, that poor little thread of straining and wrangling speech amidst the shadowy mysteries, he did so.''

Secure in this ''new Absolute Bulpington of his in his new-found Blup beyond space and time,'' Theodore is proof against the jeers and denials of his scientifically oriented friends, Teddy and Margaret Broxted, the Professor's son and daughter. When Margaret insists that we live and we die, that we are selves rather than immortal souls, and that in proportion as we become intelligent and learn about things we want to escape from ourselves and find other things that seem bigger and more important to us, Theodore's reply is a perfect blend of egotism and spirituality: ''What can be bigger and more important than the immortal soul?'' (p. 180). The Bulpington of Blup wrestles to win Margaret away from the Inheritors seeking incessantly to undermine all established value and to preserve her as the Delphic Sibyl whom she resembles and in whose idealized form Theodore ideally loves her; but she resists and remains Inheritor, materialist, fanatic for truth, Godless Puritan. Thinking of himself, by way of contrast, as a Cavalier, Theodore lays plans to be baptized and confirmed by the Anglican church. "The Church," he tells Margaret, "stands for something—asserts something." "Your immortality?" she asks, coming perilously, if not fanatically, close to the truth. "*Our* immortality," he replies, adding characteristically, "And I stand for the Church." It is a fine stroke for this section of the novel to be titled "Intimations of Immortality," for Theodore's quest for, and appropriation of, eternal life has the same elusive, unreasoning, incommunicable quality as his earlier Wordsworthian ecstasy.

Wells seizes the occasion of the baptism to sum up Theodore's religion, egotism, retreats, and young manhood in that moment before the outbreak of World War I when such a tissue of indulgences had a certain plausibility, even representativeness. Again the matter is important enough to Wells for him to make explicit what he has hitherto presented for the most part implicitly and dramatically:

> So by the spring of 1914 Theodore's brain was going about the world in a state of reasonable contentment, equipped with an attitude of honourable scorn for, and a practical acquiescence in, social inequalities, a complete indifference to contemporary political, social and financial processes. . . . And he was a member of the Established Church. His apprehension of our corporeal mortality had led his thoughts to God, he had booked himself for eternity and achieved as delicate and impalpable an Anglicanism as ever protected a human brain from the harsh assaults of reality. He had got a soul just as he had got a moustache, as a most natural adolescent outgrowth. He had successfully evaded too close an identification of himself with his actual self, and if his feet walked on the firm grounds of material satisfaction and security, his head was pleasantly beclouded by the nobler conception of that ideal personality, the Bulpington of Blup. He pressed no further questions either into himself or into the appearances of things around him. [Pp. 184–85]

For all of the intricacy of theological debate in the novel, Wells clearly wishes us to understand that for Theodore religion, like art and history, is but an adjunct to a realm of private fantasy, founded and ruled by self-absorption, need, and fear. The posture and dynamics are simple and familiar enough, but the conflicts, issues, and ideas that Theodore must traverse on his way to solace and refuge are not. In their complexity, and in Theodore's resourceful and subtle, if self-deluding, manipulation of them, Wells gives us a compelling sense of the ways in which a capable, even sophisticated mind leads itself on childish errands. The pattern of self-delusion, of escapism is universal, but the terms are always particular. Out of those particulars, as Wells is thoroughly aware, come persons, characters, interest, fiction, and life. Out of them comes Theodore, who in the imaginativeness of his withdrawal, the intensity of it, becomes interesting.

The intricacy of a number of the religious, historical, or aesthetic ideas in *Bulpington* and Wells's practice of presenting them in debate also serve to remind us that these ideas, regardless of Theodore's employment or distortion of them, are real for others. Theodore does not discredit religion, art, or history by making them elements of his romance. They remain honorable pursuits for other characters, for Wells, for us as we read. What the novel does is to make them momentarily suspect, or, better, momentarily more difficult to honor. If an Anglican reads the following passage, he must reckon with Theodore's folly and Wells's mordancy; his Anglicanism will survive, but it will be slightly modified by its brush against Theodore's dramatized Anglicanism: "Romanism still wants to judge the faithful and does so whenever it gets a chance, but the Anglican God was ever so much too much of a gentleman to judge anybody, much less to be the Judge of All Mankind. A God with *tact*, that was Theodore's idea of a God" (p. 176). It is a tribute to the intellectual and dramatic validity of *Bulpington* that Wells achieves the same effect with those commitments— science, sex, and social consciousness—which oppose Theodore's romanticism and which come closer to Wells's own view of things.

Wells certainly deserves his fame as scientific romancer, scientific prophet, scientific apologist, and scientific popularizer, but his attitudes toward science, even from the time of such romances as *The Island of Dr. Moreau* (1896) and *The Invisible Man* (1897), were quite complex and far from uncritical.[3] They prove to be so once again in *Bulpington*, although at the same time there can be no question that Wells sets science in dialectical opposition to Theodore's dreaming.

The science in *Bulpington* is entrusted to the Broxted family, with, as we have seen, occasional speculative assistance from Clorinda. When he has just turned fourteen, his head filled exclusively with Blayport aestheticism and Blayport Varangians, Theodore meets young Teddy Broxted and his beautiful Sibyl-like sister, Margaret, and is introduced to the wonders of the microscope by Teddy in Professor Broxted's laboratory. After viewing a drop of blood and some other specimens, the imaginative Theodore is overwhelmed by a "vision of the whole world magnified in texture and teeming with unfamiliar particulars" (p. 34). It is borne in upon him that the world about him is a "mere summary of the material multitudinousness of reality" and that under the microscope that "world disappears and a swarming infinitude of cells and atomies, corpuscles and fibres, replaces it." The experience is profoundly unsettling, invading as it does the very terms of his existence, the romantic dream in which he has been reared. When it is over he remains "aware of a threat to the particular universe he had made for himself to live in" but is on this particular occasion unable to discover "the counter-thrust needed to restore one's self-respect" (p. 35).

The episode is an epitome of Theodore's relations with science throughout the novel. Science always threatens to bring a strange, unassimilable, intimidating reality to bear on Theodore's fantasies, to displace his comforting, exquisitely elaborated dream world with a world he never made and does not choose to live in. If mankind cannot bear very much reality, Wells's Theodore can bear less than others. Under the threat of the Broxteds' scientific understanding of things, his impulse is always to strike down, or at least strike back at, everything they say. The one unusual feature of this first encounter is Theodore's speechlessness, his failure to produce a suitably self-preserving counterthrust. This we may take to be Wells's tribute to the legitimacy of Theodore's wonder as he actually sees for the first time a world that he has hitherto only talked about—a wonder which puts us in mind of Keats's watcher of the skies or stout Cortez rather than Wordsworth.

In any case, Theodore is never speechless again with his scientific antagonists. A little later in the same day, having recovered himself by discoursing extensively on the Varangians to Teddy, Margaret, and their mother, none of whom know very much about them, Theodore has an exchange with Teddy which is a paradigm of those to come. On this occasion Theodore calls upon history to fend off science. Mrs. Broxted begins the conversation by asking Theodore hospitably and rhetorically whether among his histories and books he has any use for microscopes:

> "None, mum. It's life-size we do—life-size human beings we are thinking about. No historian wants a microscope. Microscopes wouldn't be any good to my father."
> Teddy objected to that. "But how can you understand human beings unless you understand life, and how can you understand life without a microscope?"

"But human beings *are* life," said Theodore. "And you don't
want a microscope to see them."

Teddy's face flushed for controversy; his ears got red. "I didn't
say you couldn't *see* human beings, I said *understand* them. How
can you know what human beings are, unless you know how they are
made?"

"You can watch what they do."

"That doesn't explain how they do it."

"Yes, it does. If you—"

"No, it doesn't."

"History explains."

"History tells a tale. History is all tales. You can't check it back.
It isn't Science. It isn't Real."

"It is."

"But it isn't. Your old History—"

The discussion was degenerating. Mrs. Broxted intervened.

"Have you lived long in Blayport, Theodore?" [P. 41]

Wells has certainly made much of his microscope prop and much, too, of
his fourteen-year-old's wrangling. Before the discussion degenerates, it
has touched on the significant epistemological question of how we may
best know what is most worth knowing. *Bulpington* is about the pursuit of
reality and the flight from it. Theodore and Teddy—their sharing different
forms of a single name is surely a deliberate touch on Wells's part—are
debating about the best modes of pursuit. Yet we are aware as we listen to
Theodore that for him, as for his father, history is really a mode of flight
from the real. Still, what he is *saying*—and in any dialogue this must be the
first, if not the last, consideration—is on the whole more persuasive than
what Teddy has to say. Despite Wells's ostensible sympathy for science,
he obviously intends Teddy's questions—"How can you know what
human beings are, unless you know how they are made?"—to sound as
puerile and misdirected as they do. In the interests of real debate and
drama, that is to say, of such modulation and modification of ideas as
comes of incarnating them in living persons, Wells here casts doubt on the
scientific reality which he will elsewhere employ to cast doubt on
Theodore's subjective world. He can do this because within the intellectual
structure of *Bulpington* some scientific realities are more real, or at least
more pertinent, than others. As for the impasse that the boys come to, that
too has its importance in the novel. Speakers in these Wellsian dialogues
are not so much in possession of the truth as they are in possession of a
relative desire for it, a relative accessibility to it. Debates, characteristically, are not resolved; dispositions are revealed. Nonetheless, on

this basis there are important discriminations to be made. In the end, it is
these that go against Theodore.

Professor Broxted himself, for all of the warm Huxleian associations, is
guilty of a disquieting intellectual and moral narrowness. Wells's irony
extends to him almost as readily as it does to Theodore's daydreams:

> Broxted was a propagandist of experimental science—in ed-
> ucation—in public life. For him modern science was light invading
> obscurity; it was the dawn of Truth, in a world that has hitherto
> muddled along in a picturesque but dangerous twilight. Everything
> else, he held, must adapt itself in the long run to scientific truth.
> Everything else was secondary—systems of morals, social ar-
> rangements; the primary matter was to know what things were,
> ourselves, life, matter and so forth, and then afterwards to discuss
> how we were to deal with them or behave with them.
>
> "It isn't the business of a man of science," said Broxted, "to
> consider whether his facts lead to conclusions that are morally good
> or bad—or shall I say beneficent or evil? Such values come
> afterwards. For him there is nothing but the truthful ordering of
> facts. He has to follow his facts to whatever conclusions they point
> towards—however startling, however unpalatable." [Pp. 59–60]

The passage is rather delicately nuanced. The Professor is a little more
plausible than his young son, but only a little. His position is both right and
wrong—right in its essence, yet wrong in its purity and rigor. Despite
Wells's submission to the wonder of scientific exploration—and we must
remember that for him it was largely an imaginative experience, the
excitement of the spectator rather than the participant—he was always
sensitive to the danger of conceiving scientific responsibility and
accountability too narrowly. What he offers us in Broxted's science, as he
has been offering it to us in Theodore's aestheticism, is the sort of luxury
that the world could afford, or thought that it could afford, prior to 1914.
When the war comes it discredits the Professor as much as it does
Theodore.

As Theodore's friendship with Teddy and Margaret grows, the debate
between them flourishes. Theodore pits not only history but also religion
against their inexorable scientific enlightenment. He continues to identify
them with the Inheritors intent on destroying all established value, but
Margaret, whom he is coming, in his fashion, to love, poses a dilemma as
an advocate of Broxted ideas. Can she be an Inheritor if she is, in her
beauty and grace, the Delphic Sibyl? Do the Inheritors have souls? Or is
she like Undine, the water nymph who could obtain a soul only by

marrying a mortal and bearing a child (p. 49)?[4] At the beach on one occasion of their endless dialogue, a dialogue so much more painful and complicated than Theodore's dreams, after Teddy has hurled socialism— an adjunct of his scientific views—at him, and Margaret has hurled feminism, Theodore shifts to aesthetic resistance. "The world exists for Art," Theodore declares. "That is the greatest thing in life" (p. 73).

When Teddy disparages Theodore's Art, Theodore uncovers the fountainhead of his, and his father's, aestheticism, the gray eminence who presides over his deepest disposition:

> "Interpretation," expanded Theodore, quoting Raymond quoting Henry James; "*rendering*, giving it a form—the only thing that matters."

But Teddy is resolutely fundamental and ultimate, and Margaret, if anything, more so:

> "Here we are," said Teddy, getting back to his own question, "we three, chucked from nowhere into—*this*. And we don't know How and we don't know Why."
> "And we don't know What For," added Margaret with her chin on her fists and looking out to sea.
> "If there *is* a What For," said Teddy.
> "I thought your old Evolution explained all that," Theodore commented in the sly Wimperdick style.
> "It describes, it doesn't explain. Who said science or evolution *explained*? Science makes one thing consistent with another, or tries to. That's all science claims. Nothing in the world is really explained. Perhaps nothing can be."
> "But when the artist comes in things are—illuminated."
> Teddy was struck into a scowling meditation for a moment or so; his lips repeated the words noiselessly; then he turned over and scrutinized the face of his friend. "Bulpy," he said, "that last sentence of yours doesn't mean anything at all."
> "It means as much as your universe," said Theodore, and felt he had scored again. [Pp. 73–74]

Once again, impasse. Margaret ends the silence that follows Theodore's last remark by suggesting that they all go for a swim. But the impasse is instructive. This time the exchange has bite and rhythm. In Teddy's distinction between describing and explaining and in Theodore's dexterous, if factitious, claims for illumination we sense the sheer delight in argument that governed so much of Wells's intellectual and creative life—a delight that led him inexorably to the dialogue novel. But beyond this, we discern the major impasse with Henry James that lies so close to the heart of Bulpington.

Wells remarks, before presenting this argument over science and art, that he is sketching the "scenes and circumstances amidst which these three young minds acquired form and substance and played upon and educated one another." The words are well chosen. As we read the dialogues between Teddy and Theodore, with Margaret's increasingly touching and prominent obbligato, we come to see that there will be, can be, no resolution. The three young minds play upon and educate one another not by enlightenment and accommodation but by a hardening of defenses, by downright aversion. What we witness is not a Socratic triumph—and here Wells's analogy with the Platonic dialogues breaks down—but a growing determination to be unreconciled. What we witness is that agreement to disagree, to be perpetually at odds, that governs three quarters of the intercourse among men. There is no more reason for Henry James's champion, Theodore, and his friend, Teddy, to compose their differences in the novel than for Wells and James themselves to do so in life. And it is an aspect of the living quarrel between Wells and James that comes close to the heart of *Bulpington*.

Wells's whole career is based on the idea that the world can be, must be, changed for the better by the application of intelligence and good will. As we saw in Chapter 1, art and literature figure for him as part of that process. Fruitful change can be projected and achieved in his view only by those who have an adequate apprehension of reality—real needs, real desirabilities, real possibilities, real means—and it is a function of the art of which he approves to inculcate this reality. In addition, because Wells is urgently interested in changing the world, he is passionately interested in the forces that on the one hand resist, and on the other encourage, change. For him these forces are largely incarnate in persons. That is why he continued to write novels; and that is why, as the prospects for salutary change grew dimmer and dimmer late in his life, he wrote novels dominated, for the most part, by characters whose casts of mind and temper oppose change. In Wells's view, James had such a mind; as a pure artist, James's impulse is to keep the world what it is, to get it to hold still long enough so that it may be exquisitely, profoundly, lovingly portrayed. Theodore embodies this impulse in *Bulpington*, but in a thoroughly antiheroic way, for he has none of James's command of even a static reality and none of James's genius. Indeed, he has no genius at all, only a number of pretenses. The Broxteds, on the other hand, for all of their foibles, are receptive to the idea of change; it is inherent in the very discipline of the science to which they subscribe. It is this receptivity, this capacity for discovery and emendation, rather than their biology or methodology, that Wells commends. And on the whole he is less interested in commending it than he is distressed by its utter absence in Theodore.

Wells does not stint in seeking to make Theodore's resistance to science and change the formidable thing it must be to sustain the novel. There is a slightly mad plausibility in Theodore's meditations and maneuvers that is precisely the right note. For years after first meeting them, Theodore struggles against his only half-admitted growing fear and respect for the Broxteds, father and son. "They were destructive of something he could not endure to have destroyed. They were like hunters who never tired and who were driving him patiently and incessantly towards their corral of harsh realizations. They were spiders perpetually spinning fresh threads in the great web of science to catch and hold, discipline and dessicate, his imagination. They were under an urge to draw out slowly and certainly a compulsive map of the universe for everyone. It would show inexorably what was what, how all things were, what could be done, what could not be done, and even at last what inevitably should and would be done. For the truth is the ultimate and most rigid of dictatorships" (p. 103). But at the Rowlands School in London where he has gone to study painting after Raymond's death, Theodore discovers a powerful new word, "values," with which to arm himself in his struggle against the Broxteds. "Now across this formidable rigid plan of theirs Theodore could flourish a nice loose versatile Scheme of Values, and immediately this fact became greater and that less, unpleasing things ceased to dominate and frail and fading concepts rose again with all their ancient charm and vigour restored." So armed, Theodore can dismiss Teddy's concerns as unimportant. The standard of importance becomes totally subjective, and a lack of agreement becomes a lack of discernment on the part of others. The "values" that Theodore invokes are largely artistic and they allow him to aestheticize his debate with science with great abandon.

At this same juncture he has considerable success in aestheticizing yet another troublesome challenge to his willful neglect of things. Theodore's sense of history had always been, like Raymond's, a romantic flight into a past both remote and idealized. But there is another sense of history in *Bulpington* espoused by Theodore's antagonists and having connections with such dread things as science, social consciousness, and politics. To this intractable stuff too Theodore must bring his peculiar order.

Lucinda Spink is the oldest of Clorinda's sisters, a spinster, a nonmilitant suffragist, a leader in the Fabian Society, and a member of the London County Council. As such she offers Wells a dual opportunity. She is one of the major voices summoning Theodore from his Palace of Art to the streets below, where he may fulfill his obligations to society; but at the same time, her genteel ineffectuality allows Wells to ridicule his old enemies and former friends, the Fabians. The other voices in this rather mixed social and political chorus belong to Teddy and Margaret Broxted and their friends, Rachel and Melchior Bernstein, a brother and sister several years older than Theodore. Theodore, with his Art, and his Values, is proof against them all, of course, but they press him hard and force him to define his pretenses more subtly than ever. They help him, thus, to become the redoubtable derelict to the present and the future that he is by the end of the novel, and they help Wells to establish yet another plane, or succession of planes, of the reality which Theodore banishes from his life.

Aunt Lucinda has been charged with keeping an eye on Theodore while he attends the Rowlands School of Art in London. At tea one day she assaults him with a very high Victorian seriousness. When he mentions his evening classes in drawing the nude, she says augustly, "The nude is not everything" (p. 87). When he says that he makes studies of draperies as well, she says, "No doubt you work at your art. But there are other things. Do politics, does social life mean *nothing* to you?" When he replies rather preciously that politics seem such an *excrescence* on life, she becomes formidable: "No," she says flatly, "Art is the excrescence. . . . At bottom all artists are parasites and prostitutes." Warming to it she insists that Theodore, economically privileged as he is, owes something to the world; that in addition to working at his art he must study to understand its relation to "the political and social scheme." "Every citizen," she continues, "is responsible. If you shirk your duties, and if everybody else did the same thing, who would keep order, who would keep the streets clean, who would prevent our being murdered in our beds? Even now don't you realize there is a great lot of social injustice in the world? There are old laws, bad institutions. Poor people are oppressed. Women are oppressed. India is oppressed" (p. 88). Going to the window she presents Theodore with a vision of the street below ruled by Social and Economic Forces and insists that it is Theodore's duty to read, to learn, to know about it all: "Surely economic and political science is interesting enough when you see it that way! All London, all the world is realized sociology in movement. Realized sociology in movement! You know a lot about Vikings and the

Troubadours and the Crusades; but isn't all this just as living? Seeing that it is actually alive! There it is—sociology going on.'' Then, without argument, indeed without even asking, she settles it that Theodore will attend a meeting of the Fabian Society the following week.

Wells's ironic touch here is quite delicious. Once again he places necessary, corrective sentiments in the mouth of a speaker who somehow manages to make them comically suspect. Lucinda is quite right about Theodore's selfish obliviousness to every form of human need, social, or political, or economic, which does not bear directly on his own well-being, quite right about his specious aestheticism and his escapist history—quite right from Wells's point of view and the reader's. Yet dear Aunt Lucinda is too quirky, too elevated, too righteous, too humorless, too naive to express the reproach without modifying it by her own person. Her correction, while real enough, becomes through Wells's artistry itself subject to correction.

This intimation is corroborated and fulfilled at the meeting of the Fabian Society itself. With Aunt Lucinda sitting on the platform next to Sidney Webb, Theodore listens inattentively to a paper being read. The atmosphere is reminiscent of Wells's critical and satirical accounts of the Fabians in the *Experiment in Autobiography* and *The New Machiavelli*. It is just the right sort of home for Aunt Lucinda: "The paper was called *Marxism; its Virtues and its Fallacies*, and sometimes it was vividly interesting and sometimes it was incomprehensible and sometimes inaudible. (Then impatient voices at the back cried, 'Speak UP.') The debate was rather fun because it sounded wildly incoherent; with a passionate storm from a German comrade at the back, a scene between the Chairman and a deaf old lady who wanted to ask questions, and an entirely irrelevant side speech from a consciously Irish Catholic'' (p. 91). Fortunately, Teddy and Margaret are there as well with their friends the Bernsteins, and Theodore joins them after the meeting for beer, sandwiches, and talk.

In the conversation that follows, Wells gives us evidence of Theodore's growing capacity to deal with the whole political-social-economic threat to his existence. Once again Theodore recovers from the initial shock, as he had done with the microscope; and this time he exhibits enough intellectual flexibility not only to engage but to assimilate the new ideas. Wells's Theodore is no dreaming fool but a demonically ingenious casuist; on this occasion he is adroit enough both to save himself and score points against some of Wells's own political and social bêtes noires.

Rachel Bernstein begins the conversation by commending the extraordinary cleverness of the man who had read the paper on Marxism. She says that he is actually a Communist who posed as a critic of Marxism in order to get the Fabians, who otherwise would not even have listened to him, to defend Marx. Rachel is also a Communist; Theodore's reflections on this speech of hers are not very far removed from Wells's own views of the Marxist mentality: "As his acquaintance with the Socialist movement increased, Theodore was to find this sort of cleverness and these imputations of subtlety pervaded it from top to bottom. Everyone was being cleverer than anybody else and manoeuvering the unsuspicious into the unanticipated" (p. 92). Moreover, Theodore is himself clever enough to charge the Marxist revolutionary movement with being as much a fantasy as his own habitual fantasies. He meditates on the solid, irresistible reality of the restaurant, counters, attendants, tables, customers, amidst which he and his friends sit, and of the crowds, cabs, omnibuses, and buildings outside, and he marvels at the hallucinatory presumption of reform movements. "The five of them sat round the white table-top and talked as though that little meeting they had attended of four or five hundred people in a hired hall was going to take control of these torrents of movement and these solid cliffs of matter, and do some extraordinary thing to them, the Social Revolution, which was to alter—what could it alter? Alter the immutable? Divert the implacable?" (p. 93).

When Theodore finally speaks to the group, telling them that after their Social Revolution everything will be very much as it is now, he assumes the odd, the rather startling role of proponent of reality. Our epic dreamer denounces the dreams of others: "Reality is stronger than theories. There will never be a Communist State. Marx was an impracticable dreamer," he says. Of course, Theodore's appropriation of reality is a misappropriation. He knows little enough about it, and by the time Wells published *Bulpington* in 1932 something like a Marxist revolution had occurred in Russia and something like a Communist State had been formed—enough like to discredit Theodore's skepticism. Yet Theodore's consciousness of the real world is extending itself here, so that when Rachel dissents by asserting that reality is "economic forces" and Melchior chimes in declaring that Marxism is not a theory but an "analysis and a forecast," we are interested in Theodore's reply. For the moment, at least, he strikes us, in his groping toward a solution to the social-political threat, as a more reliable witness than those who merely serve up the slogans of Marxist doctrine. He makes two points, neither of which is satisfactorily answered by the Bernsteins or Broxteds. Why, he asks, if Marxist theory is a forecast, need anyone talk and work for the Social Revolution that is bound to happen? Then, graciously assuming that the capitalist system will crash on some such terms as Marx predicts, Theodore gives the group a start by inquiring what will happen to the physical reality of London—houses, traffic, crowds—when the Revolution takes over. Teddy joins him by asking the Bernsteins what the Communist countryside will be like, and Margaret wants to know about women under the new order. Melchior dismisses such speculations as the pretty pictures of Utopianism, a fallacy to be avoided, but his refusal to enter into details decidedly weakens his position, and the evening ends with Teddy and Margaret, momentarily allied with Theodore, refusing to give a blank check to what has now become the Bernsteins' Social Revolution.

But despite the outcome of this conversation, Theodore soon finds the vagueness of the Bernsteins, as he finds that of Wimperdick, beguiling and seductive. Their formless Social Revolution is for him of the same order of being as his reverie of the Bulpington of Blup. The two, quite readily, mingle in a daydream that harmonizes them by allowing Theodore all the latitude that his fantasy life requires: "Sometimes the Bulpington of Blup led this revolution; sometimes he was the great counter-revolutionary who saved the ancient order of the world" (p. 96). He finds this far more rewarding than contemplating the poor whom Aunt Lucinda is forever commending to his attention. He thinks them a dreary, dull multitude whose circumstances are unlikely to alter. Like Wells's Henry James, "At the bottom of his heart, [Theodore] believed that the appearances of the present were invincible." He also finds his Bulpingtonian revolution far more satisfying than Aunt Lucinda's Fabians, who can never answer Theodore's—or Wells's—questions without raising further questions. It is certainly more satisfying than Teddy's determination to learn what he can in order to change as much as he can the beastliness of conditions. For the truth is that Theodore does not, fundamentally, want to see how beastly things are for the needy, and he has a perfectly adequate means, supplementary to the Bulpingtonian reverie, of preventing himself from doing so:

> Meanness was not mean; it was humorous, it was pathetic. Frustration had its comic side; a starving man is not so much starved as mentally exalted—or why should the saints abstain?—and a cripple is privileged to grotesque effects denied to normal creatures. The great artists preferred to paint cripples and old women because if

you get your values adjusted properly there is something insipid about normal health and grace. And when his mind was unable to go all that way in evading the indigence and indignity of the slums, it could always step neatly into the dimension of dreamland and a world transfigured. [Pp. 99–100]

Thus Theodore's ultimate answer to the claims of social conscience is perdurably, inhumanly aesthetic. Just as he had invoked his new-found term "values" against the "hard materialism" of the Broxteds' science, insisting on the primacy of artistic values over scientific ones, so can he now turn away Lucinda's—indeed, anyone's—high summons:

> Moreover he could evade his Aunt Lucinda's sociological pressure with a good conscience. "My dear Aunt!" he would say with a note of protest, and that was all; as though she scandalized him; that sufficed; and he could go through the Saturday-night slums, admiring the dancing lights and shadows of the paraffin flares, the hard high scream of a woman against the general rumble, the chattering and clattering of the marketing swarm, the shining erubescence of a drunkard's face, the narrow brownly sombre emptiness of the mean side-streets, without a troublesome thought of responsibility for the squalor and degradation of the under-folk, without even a thought of their squalor and degradation. [P. 104]

The intensity of Wells's distaste for aesthetic evasion is clearly discernible in the essential exaggeration of the passage. Theodore emerges in it as a depraved and sinister fugitive from the decadent nineties. Yet there was a nineties. And implicit in aestheticism, there has always been a willingness to let art feed on, come of, suffering. In any case, Theodore, for all of his intellectual and emotional substantiality—and the whole novel derives from this—is conceived by Wells as an exaggeration of tendencies that are real and perverse. Wells speaks of *Bulpington* in *Experiment in Autobiography* as his most elaborate treatment of the "theme of the floating *persona*, the dramatized self," involving a high level of complexity and self-deception, and goes on to say that the book "is a very direct caricature study of the irresponsible disconnected aesthetic mentality."[5] The degree of Theodore's late adolescent aesthetic disconnectedness is breathtaking. He transmogrifies, trivializes, and neutralizes the vital social, historical, and political concerns of others by setting them in the context of his art. As a Bulpingtonian revolutionary he speaks of putting revolutionary feeling into his line, of seeking novel and rebellious color effects. And having appropriated the word "bourgeois" from the Bernsteins, he employs it with the same successful arbitrariness that had attached to his use of "values." The Fabians are "bourgeois," Professor Broxted and all science are "bourgeois." So too are Florentine art, the Royal Academy, most portraiture, comfort, bathrooms, punctuality, duty. With this mighty lexical weapon, with his values, and with his art he frees himself in triumphant irresponsibility from the nets of social obligation cast by Lucinda, the Fabians, the Broxteds, and the Bernsteins. The self-scrutiny that his dialogue with the young Broxteds had sometimes made unavoidable is now avoided. So adroit does he become in the use of his aesthetic tactics that he can now deal with that most difficult of problems, flux: "His mind was making the transition from the acceptance of a static to the realization of a changing world with a brilliant evasiveness; he was growing up and still he was keeping the freedom of his imaginations" (p. 105). Wells makes it clear that neither religion, science, nor history is any match for the floating persona of Theodore. There is very little room for others on the stage where the drama of the Bulpington of Blup goes forward.[6]

The debate structure of *Bulpington* is neither an innovation nor an eccentricity. We sometimes forget how central and powerful the tradition of argument, of rhetoric in the classical sense, has been in western imaginative literature. Achilles and Agamemnon, Antigone and Creon are masterful debaters, and not only the Book of Job or *Troilus and Cressida* but *King Lear, Paradise Lost, Absalom and Achitophel, Rasselas, Pride and Prejudice, Middlemarch, Père Goriot, The Brothers Karamazov, The Portrait of a Lady*, and *The Magic Mountain* would be unthinkable without rhetorical, and rather dialectical, confrontation as a major means of creating, elaborating, and consummating drama. Nothing, after all, is more characteristic of drama than the voicing of differences. In *Bulpington* the debates may initially appear to concern more abstract, less personal matters, but we have seen already how often this appearance is misleading, how closely tied to each speaker's temper and situation every utterance of his usually is, and how ready Wells can be to surrender ideas to more subjective delineations and intimations. But even in *Bulpington* there comes a point where debate rather noticeably gives way to action, where issues that have occupied Theodore's mind as speculations become experiences that he must live through. And it is altogether fitting, in view of the subject and design of the novel, that this should occur with the outbreak of World War I.

We have traced at length Theodore's considerable success in overcoming the more or less theoretical challenges that spiritual, scientific, and historical considerations pose to his retreat from the world. We have even watched him subdue the threat of death when his father dies. There are, however, two realities with which he fares far less triumphantly. One is the war, and the other is love, particularly love under the conditions imposed by the war. These are matters that he must undergo and cannot evade by means of talk or fantasy. He manages to live them through, but on terms that render him both pathetic and repulsive. They are tests that he fails on all but his own bizarre terms. Wells has carefully shaped the novel so as to make these failures climactic and definitive, the disastrous measure of all the pretense and self-deception that have governed Theodore's life from the beginning. Had there been no war, Theodore might have escaped reckoning; but it is part of the intimation of the novel that given enough Theodores, there had to be a war, and inevitably the war had to call in question much of what Theodore represents.

Wells introduces the war in Chapter Six with observations on the way in which it made the old private life, the indulgent pursuit of one's own ends and pleasures, impossible. Prior to 1914, Theodore and his like might ignore history, politics, business, society, the whole public sphere, with impunity and leave the management of the world to those foolish or ambitious enough to be absorbed with it. A life devoted to art and criticism, and nothing else, was tenable in those privileged years, even if it might earn the scorn of a Lucinda or a Wells. But the coming of world war in 1914 ushered in the conditions of inescapable involvement that have since become the basis on which all life in this century must perforce be conducted. Like everyone, Theodore is swept up in the excitement of the conflict.

Surprisingly enough, he responds eagerly. Both his newfound flexibility in the face of change and the essential trivialness of his aesthetic dabbling make him emotionally available. For him the war is not so much the end of productive and serious private labors as it is the offer of a new sphere of operations for his old heroic dreams. Speaking unmistakably in the accents of the Bulpington of Blup, he greets the conflict enthusiastically as an opportunity to restore the soul of England under the discipline of struggle. The honor of his country, he tells the Broxteds, impels it to fight. A great romantic victory is inevitable for dear England, his England.

The Broxteds too are swept up in the swift march of events. Despite all of his earlier advocacy of the supreme disinterestedness and purity of science, the Professor now passionately seeks to mobilize every man of science in England to further the war effort. He is convinced that Germany is launching an attack on civilization itself and must be defeated. In his

view the overthrow of German militarism and armament would inaugurate
a World Confederation, the Parliament of Mankind, the World State; this
was, consequently, the War to end War. His son, Teddy, disagrees totally.
For him the outbreak of war "was only the necessary culmination of the
long stupid game all the Foreign Offices of the world had been playing in
despite of the welfare of mankind. Germany had been played into the
position of firing first. That was all" (p. 201). He views the conflict as a
piece of childish irrationality. Margaret comes closer to Teddy's outlook
than to her father's. She is appalled by her vision of the suffering,
bloodshed, and death that must ensue and that in the end will prove largely
meaningless, for she has little hope of a new world emerging from the
struggle. Wells manages to distribute among the Broxteds ideas and
feelings that he himself entertained at various stages of the war. The
Experiment in Autobiography traces his progress from patriotism like the
Professor's—Wells published a pamphlet entitled *The War That Will End
War* in 1914—to disillusionment like Teddy's and Margaret's, though in
Wells's case, of course, the World State remained as the only possible
solution. But Wells's case, once again, does not matter. *Bulpington*
explores these positions for its own sake in order to project and motivate a
dramatic action.

Margaret's vision of the horror to come, for example, moves her to
plead with Theodore not to go off to war. By this time, despite the
profound intellectual and moral differences between them—she still
hovers, for Theodore, between Inheritor and Delphic Sibyl—and despite
the hard little sexual interval with Rachel Bernstein that Theodore has
found necessary in coping with the reality of his body, Margaret and
Theodore are officially in love, although he has not yet succeeded in
persuading her to go to bed with him. Her plea that Theodore not join up,
however, is not nearly so necessary as Theodore's brave talk of the honor
of England leads her to think. Typically enough, it is merely talk, the voice
of his dream. The fact is that while almost all the young men of his
acquaintance, except for Teddy who is ideologically opposed, rush to
enlist, Theodore carries on his customary artistic activities for upwards of a
year after the outbreak of hostilities. In the face of the most embarrassing
encounters with those who accuse him of shirking, he hangs back, exalting
the heroic enterprise, yet discovering a series of motives for not joining it.
First he imagines, with no evidence whatever, that his heart and
lungs—there is his poor father's untimely demise for precedent—would

prevent him from qualifying for service. For a time he even imagines that he has had an army physical and been turned down. Then there is Clorinda; surely he cannot take from her her only son. And Margaret, who had indeed pleaded with him not to go. How can he violate their feeling for him, jeopardize what they hold most dear? Besides, the war is not likely to last more than six months, and if he enlisted, by the time he finished the tiresome training he would face the frustration of having no one to fight. In the end, however, Margaret is decisive. Her assumption that he is staying out because he rejects the war in terms similar to hers becomes intolerable to Theodore. "It was the obscure necessity he was under to justify his attitudes to Margaret that at last tilted the delicate balances of his mind and drove him, stammering again slightly, to the recruiting office and into the war" (p. 220). The Bulpington of Blup can do no other, at least not indefinitely.

From this point on action dominates the novel, allowing dream and reality to clash and regroup. The war becomes a context of verification for all that Theodore represents or suggests. Writing with an economy and vividness that recall the imaginative achievement of another noncombatant, Stephen Crane in *The Red Badge of Courage*, Wells traces Theodore's experience in the trenches. At his first sight of blood, dismemberment, and death Theodore goes to pieces, retching and weeping. A short time later on watch he imagines that his line is being attacked by a monstrous black dog approaching over no man's land and fires at it, only to be ridiculed by his fellows for seeing things. The dog becomes a recurring nightmare. Along with this hysterical behavior, Theodore is guilty of constant heroic chatter, meant to encourage others and quiet his own anxiety. Its effect, however, is only to make him unbearably obnoxious. At this juncture his lieutenant suggests that Theodore apply for a drafting job at division headquarters in view of his art training and the need for draftsmen. Agreeing to serve where he is most needed, Theodore applies and is swiftly transferred. So ends his first ignominious brush with the war that he had been commending fervently to others in London for more than a year. Through it all, Theodore manages to sustain the illusion that he is a good soldier. The more cowardly his behavior, the more adroit his pretense and hypocrisy. His self-delusion is exported to Clorinda and Margaret in fine brave letters filled with manly duty and courage. Nor does he forget to write to his aunt, Miranda Spink, now Lady Brood, the wife of Sir Lucien Brood, Minister of Munitions,

putting the same brave face on things in case of future need. In one
particular he has profited extraordinarily from the war. Margaret, out of
compassion and fear for his life, has become his mistress.

The pattern of cowardice, self-delusion, and heroic posturing
established in this first segment of Theodore's military service persists
throughout the war. He wrenches his knee at division headquarters
climbing some stairs and is sent, through Sir Lucien's intervention, to yet
another safe assignment in Parville. Here, however, an osteopath named
Barker indicates to Theodore that he can easily repair the knee injury and
render Theodore fit for the front lines; out of war-weariness and compassion Barker offers to leave Theodore lame temporarily, but Theodore
refuses the offer. Sir Lucien has already arranged for Theodore to return to
England to train for a commission and there is no need for so blatant a form
of connivance as Barker proposes. During surgery, however, Barker hears
Theodore's muttered accompaniment to the black dog nightmare and gains
rather a thorough understanding of his patient and his history.

Once back in England for officer's training Theodore persists in
advocating the glorious, exalted necessity of the war to Margaret at the
same time that he makes love to her. He goes so far in his soldierly pose as
to call Teddy, who has been imprisoned for resisting the war, a coward.
Margaret, now studying medicine, becomes more and more troubled by the
extent of the differences between herself and her lover: "If we could strip
souls as easily as we strip bodies," she says. "So much love-making. Like
a desperate attempt to dissolve another person into oneself, to get close and
near. And one doesn't get close and near. I'm tired. You've tired me out"
(p. 276). In their endless quarrel about the war, as in their endless quarrel
about life, we witness the eerie spectacle of Theodore living the truths that
she proclaims—the unassimilable horror of modern war—yet adamantly
denying them to her face, and through her, to himself. When, before
leaving once again for Paris, he asks her to marry him, she refuses. Though
she has always found him attractive, even loved him, the war makes it
impossible for her to overlook things about him that were mere oddities
before. The new context has changed his self-indulgence to unendurable
enormity.

Theodore's experience of war and of love under the stress of war now
moves swiftly to its inevitable, climactic revelation. He learns that Sir
Lucien has fallen from power and that nothing, consequently, can keep
him from being returned to the front as an officer. While contemplating this
prospect with dread, he learns also that Clorinda has died and receives a

last letter from her in which she speaks with the conviction and regret of her imminent death of Theodore's life-long retreat from reality: "I have watched you growing up, spinning threads of imagination out of your head like a spider, and catching them up and weaving them into a bandage. A mist bandage. So that you fall against things and hurt yourself and others. . . . Stop telling yourself fairy tales about yourself. Life isn't a fairy tale" (p. 286). Theodore deals with these home truths by concluding that his mother has never really loved him, that no one has, that there is no such thing as love in the world, only death awaiting everyone, awaiting him especially now:

> All human beings, he realized, want to be conquerors in love and none will be the slave that everyone desires. So Clorinda, it seemed, had failed him, and Rachel and Margaret had promised and failed to perform, had seemed to give unreservedly and yet had made reserves. He had been lured into a promised Paradise of indulgences and he had found it a harsh testing-house, a place of peculiarly intimate scrutinies. Love exalts us, strips us bare, and then looks at us without mercy.
> And so shows that it is not really Love.
> A vast self-pity arose in him, so love-eager, so love-worthy, a loveless being in a loveless world. And now going unloved and lonely to danger, hardship and perhaps death. [P. 290]

Lovelorn and unlovable, snatching at life in the face of death, Theodore for the first time spends a night with one of the prostitutes who have been importuning him throughout his stay in France. The next morning, filled with hatred for Margaret and her allegiance to Teddy and his ideas, he sends her the rash note which effectively releases her from all further obligation to him: "You have never loved me. . . . You do not know what love is. Why, the very prostitute with whom I spent the night before I went up to my death knew more of love than you" (p. 297).

Shortly after this, his war service comes to its climax in an episode that Wells contrives to make immensely appropriate. Back at the front once again, Theodore undergoes a furious bombardment, far in excess of anything he had experienced or seen during his earlier tour. He represses his memory of what occurred and what he did almost completely, but it is clear that he fled from the scene and sought safety in the rear, leaving his men to face the danger without him. Yet another compassionate medical officer intervenes and designates Theodore a victim of shell shock although he is in fact guilty of total dereliction of duty. Summoning his powers of self-deception, Theodore persuades himself before long that he was actually wounded in the shelling. By the time he is qualified for discharge, he has set his military house in good Bulpingtonian order by totally eradicating the truth. Wells's handling of this entire sequence is a remarkable adumbration of the delicate and arcane modes of self-delusion. Dream and reality, as in the erotic fantasies of Theodore's puberty, when his awakening sexual urges were forced to express themselves only in sleep, are suggestively reversed: "The Theodore who had fled through the trenches had passed altogether out of his waking life, was a reality only in his dreams" (p. 310). In the waking dream of Theodore's life, fashioned by the spidery threads of his imagination, he has quite a different history: "The closing phases of his war services were effaced from his mind and replaced by vague and fluctuating legends of heroic service. He was a war hero returning to civil life. He had served and suffered. The Bulpington of Blup had played his part, done his bit in saving this dear England . . . ."

But these powers of invention prove helpless against Margaret's determination to end their affair and marry someone else. Having decided to relinquish painting for literature and join the exciting artistic quest for a "new language, a language richer and more subtle, reforged for the new needs" of the postwar world, Theodore bombards her with tasteless, posturing, raving letters seeking to change her mind. His reward is a visit from her fiancé, who turns out to be the former medical officer that certified Theodore for shell shock when he knew better, and who, in a remarkable scene, forces Theodore to withdraw all his claims to Margaret.

There are, then, intractable realities for Theodore. But he has his ways of moving past them, on into his dream. On this occasion he seeks out the darkness and stillness of the Westminster Pro-Cathedral, where, in a reverie, he sees himself, a suffering Byronic figure, taking refuge in a Trappist monastery, then emerging from it years later as the indefatigable Father Theodore to be reunited with his beloved Margaret in snowy death. The sound of the religious service makes the old aesthetic-religious emotion work in him and he responds gratefully to the church's offer of comfort and refuge. "It was an immense 'Never Mind, my Poor Child' in architecture and carven wood and stone" (p. 336). In a moment, the whole atmosphere takes on ideological implications which sort with his mood and his hurts. He entertains the idea of a religious retreat from the cold, hard spirit of modern life, the spirit of science which had poisoned Margaret against him, made her skeptical of his "devotion, his patriotism and courage and love" by first robbing her of all "mystery and romance." "If science had its way," he thinks there in the darkness, "if Teddy and his father had their way, they would in the end rout out the last refuges of the human spirit, expose the whole world to that desiccating soul-destroying blaze, that scorching questioning, which they called light'' (p. 336). Once again he sees the Broxteds as Inheritors, bent on destroying all the eternal human values. He sees himself, on the other hand, as a modern St. Ignatius:

> The figure of St. Ignatius of Loyola floated into his mind. What a marvellous career that man had made for himself! Ex-soldier like himself, ex-lover like himself, turning his back on the empty gratifications of courage and gallantry, to give himself to a mightier task! In those days too, everything worth while in human life had seemed to be crumbling. Faith failed and society trembled on the brink of dissolution. Everything was questioned. Everyone did what seemed right in his own eyes. The waves of the Reformation beat pitilessly upon the defences of the Church, rising continually like a tide that would never turn. Every day saw new extravagances in religion and new violences. And then one simple resolute man stepped into the breach, arrested the torrent, raised up a bulwark against it and turned it back. Always that story of the Counter-Reformation had appealed to Theodore's imagination. Now it came back to him with irresistible force. He too would be a Loyola. [Pp. 337–38]

The deluded grandeur of the aspiration is altogether fitting. Arising from Theodore's bitter personal disappointment, it once again testifies to Wells's concern in *Bulpington* with the emotional sources of ideology. We recognize, under the stress of Theodore's defeat at the hands of the real world, the return of the antiscientific, loosely religious assertions. Now, however—and this marks a new emphasis—they are explicitly linked, for Theodore, with culturally, politically, and intellectually reactionary impulses. He does not enter the Church and he does not become a modern Loyola. These are momentary whims. But he does, from this time forward, align himself with a number of rather ultramontane tendencies in the postwar world of art.

For ten years following his loss of Margaret, Theodore wanders in wounded Byronic exile through Europe. In Paris he changes his name to Captain Blup-Bulpington and invents a new past for himself: he is now the only surviving scion of an old English Catholic family, a conservative even among Catholics. "He was saturated with ripe, old traditions, a fine and gallant gentleman picking his fastidious way through the bulks and noises of a crude mechanical age. He condemned the times. The vague incalculable onward thrust in things had not, it appeared, rejected him and pushed him aside. On the contrary he had rejected it'' (p. 344). He finds friends who have similarly turned in fear and loathing from the present and who, being too ineffectual to try to impose their reactionary ideas on the world, turn instead toward ''those creative and consolatory universes of unreality to which art, in its endless diversity, offers keys'' (p. 345). Haunted by Materialism, the Delusion of Progress, the Mechanical Spirit, and the new Pragmatic Irrationalism of Science, and seeking the comfort of art, Theodore becomes editor and part owner of a little magazine, *The Feet of the Young Men*, which gives perfect expression to both concerns. Despising the pretensions of science to rationality and lucidity, it is printed entirely without punctuation marks, employing instead gaps of varying length; and all its capital B's and P's are put backside foremost. To mock all the utopians' hopes for a universal language, a kind of basic English for their projected World State, Theodore makes certain to include in every issue a short lyric in Bulgarian, Estonian, Czech, Erse, or a mixture of them all. Occasionally there are five or six pages of universal, symbolic prose using no words at all. Since Theodore is now in open Don Juanian revolt against the restraints and decorums of sex, a good deal of indecency, in both word and picture, is featured as well, although it regularly offends the Catholic divines who contribute brief devotional or briskly controversial papers. Theodore finds it hard to make the churchmen understand ''the deep Reactionary purposes'' of this other material. The overall tone of the magazine is high-spirited and defiant. ''It was,'' says Wells, ''the very latest thing in reaction'' (p. 347). Eventually, however, Theodore comes to feel that the work of *The Feet of the Young Men*, whatever it was, has been accomplished. He sells his half-share—''it was the third half-share he had disposed of altogether, but he was never very good at arithmetic''—and turns his face toward home again. Yet another of the Spink sisters, Belinda, has died, leaving Theodore a lovely little cottage in Devonshire to which he is now disposed to retire.

The last full-scale debate of the novel takes place on Theodore's homeward bound train. He has the bad luck to take up with a young man whom he had seen buying a copy of *The Feet of the Young Men*, but who is actually a disciple of the Broxteds. Teddy, whom Theodore loathes and holds responsible for everything in the modern world that he finds distressing, including Margaret's defection from him, is now a Professor of Social Biology, the youngest Fellow of the Royal Society, and ''all sorts of brilliant things." The news of this is terribly disquieting to Theodore and he argues with intense urgency to preserve his reconstructed world against all the old challenges. After an exchange on the war, which the young man dismisses as folly and confusion and Theodore exalts as the salvation of civilization, the two settle down to the present and the future. Theodore attacks Materialistic Utopianism, cites Soviet Russia and Fordized America as "two gigantic demonstrations of the failure of large-scale modernity," and advances France and Britain as "the two surviving exponents of balanced sanity in a distraught world" (p. 355). The young man proclaims the new revolution in the making, the coming of a "planned world" for which the Russian Five Year Plan is but a preparation. The dispute rages as they move from train to channel boat and on to their London train. When Theodore points to his antagonist's copy of *The Feet of the Young Men* and says that in it there will be found the true voice of the Young, the reply is devastating: "Oh *this* stuff! . . . Rich old women in Paris—middle-aged muck-abouts—art shops—falsetto. *These* aren't the young."

Rallying his forces, Theodore makes an accusation that we have heard him make before in similar circumstances. The archdreamer of the novel accuses his opponent of dreaming, of ignoring "the eternal primary facts of human nature" in contemplating his planned world. When the young man replies that people can be made different by education, Theodore calls this a dream as well, since it ignores all the tendencies and forces pulling the other way. Gathering himself together, Theodore issues one of his most grandiloquent formulations of the problem, a strange mixture of the poignant and the pigheaded which bespeaks Wells's recognition of the intractable other side of things:

> "The really active and vigorous people of the world have quite other ideas than these fancies of yours. This mixture of scientific humanitarianism and Bolshevism you and your Professor affect is just nonsense—forgive me if I speak plainly—nonsense to the normal live-minded man, the man who is by nature soldier, master, ruler. We have other values. It's all too high and thin for us. We believe in pride and domination. We believe in individual devotion to an individual. We believe in the narrower intenser loyalties, in the passionate extravagances of personal love, in kingship, in the strenuous pursuit of war, in the beauty of noble endeavour and high tragedy." [P. 357]

The case for the old order has seldom been put better, but we are conscious, of course, as Theodore makes it, that he has proved quite

incapable of living by such a code himself. The young man, however, does
not know Theodore as we do. He closes the conversation on a touchingly
yielding note, impressed by the time-tested authority of Theodore's words
and by his glimpse of the dreary, unpromising crowds on the streets as the
train passes through the outskirts of London. His is a speech of
extraordinary revolutionary candor, in which, once again, we sense
Wells's refusal to simplify or propagandize along with Wells's desire, as
novelist, to create a plausible honesty in the young man as a dramatic
contrast, at once subtle and vivid, to Theodore's performance:

> "This hope of seeing the world leavened with sound knowledge.
> . . . A world community. . . . It *may* be a dream—thin and high,
> you called it. Oh, probably it *is* a dream. Still—it happens to be the
> dream in which I live. My kind of people—whatever we stand for.
> . . . Don't you think that perhaps . . . after a few more economic
> messes like this present one, and after the revolution that is bound to
> follow, and after another war, and a famine and a pestilence, the
> crowd may come to the realization that our kind of thing is worth
> attention? With us, you know, my sort, Broxted's sort, pegging
> away at it all the time—what was it someone said?—without haste
> and without delay. Telling the truth—incessantly. It won't be over in
> our time. It won't be over when you and I are dead. I believe the
> great revolution, the real human revolution—I'm a poor specimen I
> admit—has begun now *for good*. Defeats won't matter. It's going
> on, you know. We're going on." [Pp. 358–59]

The dialectic between romantic dream in Theodore and revolutionary
dream in the Broxted circle comes to a head here, and we recognize, aided
by the winning frankness and waivering of the young man, that distinctions
can be made. One dream is large, one is small; one is generous, one
selfish; one functional, one useless; one brave, one sniveling. Yet Wells
has not needed to intervene at all in order for us to come to this point. In the
latter half of the speech, the young man's voice comes very close to what
we may conjecture as Wells's view of the inevitability of revolutionary
change, but the total effect of the debate is a standoff. Theodore has spoken
well enough to remain formidable. And the business of the novel, we must
not forget, is to persuade us of just how formidable he is.

Formidable or no, however, Theodore spends a sleepless night in
London rehearsing his conversation with the young man and concluding
that the young man had had the best of their argument. It is a rare moment
of revelation, of self-knowledge for our hero, even if it doesn't last long.
Wells presents it to convey the magnitude of Theodore's perverse task, the

heavy burden of truth that he must subvert or ignore at this historical juncture in order to continue his life on his own terms: "While he was talking and writing of those contemporary movements in art and literature which, in such rare phases of despondent realization as this, he knew to be no more than a confusion of folly, quackery and pretentiousness, were Teddy and his friends, were Margaret and that bully bully of hers, and this young man, and all sorts of people, beastly outsiders of course, but more and more of them, really getting on to something real, getting something prepared, laying a train to blast the road of mankind out of its present perplexities to this new order that they seemed to know so surely was possible, blasting away, among other things, the whole world that Theodore had made for himself?" (pp. 361–62). This prospect is disconcerting enough, but more disconcerting still is Theodore's recognition of the possibility that they are right and he wrong, that their dream is no dream at all but an incipient reality, while his whole life has been a delusion:

> Suppose after all that something was going on in this old world finer than had ever been tried before? Something that had hardly been thought of before? Suppose these people really were more than visionaries; were getting their eyes clear and their minds clear and their purposes clear? Suppose they were *right*! Suppose that at last the world's "awakening" was at hand? Suppose a mighty page was turning over—now!
> He lay helpless, unable to make head against these disconcerting suppositions. Had he taken the wrong way with life, or at least had he failed to find the right one? Had he—was it possible—had he made a mess of his life? For some searing moments he saw himself bare. [P. 362]

It is indeed a searing moment for Theodore and a time of cumulative assessment for the reader. Like all novels, *Bulpington* is centrally occupied with the relation of its characters to reality—to the reality, that is, that Wells defines as reality. As readers we must assess both Theodore's failure to come to grips with the actual circumstances of his time and Wells's success in persuading us that they are the actual circumstances. Wells's delineation of Theodore's shrinking from actualities is clear enough when it occurs on the level of personal action, like Theodore's quite unmistakable cowardice and desertion during the war and his subsequent falsification of it. But the level of ideas is more problematic. In order to see Theodore precisely as Wells does, it is probably necessary for the reader to be more sympathetic to the revolutionary young man's hopes and

anticipations of a new world a-coming—and the Broxteds' as well—than
the reader might be disposed to be. Yet, because it is a novel, and a very
artful one, we need not see Theodore precisely as Wells does. It is quite
enough for us to feel not that the young man and his friends are right, but
that for one terrible moment Theodore feels that they are. By the same
token, it is enough for us to feel not that Theodore is wrong about
everything, but that he represents real impulses abroad in the world. The
reality of the novel itself is that both attitudes exist and have consequences
which the novel traces.

In any case, we know that it is not like Theodore to see himself "bare"
for long. His fantasizing powers soon reclaim him. He imagines a scene in
which he wins Margaret back by dint of sheer bold eloquence, disposes of
her fiancé, and then, in a truly dazzling ideological maneuver, triumphs by
acceding to the truths that his enemies subscribe to and becoming their
leader. It is one of his canniest Bulpingtonian dream visions: "And then
with Margaret indissolubly his, he would face facts, adopt the proper
Inheritor attitudes, join their ranks and work with a steadfast grim
persistence. Presently become of dominating importance among them, the
Inheritors' Mirabeau . . . ." It is a splendid, daring escape from the
problem, and the next morning he is quite at peace with himself once
again, without a trace of concession or compromise.

The last part of *Bulpington* traces Theodore's consolidation of this
peace. He achieves it with a sweeping intensity and finality that is to
madness near allied. On his way down to his new cottage in Devonshire he
reads a witty little booklet by T. S. Eliot on the Lambeth Conference and
finds it "impossible to resist Eliot's implication that all's well with the
Anglican world." Having arrived and discovered his new home to be all
that a cottage in Devonshire should be, he begins to dream, in this
benevolent atmosphere, of changing over to the attack in his war on
modernity, of enunciating positive ideals instead of merely parrying the
Broxted circle. He entertains a vision of creating a New Historical
Romance which "would do for the nineteenth century what Sir Walter
Scott had done for the eighteenth," which is to say, he would inaugurate a
second romantic movement and make possible a great cultural
recuperation, just as "Scott and Byron had rallied the latent aristocrat in
every man and so burked the worst possibilities of revolutionary discontent
that followed the Napoleonic wars" (p. 368). But it would be even a larger
canvas than the Waverley scene, quite Elizabethan in its breadth. Its

knights and explorers would be the Empire-builders, its goddess, Queen Victoria, its King Arthur, the Prince Consort; and Melbourne, Palmerston, Gladstone, Disraeli, Cecil Rhodes, and General Gordon would all be secretly in love with their queen. The arts, of course, would lend their sanction and color: "Edward VII might be another Prince Hal and here would come in glimpses of the night-side of London in the nineties with Beerbohm Tree, say, as Falstaff, and Oscar Wilde, Arthur Roberts, Frank Harris, George Moore and so forth, a brilliant rabble, in his train." Theodore's vision has all the large promise of his father's projected work on the Varangians.

The only discord in his happy contemplation of the great work before him is a reproduction of the Delphic Sibyl that hangs on the wall of the dining room and reminds him unbearably of Margaret. His feeling for the Sibyl has changed dramatically with his final rejection by Margaret. As she looks toward the future with her presumably secret knowledge, she now strikes Theodore as knowing nothing. "Just a simple-minded peasant girl," he tells his housekeeper. "Looking for something to turn up. Because you see as yet there *is* no Future. It is nothing. It hasn't arrived. It is all a bluff about our inheriting the future. Don't you think she *has* an empty face?" (p. 372). Ensconced in his country retreat, dreaming of his New Historical Romance, Theodore has disowned any future which is not limited to merely recapturing the past. He has come to terms with the world by shutting the world out completely.

His last encounter with people in the novel comes when his new neighbors, Miss Watkins, a retired schoolteacher, and Miss Felicia Keeble, "essentially a poetess," invite him to dinner. All debate and dialogue has now disappeared from the novel because Theodore has fled from it, and we are left with the half-demented, thoroughly self-intoxicated, rather pathetic monologue which the hospitable ladies elicit from him with good food, far, far too much good drink, and naive adoration for the heir of all the Spinks, who has returned a wounded hero from the wars. In the hallucinatory egoism of Theodore's talk on this occasion, Wells brings to fruition all the disastrous implications of a lifetime of flinching, shirking, fleeing, and dreaming on the great preserve of the arts. Here Theodore comes most fully, most repulsively, into his own.

After several martinis, and at least three vodkas with his caviar, Theodore offers the ladies, at their request, advice on their investments, a matter about which he knows nothing. He counsels them to leave their money where it is. "Recovery," he says, "is simply a question of time. I happen to know." This last is a phrase that rings egomaniacally through the whole evening.

After turtle soup and *Petites Bouchées à la Reine* comes an excellent bottle of Liebfraumilch. Wells makes superb use of the elegant succession of courses and spirits to render Theodore's discourse hateful, for the voice proceeds from a mouth perpetually filled with the most elemental forms of privilege and luxury, *haute cuisine* and plentiful, choice liquor. The voice is next heard defending the government's economic policy: "The King was in a difficult position. I happen to know." When the lamb arrives along with a splendid Chambertin, however, Theodore's utterance really takes flight. He tells the fascinated ladies how a mere handful of men and a mere nine guns, in a truly Homeric rear-guard action, saved Amiens from the German breakthrough, from an advance by the entire German army, in the spring of 1918. He happens to know—it was never reported anywhere— because he was there. And when, the epic struggle concluded, he ordered his men to leave the danger area so that he might fire the dump, he tells how they refused: " 'Would you believe me,' he said and suddenly there were manly tears in his eyes; 'not one of those fellows would leave me. Not one. Ah!' " (p. 389). It is an extraordinary inversion of his own flight from his men under bombardment, and the emotion has a strange pathological appropriateness. The ladies are hushed with adulation. They pass the chicken to their heroic guest. "He chose a wing," says Wells, "with sacramental concentration." But the end of the tale is better still. With all the instinct of a mad failed artist, and an artist who is shrewd enough to quote from Yeats, Theodore concludes:

> "But the dreadfulness of war! And the beauty! The terrible beauty! Dawn. . . . And then— Out of nowhere comes a young blood of an officer clean and smart. And he said these words—I vouch for it—he said, 'What are you stragglers doing here?' *You stragglers!*"
> "The idiot!" said Felicia, deeply moved. "The young *FOOL!*"
> " 'Some of us are waiting for stretchers,' I said, 'and some of us are waiting to be buried. And there's a lot of Germans here you'll have to bury too. We were holding them up, you see, until you had had your bath.' And that was *that.* But you see, dear ladies, how it is that some of the best war stories do not appear in the official histories. Reality is one thing and history is another. [P. 390]

Certainly Theodore's reality is another thing from history. But the best is yet to come. After some of his Aunt Belinda's port, Theodore pays tribute to the System of Values enshrined in Christianity—the Family, the Community, the Nation, the Monarch, the Church, the Faith—which alone holds mankind together, and to which alone we owe "all the decencies of life, loyalty, honesty, solvency, stability; everything that rose in the mind when one said Civilization" (p. 392). Opposed to this, he says, is the great Antagonism, the Darkness of Persian theology: the heretic, the infidel, secret societies, the Black Mass, the Rosicrucians, the Templars, the Free Masons, the great outbreaks of unbelief and dissent, schisms, insurrections, "and so on down to Socialism, Bolshevism, Anarchism, Infidelity." The word Inheritors falls from his lips, but he abandons it, realizing his listeners could not understand its special meaning.

Moving with their visitor to the hall parlor for Old Brandy and Egyptian cigarettes, the two ladies are visited by a sense of their blessed exemption from all this horror: "There they were, they realized, deeply and snugly embedded in the fundamental human values. . . . Yet all the same, there was a thrill in thinking of those prowling forces of the outer world, those machinations, Bolshevisms, rapes, murders, haggard discontents and giant dark threats, so remote, so held off them, and yet so actual and powerful" (p. 395). Elaborating the actuality and power of these forces, Theodore unveils some of his private Broxted resentments: "Fanatics. . . . The riddle of fanaticism. Types! The wild-eyed visionary. The stubborn radical. The pretence of scientific thoroughness. Some, purely malignant. Anarchists. Enemies of society outright. Destroy! *Our* sort, they say. A great anti-religious organization, secret, dark, unseen, holds them together. There are souls—it is dreadful to admit it—who are really and inherently hostile to human things. A Great Conspiracy. Anti-Christian. Anti-human." For a moment the fire in the hearth suggests to Theodore the face of the young man on the train, and then a ruddy glow suggests that "Teddy Broxted was burning to say something." "Well," thinks Theodore triumphantly, "he couldn't." Gone forever are the days of dialogue. Now for Theodore there are only the voices alive to the Great Conspiracy. He commends Nesta Webster, the authoress of *World Revolution: The Plot Against Civilization* (1921), *Secret Societies and Subversive Movements* (1924), and *The Socialist Network* (1926), to his rapt listeners as "a great invigilator." And T. S. Eliot:

"You should read T.S. Eliot. One of the Master Minds of our age. A great influence. Restrained, fastidious, and yet a Leader. The Young adore him. He has taken over the message of Nesta. Made it acceptable. Dignified it. He has put the choice before the world, plainly and simply.''

For a while he dwelt on the merits of T. S. Eliot. ''Anglican Monarchist,'' he mused. ''Never has any man fought so nobly against his birth taint.''

''You don't mean he is—well—*ill?*'' asked Miss Watkins, haltingly but eagerly.

Nothing of *that* sort, no. But he was born in America. His grandfather was a Light of Bostonian Liberalism. That faded dream of Progress! How splendidly he is living it down!'' [P. 396]

The comedy, delicious as it is, does not obscure the portentousness of Theodore's artistic and intellectual alliances. Where his aestheticism was once merely a refuge from unpleasantness, it has now become an active principle of what Wells takes to be social and political ill-will. Theodore's sympathies are all with the antidemocratic impulse of writers like Eliot, T. E. Hulme, Pound, Wyndham Lewis, and Yeats.

Musing on kingship, which the modern world has forgotten ''admidst its noise and vulgarity and competition and sordid self-indulgence,'' Theodore offers the ladies his final, his most incredible fantasia of the evening. It is a story about the Kaiser, the ''most misunderstood of men,'' a ''Mystic,'' a ''man with a real sense of his God on the one hand and of mankind on the other.'' Theodore happens to know that the Kaiser did not want war, that it was forced upon him, that the Kaiser said, ''I had to draw the sword, don the shining armour, strike my blow. But beneath that armour I was a Prince of Peace. All the time, most desperately, even before 1914 was out, I was seeking Peace, seeking to save the Old System and the world'' (p. 398). Theodore happens to know, he tells his hosts, because for forty-four hours the Kaiser was his prisoner. At the very end of the war during the German collapse, the Kaiser and his party, having run out of petrol, were taken into custody by Theodore's men. Theodore recounts the consternation of his superiors all the way up to the War Office, with which he was in touch by telephone, about what to do with their transcendent prisoner. Finally, he says, he was asked what he would suggest.

''And so it came about that the Kaiser was taken as a prisoner to the Dutch frontier by a party of English troops. We saw him safe through. . . . We took him by side tracks out of the hullabaloo to the quiet little frontier post. Never mind where. He stood for a moment looking back. There were tears on his worn and sunken cheeks. Few of us were unmoved. 'The ways of Our God are not our

ways,' he said. 'When I parted from Bismarck, Captain Blup-
Bulpington, I thought I had done with blood and iron. Let me face
the facts. I have been betrayed. I have failed. This is the end. And I
had hoped to die not a War Lord but the Peace Lord of the World!' ''

The Captain added one pensive touch. ''He wanted to give me a
decoration he was wearing, one of those jewelled affairs. I would not
have it. 'You have given me something much more precious than
that, Sire,' I said. 'You have given me a Great Memory.'

''We shook hands at last—very simply—and he walked across to
the Dutch sentinel. Saluted. Stood erect.'' [Pp. 401–2]

Theodore's whole life has been steering him toward this unconscionable
fantasy. The vast quantities of alcohol that he has consumed during the
evening explain, perhaps, his willingness to give it voice, but not his
power to conceive it. That power was born with his very first daydreams
and the aestheticism at Blayport that nurtured them. The novel now ends
with his reaffirmation of the total lie that his life has since become.

On his way home, out among the stars, Theodore is sufficiently aware of
his conduct of the evening to accuse himself of having become a liar, the
''sort of liar who isn't even believed,'' and of having misspent his whole
life. Here Wells recalls the Wordsworthian ecstasy that Theodore had
experienced at the beginning of the novel. The moment is ripe for such
ultimate spiritual review, for Theodore is both arraigning the universe and
being arraigned by it:

> The universe became a single silent presence. It became one
> simple interrogation. Long ago he had had that same sense of a
> presence. But then he had felt one with it and deeply identified and
> sustained. Now he was outside it, confronting it in the dock. It
> penetrated him and searched him indeed, but it left him unassim-
> ilated. He felt called upon for his defence. [P. 405]

His first line of defense takes him back at least as far as Pilate. Since the
truth is unknowable—''What is truth?'' he says, quoting very accurately
indeed—everything is a lie, including science, for all its pretensions.
Religion and history, too, are lies. ''But *working* lies! Mark that!'' says
Theodore. ''Lies that have worked, lies that have held lives together. Lies
that have made men heroes. Lies that have comforted the dying. Lies like
the whispering of angels in the ear of despair. Grand lies I tell you,
Grand.'' Man is the one animal that ''can make a falsehood and keep off
the beasts of despair.'' No man can look at himself stark and plain—not
even Teddy. Theodore's next line of defense is the admission that he is a
lie, a ''liar in a world of lies.'' But he catches himself: not a world of lies,

but a world of dreams, a "world we've made to hide from you
in"—"you" being God, the universe, reality, the silent presence that he
confronts in this eerie arraignment which is at once monologue and implied
dialogue. For everyone, then, it is a world of self-delusion, but most
people do not ever find that out. Theodore, however, happens to know, and
that makes all the difference:

> "And because I know it, I shape my life as I like, past and future,
> just as I please. What wasn't true is true now. See? I *make* it true. I
> enlisted by a trick when the doctors had rejected me. Yes, I did, I tell
> you. I led that rally before Amiens. I—your humble servant. I took
> the Kaiser prisoner. I talked to him for hours. And so forth and so
> on. If I wish it, it has to be so." [P. 408]

And with grand defiance he asks the universe, "Who will object? *You*?"
For a moment he wonders almost pleadingly, "What *are* you?" but
recovers in a thrice with the realization that it doesn't matter, really.
"You're too rigid; you're too hidebound to prevent me. . . . I dismiss
you here and now." Trying out a few formulations that prove biblically
inappropriate—"I am what I am," "I am *that* I am"—he comes to his
crowning affirmation: "No—not what I am, that's *your* affair, perhaps.
No, I am what I choose to be." Now, having reached the very pinnacle of
romantic solipsism, just as he is about to secure his vast kingdom of the
self, he finds himself, fittingly enough, alone:

> He was about to speak again. He was about to declare that his Will
> had triumphed over Reality, that there he was at last, the Captain of
> his Soul, the Master of his Fate, and then abruptly he became aware
> that he was talking to nothing, to nothing whatever. [P. 409]

Or talking, in this final phase—it comes to the same thing—to himself.
   Returning to his cottage, he removes the Delphic Sibyl from the wall.
Viewing its expression of gentle wonder and slight surprise as a sneer
directed at him—" 'Always,' he said, 'you stick that Query of yours into
everything I say or do' "—he tries to cram it into a drawer. When this fails
he becomes violent, dashes the picture to the floor, and stamps it with his
boot. On the verge of sobbing, he pours himself a stiff whisky and grows
calmer. " 'That's *that*,' he said at last." Once again, he consolidates the
idea of himself as a good soldier, as the thing that he chooses to be: "He
had made an end to weakness and sentimentality. He had established his
own world. There he was, a military man, rigid, disciplined, limited if you
like—if you choose to consider honour, courage, service, limitations—but
himself. Brave, to the marrow. Master of his Fate, and above all supreme

master of his past" (p. 412). After another whisky, he banishes all the
nagging impedimenta of his life—the Sibylline Margaret, scientists,
reformers, utopians, revolutionaries—and proclaims his culminating
phantasmagoric faith:

> Those Inheritors! What a dream it was! What a flimsy sham! As
> the world had been, so always would it be. Let them dither about
> their New World. Brave strong men (more whisky) would hold to the
> ancient values. Peace indeed! Unity indeed! Read the newspapers!
> Uncertainties. Convulsions. Disasters. But against it all—*Romance*.
> Endless Romance. So life had been; so life would be. To the end.
> Bravery. The call for manhood.
> "Adsum," he said aloud. "Adsum."
> The grand old human story!
> He lifted his third whisky. "To our next war, mon général!" He
> drank solemnly. [P. 412]

With a final whisky, accompanied by a bold "Skald!" that puts Theodore
in mind of his father's dear Varangian Guards—"Hefty lads with a
bottle"—followed by a meditation on the blessed powers of alcohol,
which shuts out "all those limitless outer alien worlds that engender
distresses for the soul," Theodore is off to bed. Receiving the salute of the
grandfather clock on the landing—"the very symbol of unquestioning
discipline and duty"—Theodore reflects on what a fine, satisfying evening
it has been. Thoroughly at peace, thoroughly vindicated, he moves forever
past us, through the ironic exultation of the last line of the novel, into
romantic eternity:

All his values sang together within him. [P. 414]

In *Bulpington*, then, Wells has devised an intriguing form—the
anti-*Bildungsroman*. Instead of growing from an inadequate subjectivity to
a mature consciousness of the objective world and his own place in it, the
putative hero reverses the process, progressively embracing and inventing
illusions, more and more determinedly resisting alternatives and voices
that clash with his own. The reason, Wells keeps insisting, is not in
Theodore's stars but in the arts, or in such special and dubious forms of the
arts as *fin de siècle* aestheticism, escapist romanticism, and the reactionary
poetics of the twenties. The range and depth of the indictment is
disconcerting. It is one thing for us to consent to the presence of moral or
social irresponsibility in the art of Oscar Wilde, since he was himself quite
deliberate about putting it there, or to agree with Wells that on the whole it
is better to face life than to run away from it. But it is quite another thing to

find Theodore mouthing approximations of such twentieth-century articles of aesthetic faith as Conrad's belief in saving illusions, or Yeats's commendation of war as a glorious and, in any case, perpetually inevitable enterprise. For what *Bulpington* does is to take such assumptions of modern romanticism and set them in a context of personality and events which renders them heinous. It is at this point that Wells makes us wonder, as he does so often in his quarrel with James, if he has not, indeed, hit upon some rudimentary human flaw in the modern artistic sensibility which leads it into strange postures and admirations. One may balk at *Bulpington*'s intimation that since an unreality principle governs romantic art, romantic art is largely responsible for sanctioning the lie of World War I, as it will be largely responsible for sanctioning the lie, or the madness, of World Wars II and III; but one balks slowly and thoughtfully. For the book makes its case with persuasive, patient, cumulative power, and that case is authenticated by an adroit, unstated psychology: the sound compensatory link between Theodore's heroic dream and his utter heroic incapacity.

Theodore the antihero, the solipsist and egoist, is the first of a series of extensive portraits in these last novels of precisely what in human personality Wells sees as impeding the coming of a new order. Although he had achieved fame through his power to envision the future, by the time Wells reached his late sixties he had come to a very full recognition indeed of the stubborn, unyielding elements in human nature that stood in the path of any future he could still imagine. The burden of these novels, their common theme, is not Wells's affirmation of a new, and rational, and just world order but, regrettably enough, his sense of the difficulty, the improbability of ever securing it. The self-absorption and egoism of such grown-up spoiled children as Roland Palace of *Brynhild*, Dolores of *Apropos of Dolores*, and Edward Albert Tewler of *You Can't Be Too Careful* constitute Wells's imaginative admission of utopian improbability, his tribute to the present, to the maddeningly uncooperative, refractory denizens of the real world. Not all of them are, like Theodore, abetted by the arts—though Palace is—but all of them share Theodore's strange, formidable, selfish impulsion. And in each case, it is an impulsion that Wells is forced to meet, as he is forced to meet it in *Bulpington*, with one degree or another of satire, often, again as in *Bulpington*, rather a fierce degree of satire.

The satirical novel—the novel which is genuinely a novel and genuinely satirical—is a difficult form to sustain. The mimetic and empathic tendencies of fiction do not usually sort well with the admonitory, repelling function of satire. The one draws us in, the other pushes us away. Wells's solution is sometimes to divide the novel between clearly sympathetic and clearly repugnant figures, as we shall see him doing in *Brynhild*. In *Bulpington*, however, he sets himself a more difficult problem, that of centering everything in a figure—Theodore—who is at once protagonist and chief object of satire. That such a negative procedure works, that such a satirical rogue can sustain a great fiction, we have the example of George Meredith's *The Egoist* to attest. Both Meredith and Wells bring it off by employing a brilliantly poised style, capable at once of malevolent exposure and irresistible evocation. The prose of their novels allows Sir Willoughby and Theodore to live vividly, plausibly for us in the mad fullness of their conceit, even as it insinuates, excoriates, and shatters the madness. Wells's style in *Bulpington* is thus equal to creating Theodore before it destroys him, or, to state it in terms of the paradoxical intention of the satirical novel, the style is equal to creating Theodore in order to destroy him. The novel at large ordinarily knows only creation, and satire only destruction.

Such prose and such a mode of delineation, such fullness of knowledge and such restraint in its deployment, suggest a patience and balance in Wells that is remarkable, for it is the patience and balance that we ask of the arts and of artists, even in their anger and frenzy, in order that they may beget a temperance that gives their work smoothness. Wells was never more an artist, in this sense, than he is in *The Bulpington of Blup*. This novel represents the extraordinary willingness of an essentially· visionary writer, whose impatience with James's inexhaustible interest in the unredeemed life is well known to us, to body forth with tireless delicacy, empathy, and fullness the workings of a temperament that he loathes—a temperament that not only is incapable of Wellsian redemption but that goes a long way toward defining the flaw in the vision itself. Wells had been over some of this ground before, but his earlier fictional roadblocks in the march of civilization—Ponderevo, Mr. Polly, or Kipps—were comic, endearing fools. After World War I and the failures of Versailles, however, the novelist was no longer amused. In these novels of the last phase he set out, with deadly satirical earnestness, though not without bitter laughter, to hold the mirror, steady and whole, up to egoism.

There is nothing quite like *Bulpington* in the fiction of this century. Aldous Huxley and Evelyn Waugh come closest to it, but there is too much obvious, pure virulence in *Crome Yellow*, *Antic Hay*, and *Point Counter Point*, too little of the extraordinary remorseful verity that Wells achieves;

and the heroes of *Decline and Fall, Vile Bodies*, and *A Handful of Dust* are likeable simpletons in a mad world, with none of the intimidating power and responsibility of Theodore. The black comedians of our own era characteristically offer a more general, scattered indictment of things as they are, forgoing the concentration of *Bulpington*, as they forego, as well, its essential rationality.

There is only one *Bulpington of Blup*, and one hopes that it will come to notice in this age that has not yet outlived—nor ever will, if we accept the book's premises—its concerns. For an illustration of how Wells himself, however, could employ his artistry very differently, and quite surprisingly, in treating the aesthetic temper, we may turn next to *Brynhild*.

CHAPTER III

Brynhild

Brynhild (1937) REPRESENTS a startling departure from the critical positions that Wells had maintained for almost forty years in his battle with Henry James. It is, within the framework of that battle, a Jamesian novel, or at least the most Jamesian of Wells's novels. Perhaps the five-year hiatus between it and Wells's last full-length work of fiction, *The Bulpington of Blup*, in which he had vented his distaste for an aestheticism that James always partly embodied for him, disposed Wells to feel that he should now, if he was to return to novel-writing at all, put the more strictly imaginative side of his talent to a test, if only to see what was in it, what he had all along been denying, and what he might hope to find or convey in the novel as James understood the form. The deepening interest in character that he confessed in the *Autobiography* must have made the occasion, since he had already moved significantly in this direction with the fashioning of Theodore Bulpington, seem all the more propitious. So too, no doubt, did his last major love affair, beginning a few years earlier when he was in his mid-sixties with the woman upon whom Brynhild, his heroine, is modeled.[1]

In any case, there are numerous accommodations to James's procedures. The time scheme, for one, is not that of the characteristic Wellsian chronicle, which took the hero, and would again take him in novels that followed, from birth to some catastrophic middle of the journey of his life. Instead, we have a Jamesian dramatic transaction, centered on a single major action and requiring less than a year of narrative time. In the "Envoy" with which Wells concludes *Brynhild*, he expressly indicates that any typically Victorian interest in the ultimate fates of all the characters is quite out of place in this work, even if he does manage to provide some indications sub rosa.

In place of the life of the protagonist as the essential organizing principle, there is a Jamesian principle of theme, or subject: *Brynhild* is a novel about contrived appearances, façades, masks, pretensions and their relation to reality and integrity. Hence, not the squeezed orange of life-likeness, but a pattern of meaning lies at the center of the book, and Wells's consciousness of the shift—his pride in it too—is discernible in the same "Envoy." With uncharacteristic owlishness and aesthetic pretension he writes, "In New Zealand, as Mrs. Ettie Hornibrook showed so ably and interestingly in her *Maori Symbolism*, the decorations on a beam or a pillar may be expanded by an understanding imagination into the most complete and interesting of patterns, and so it is with this book. It is a novel in the Maori style, a presentation of imaginative indications."[2] Whether the claim is serious or playful, it points faithfully enough to Wells's unprecedented concern with imagination, patterning, and completeness in the work. For the theme of appearances, which is first announced in the subtitle of the novel, *The Show of Things*, is reinforced by symbolic charades, pageants, and Miltonic allusion, by a tight plot structure which creates thematic connections and recurrences, and by motifs linked through reflection, diction, and metaphor. Everywhere Wells seems intent on allowing art to make the life of the book.

More specifically Jamesian still is the relative absence of general ideas in *Brynhild*. There is hardly a single pressing problem connected with the survival of civilization in it; Wells seems remarkably content to portray the world instead of wishing to change it. He works within the framework of personal life and personal relations and is concerned more with the feelings that ideas evoke than ideas themselves, insofar as the two are separable. Such large ideas as do enter are always dramatically functional, serving to reveal the character and motives of the speaker advancing them. This is feasible because authorial intrusion is held to a minimum and almost everything is seen, thought, and felt through the characters. The point of view is technically omniscient, yet Wells chooses to limit himself largely to his characters' assessments of things, employing Brynhild most extensively as the observing consciousness. We recognize here the method of as late a James novel as *The Wings of the Dove*, for the master did not always use only the one central consciousness that he commended. The high point of this technique in *Brynhild* comes in the long ninth chapter, which is almost entirely given over to the heroine's meditation on her husband, her marriage, her delusions about both, and her speculations about the future. It is formally and functionally reminiscent of the famous vigil scene in *The Portrait of a Lady*, although it has none of the climactic intensity of Isabel Archer's recognitions. Like both the *Portrait* and *The Golden Bowl*, *Brynhild* is one of the rare instances, before our own vexed era, of a novel devoted more to the anguishes of marriage than to those of courtship.

The commitment to character, especially Brynhild's, as a focal interest is thus very strong and puts us in mind of Wells's declaration in the *Autobiography* that exhaustive character study is an adult and philosophical occupation. It is true that Wells had always exaggerated characterization as an end in James, who actually abided throughout his career by the rhetorical questions he asked in "The Art of Fiction": "What is character but the determination of incident? What is incident but the illustration of character?" However, the balance that James achieved, where character becomes a constituent, along with incident, of a larger design, is precisely the balance that Wells achieves in *Brynhild*, even though a new psychological astuteness, a new sensitivity to emotional disposition and interaction, is present.

That larger design in *Brynhild* is elaborated on a field of egotism, another Jamesian preoccupation. Like Dr. Sloper of *Washington Square*, Gilbert Osmond of *The Portrait of a Lady*, and John Marcher of "The Beast in the Jungle," Rowland Palace, Brynhild's husband, is obsessed with himself, a writer who sees the whole world largely as an instrument of his own well-being and distinction. It is he who after suffering an imaginary embarrassment seeks to put appearances at the service of egotism by means of that peculiarly modern instrument, public relations. Here again Wells, who had himself been one of the greatest journalists of his time, utilizes an unmistakably Jamesian horror and loathing of publicity and newspapers, the violators of privacy, decorum, integrity, sanctity, and all value, as a major element of his "subject."[3] And with a quite Jamesian delicacy, he delineates for us not only the vulgarity of the newspapers, but the vulgarity that tempts the elegant Rowland Palace into making use of them in behalf of his own egotism. In Brynhild Palace he also provides us with a figure of Jamesian sensitivity and refinement, equal to Jamesian reaches of perception, through whom to measure the tawdriness of her husband's endeavor.[4]

Palace himself fairly seethes with refinement, but it is for Wells the specious, hypocritical refinement of the aesthete, one of the more reprehensible guises of vanity. The link between aestheticism and sterile pride, though Wells associates it with James, notably in *The Bulpington of*

Blup, is not so much a personal as a categorical observation. He never accused James of personal vanity—it would have been thoroughly unjust to do so—but of futility, misguidedness, lack of proportion, the hippopotamus retrieving the pea. James himself was, of course, immensely sensitive to the dangers of aestheticism, as the cold egoism of Osmond and the Wildean frivolity of Gabriel Nash in *The Tragic Muse* amply testify. In a sense, Wells finds Palace guilty of standard Jamesian crimes—of insufficient awareness, of a presumptuous skepticism and irony that invite Wells to treat Palace with a larger, more conscious, and more just irony, which Brynhild, in turn, is privy to. The matter is complicated—again, newly complicated—by a mingling of Wellsian as well as Jamesian features in Palace's situation. Like Wells in the thirties—and like James through most of his career—Rowland Palace has a smaller public for his novels than he could wish, is being displaced by rising young novelists, and has not been offered the Nobel Prize. Yet he is treated with very little sympathy and with no significant psychic or emotional identification by Wells, who has learned in these late novels to create mixed figures. These may share situations, impulses, even ideas with him, yet not necessarily serve as spokesmen and surrogates. They are instead firmly placed and scrupulously judged. Indeed, Wells fashions for his presentation of Palace an ironic narrative voice which establishes a distance between character and novelist that almost no similarities could bridge. James had utilized the same ironic perspective in the narrative style of *The Bostonians*, though oddly enough, with less consistency, at least in connection with Miss Birdseye, who moves irresistibly through the course of the novel from some comic Coventry into the very center of her creator's heart, and with Basil Ransom as well, who stands in an ironic half-light of repudiation and approval.

The question of impersonality is further complicated by the presence of the most Wellsian figure in the book, the one character who could not be a part of James's world and is more or less charged with keeping things recognizably in Wells's, Alfred Bunter. Like young Wells he is a lower middle-class writer who has come to literary London from the provinces at the beginning of a most promising career, full of ideas—he does indeed have some—and of passions and aspirations. Like Wells, he remains an outsider even as he is fashionably taken up by the best circles, and he is eventually undone by aesthetic vanity and ill-will. At the same time, Wells's identification with him is actually rather limited: Bunter is a Welshman living under an assumed name and, it turns out, under suspicion of having murdered his brother-in-law. In fact, Bunter's wife, Freda, who figures minimally but brilliantly in the novel, is not the only thing about him that suggests D. H. Lawrence. Bunter represents, then, like Palace, a mixture of things. Nonetheless, through Bunter Wells manages to intrude some of his own characteristic reality, not of ideas only, but of class and career, upon the Jamesian one. Much of the charm of the book resides in this impingement of worlds, the exploration of what, for Wells, had hitherto been, with the somewhat different exception of *Bulpington*, the other side of the wall. This rich union of Jamesian and Wellsian possibilities, with a resulting modification of each, produced one of the best things Wells achieved in his last years.

The thematic substance of the novel, which Wells was at pains to secure on this occasion, is drawn from his four central figures and then elaborated and modulated around them. As they first appear these figures are paired socially and culturally. Rowland and Brynhild Palace, husband and wife, belong to the upper world of taste and refinement, while Immanuel Cloote, the public relations man who takes charge of Palace's affairs, and Alfred Bunter, the rival poet, come from below, bearing an odor of disreputability with them. Yet almost at once in Palace's case we are made to recognize anomalies.

Though an eminent writer with an aesthetically enviable reputation, at the book's beginning he is discovered fretting at three in the morning over some photographs taken of him in bardic costume—scarlet robe, gold fillet, and bay leaves—at a May Day festival and published around the world. Against his better judgment, certainly against his wife's as he discerned it in a fleeting glimpse, he had allowed himself to be seduced into dressing up and awarding some literary prizes by a most Jamesian invitation:

> "A bard, a soothsayer," cried the vicar. "Merlin almost. You come, *cher maître*, apt to our occasion." [P. 7][5]

Palace frets because he feels that the photographs make him appear undignified, ridiculous. "The scarlet robe wasn't a bit splendid. It was just a big dark robe obviously much too big for him and making him look stumpy—stumpy was the only word for it. The fillet of gold was askew, if ever it had been straight; it came down over his forehead and rested over one eyebrow. The bay leaves were crooked too; they gave him dark pointed ears. His genial expression was dreadfully overdone. (That perhaps was his own fault.) The harp got in edgeways—obviously pasteboard. He looked like one of the less respectable and less expensively dressed boon companions of the Emperor Nero'' (pp. 9–10). In Palace's finicky, excessive distress Wells gives us the anomolous side of his protagonist's participation in a world pretending to grace, ease, and light. He is, in fact, beset by egotism, insecurity, and irritability: ''Like so many men who make their way to positions of importance in the world of thought and letters, Mr. Rowland Palace was a man of acute sensibilities and incessant anxieties. . . . His conception of himself was of a reserved, slenderish figure, delicate but opaque, observant, amused, kindly but enigmatical. His bearing, like his work, was pervaded by a gentle irony. (But Mrs. Palace knew better.) He carried his faintly smiling face a little on one side. Few of his intimates suspected his phases of irritation and neurasthenia'' (pp. 2–3).

These passages serve to convey Palace's instinctive devotion to appearances. His concern over looking stumpy, over the dreadfully overdone genial expression, the obviously pasteboard harp, together with his mask of reserve, kindliness, and gentle irony calculated to disguise the irritation and neurasthenia within, gives us in short compass—Wells is working with great economy here at the outset—the disparity between what Palace is and what he would like to appear to be that governs his life. In addition, the May Day incident that gives rise to Palace's distress is a rich emblem of the permutations of the motif of appearance that lie ahead in the novel. Although he feels his bardic costume has gone tragically awry and misrepresented him, Palace was at least in donning it pretending to be what he actually is, a writer of some distinction. Yet even what he actually is turns out at the next moment to be elusive, a kind of appearance within to match the appearances without: ''His intellectual pose was to acquiesce in everything and believe in nothing. His dexterous depreciation could be turned left or right or where you would. He undermined and destroyed with a polished civility. His style was a witty style. This endeared him to youth, full of youth's natural suspicion that it is being dreadfully put upon and not quite clear how and why. He believed nothing; he clung to nothing. No trustful infantism for him, he intimated. They envied that tremendously ripe grown-up attitude of his beyond measure'' (pp. 3–4). As a result of this near nihilism, he gains a reputation as a liberator and comes to accept the role with characteristically meaningless, irresponsible, futile urbanity: ''But there was nothing anarchic or revolutionary about the liberation he purveyed; it was the liberation of a man of the world. It left you free to do anything—or nothing" (p. 4).

Brynhild, on the other hand, possesses the integrity and candidness that sorts with her station. Beautiful, quiet, and wise, she is the daughter of a country rector, a fine classicist who "had not so much educated her as made up his old classical clothing for her mind to wear. It fitted very loosely but it kept her out of contact with vulgar ideas" (p. 36). Her upbringing has made her a gracious antithesis of her husband, for her father had done his utmost to impress upon her "that though sin was highly reprehensible, meanness and mental disingenuousness were far more hateful to both God and man. One was in the world, of course, but that was no reason why one should mix oneself up with it in an indiscriminating way" (p. 36). Much later in the novel, the point is made even more explicitly and forcefully as Brynhild recalls words of her father that she had long ago committed to memory:

> "The one precious thing in life, my dear, is integrity—an inner integrity. The hard, clean, clear jewel, the essential soul. No matter where it takes you. . . . What I pray more and more frequently nowadays, Bryn, is this: May the Almighty damn and destroy me utterly and for ever, if I compromise in one particle when I am thinking in my own private thoughts. You think that over. You remember that. That's what I want to get over to you, my dear, somehow." [Pp. 179–80]

Consequently, though she is sympathetic with Palace in his distress over the photographs, she cannot quite agree with his estimate of the situation or the remedy that he eventually proposes. At three in the morning—the chapter is ironically called "Nocturne"—she patiently suggests that his concern is exaggerated, that writers are after all to be known by what they are and what they write. Palace, however, will have none of it and begins instead to elaborate a theory of the indispensability of façades, public identities, keeping up appearances. Warming to it, he insists that the world has always dressed up to dramatize identity and authority—crowns, robes, the wig of the judge, the mask of statesmen—and that all life is a "vast tumultuous masquerade, a clamor for attention," that "no one has ever really *seen* a human being." Having relieved himself intellectually and invited her to comfort him sexually, Palace retires. But after ministering to him, Brynhild sleeps no more that night, contemplating instead a world of artificial faces, artificial bodies, and the question of what both Rowland

Palace and she herself might really be behind the arras of their apparent selves. The "Nocturne" of Palace's song of himself and Brynhild's nightmarish brooding ends with one of Wells's rare authorial intrusions in this novel, justified by his intentness on stating the theme, the interest, the center of the whole book:

> And so the rediscovery by Mr. Rowland Palace of Schopenhauer's realization of the importance of Show (*Verstellung*) sent him and his wife off in diametrically opposite directions, for while it started him upon the idea of the extreme importance of enlarging and strengthening the façade he presented to the world, a façade obviously perilously vulnerable at present, it sent her inquiring into all the neglected possibilities that might be pining and fretting behind the façade she had hitherto unquestioningly supposed to be herself. [Pp. 23–24]

Wells here charts the course of the entire novel. From this point, Palace moves in the direction of wider and deeper appearances, engaging Immanual Cloote as his "impresario" to fashion a suitable public personality for him and to organize illusion to Palace's advantage. Cloote, a man of some genius in the infant art of public relations, is Palace's alter ego from below, his brother in vulgarity, stripped of all polite pretensions. His success in fashioning a public identity for Palace as a great man of letters and a likely candidate for the Nobel Prize is total and represents a considerable advance in sophistication and insidiousness over the promotional tactics of such an early work, dealing with such a simple time, as *Tono-Bungay*. His task is made easier by Palace's limitless unscrupulousness and essential emptiness, despite his pretensions.

As Brynhild has suspected even from the days of his courtship, there is a hollowness at the heart of Palace. On one occasion very early in their relationship presented in flashback, after hearing him declare that his aim as a writer was to release people, she asks, "Release from what?" When he replies "From all the clotted nonsense, new and old, in which they are—imbedded," she pursues him with "And, dearest, what *then*?"

Palace's aim is recognizable to any reader of Wells as Wells's own. But his reply to Brynhild's question about the next step is Jamesian, aesthetic—and hollow: "Art, freedom, a sufficient life." For what Brynhild begins to see at this early stage, and what Wells develops with great force throughout his portrayal of Palace, is the reprehensibleness of Palace's engaging in universal, "liberating" criticism, yet having nothing—certainly nothing like a Wellsian program for the salvaging of civilization—to recommend in place of what he decries. The posture is for

Wells quintessentially aesthetic; and it is the hollowness of Palace's
endless aesthetic sneering that cries out to be filled with the illusions and
impositions of a "planned, controlled, and effective publicity." Even at
this early time Brynhild, in a passage framed typically within her own
consciousness, sees more of the pretension within Palace than she quite
wishes to:

> Was he embarrassed at expounding the obvious or was he evading
> the inexplicable? Art, freedom, a sufficient life? She felt, but she did
> not know how to say, that these words meant nothing until they were
> defined. But her mind suddenly bristled with questions like a
> hedgehog's quills. And as immediately it came to her that not a
> single quill could be shot at him profitably. What was this "art,"
> what was this "freedom," what was this "sufficient life" that
> justified his widespread scorn for the rest of humanity and in
> particular the rest of humanity which wrote and practised the arts?
> She had better not ask it. Somehow it wasn't the time. And yet there
> she was thinking it. This realization gave her her first twinge of
> disloyalty. [P. 38]

On their honeymoon the difficulty arises again in another flashback as
Brynhild says with somewhat ironic humility, "Very often you seem to be
condemning. Just condemning. When really, if I knew your standards, I
should understand why you look down on so many people." Palace's
response this time is hollower still, consisting of downright bad poetry:
"Am I nothing more than bitter tongued? Maybe. I thought you understood
me better, Bryn. Perhaps I don't even understand myself. . . . The
haunting, impalpable presence of an infinite desire" (pp. 42–43). As
Brynhild stores the remark up to gnaw over in private, Palace sees, like
Osmond with Isabel, that she will never feed his egotism with the plenitude
he had envisioned: "She didn't quite know how to take things like that.
She was joining up one thing he said with another and keeping an account
for reference. He did not want her to remember; he wanted her to
sympathize and accept. And pass on."

Finally, after nine years of marriage during which he has found it
impossible to answer Brynhild's haunting question, "Liberation for
what?" Palace resolves the problem, for himself, at least. Meditating on it
he concludes, "You can't invite inspectors into the Holy of Holies." As
Brynhild had earlier resorted to Milton's "safest and seemliest by her
husband stays" to quiet her own doubts about a spouse for whom "even
the Alps never rose to their highest" and who generally "thought the sun
might have set with a better grace," so too does Palace invoke the poet. "It

is plain I am a Mystic,'' he comes to see. "Mystics cannot explain. Mystics cannot be called upon to explain. But nevertheless they can have the clearest sense of value. They are not merely justified in condemning and deprecating certain things; it is their duty. To some of us is given the spear of Ithuriel.'' Milton's angel sets him free to join sheer negation and public exploitation in a triumph of narcissism:

> And now having found his essential self and his essential function and defeated and dismissed that long-rankling doubt, that nine-year-old doubt, about his fundamental self, having assured himself that at heart he was not practically empty and envious but mystically full, he could deal with the problem of putting himself over to the public with a steadfast and confident mind. [Pp. 50–51]

Now, having released himself from all ties to reality—Wells's image, "not practically empty and envious but mystically full,'' is perfect— Palace is ready for Cloote, who will undertake to locate his employer's existence in the public mind. One overriding irony of this chapter of reflections and flashbacks tracing Palace's eventual abandonment of all integrity, all genuine selfhood, is that it is accurately enough entitled "Mr. Rowland Palace in Search of Himself.''

Even at this still early point in the novel Wells's treatment of Palace, making its amused transit from displeasure to disdain, is a remarkable instance of disinterestedness, or at least of impersonally complex comic portraiture. For Palace shares a good deal with his creator. Like Wells he is interested in women. When an extremely good-looking housemaid pauses after passing him to look back, Palace reflects, "It meant nothing. It meant everything.'' When he is suddenly kissed by a lady during the intermission of a performance of *Tristan* "in a mutuality of appreciative exaltation'' he savors it: "Such little things confirm a man.'' But later in the novel our suspicion that he is really rather different from Wells in this regard is made clear as we discover that it is precisely confirmation of his own peculiar sort that he seeks from women, or through them, and little else; and it is a confirmation that does not even require him to have affairs. This too becomes an aspect of the show of things, for what Palace wants is only the appearance of sexual prowess in order to "confirm'' an illusion about himself. Nonetheless, Wells feels free to ascribe needs and inclinations to Palace that come at least suggestively close to his own.

This is clearer still with the literary considerations that arise in the chapter on "The Science and Art of Publicity'' as we follow Rowland Palace about, "brooding still on the untilled field of his personal fame.''

Not the least of Wells's techniques for creating yet controlling distance, for making judgment hover between dismissal and sympathy, is the use of such metaphors as this, with an irony and exaggeration fine enough not to destroy all sense of Palace's plight. Wells's related interest in the mode of specious metaphor that pervades literary promotion emerges elsewhere as Cloote, groping for images, describes his aim to Palace; the genuine, incisive metaphor by which Wells himself describes Cloote's gestures affords just the contrast between reality and humbug, between Cloote's behavior and what he is saying, that Wells wants here: " 'You want building up. To me, Mr. Palace—you musn't mind my saying it—to me you have to be the Clay that I can make into a Living Speaking Image. Perhaps not exactly Clay. No—that has associations!' He cut up the space before him with gestures of his hands. It was as if he cut out bits of it and threw them away. The piece he kept was: 'Glorious living material, fine and subtle. But there it is—you see what I mean. It is an adventure which—I can only say'—he hesitated for a moment seeking the right word, and produced it at last with an air of triumph—'fascinates me' " (p. 94).

As we follow Palace about in this chapter, we find him voicing a number of complaints about the literary situation, and about neglect especially, that Wells himself expressed elsewhere.[6] It is almost as if Wells is able to exorcise his own grievances, as a novelist at least, by having the indignant but discredited Palace utter them. We have, at any rate, a complex, almost eerie, sense of home truths spoken by one whom we thought disqualified from all reality: " 'There is no longer a reading public; there are innumerable little transitory reading publics. They come and go. They are attracted with more difficulty, they forget more readily, and they misunderstand—swiftly' " (p. 58). " 'But now,' said Mr. Palace, 'a personal reputation is infinitely more exposed and precarious; it has to be sown, watched, fostered, protected from wilting, protected from parasites and enemies of all sorts, developed, guarded, magnified' " (p. 59). In this speech the satirical and egotistic color is more discernible and somewhat undermines the position as it undermines Palace; but when Palace calls on his publisher, Schroederer, to complain about insufficient promotion and publicity, Wells treats Schroederer with such open satirical distaste that the episode reinstates, rather complexly, the near-legitimacy of Palace's demands.

Wells initiates this shift by momentarily adopting Schroederer as point of view and presenting the publisher's hard-nosed fantasy: "Schroederer was a realist and his concern was with his firm. Authors were merely the

material you arrange upon your list so as to make the pattern of
Schroederer clear and bright. They rose somehow to fame and you paid for
them; they declined and you dropped them. The thing to do was to put
them all in uniform mauve-green wrappers with red and buff covers
underneath, so that ultimately the public would recognize these chromatic
signs for good reading and bother no more who the authors were. 'I read
Schroederer books,' the public would say, and then there would be an end
to authors and their airs and graces, and he would get intelligent female
labor at reasonable rates to write the stuff inside under his direction.''

The climax of Wells's involved noninvolvement comes in Cloote's
exposition to Palace of a cardinal error in the tactics of literary promotion.
Here we find Wells obtruding his own painful situation on our notice as
though his account of Palace's yearnings were being written by someone
else altogether: ''You must not harp too much on one aspect of a writer's
quality. Gissing, for instance, was handicapped by his irony; they called
him depressing; Chesterton was pigeon-holed as paradoxical even when he
was doing his simple utmost to speak plainly; Wells was pinned down by
his being always linked with 'The Future of—this or that.' (But Wells at
the best was a discursive, intractable writer with no real sense of dignity. A
man is not called 'H.G.' by all his friends for nothing.)''

Brynhild, on the other hand, is impelled by the Nocturne episode, with
its evocation of Schopenhauerian Show, truly to take the long journey into
herself in order to seek out the reality of what she is. As Cloote is Palace's
alter ego, Alfred Bunter becomes Brynhild's secret life, rising up from
below socially, psychically, intellectually, emotionally, and spiritually for
her to discover and embrace.

They meet on a country weekend at the estate of Lord Valliant Chevrell,
where literary figures like Palace and Bunter are interspersed as sources of
interest among the aristocratic guests. Wells sets the tone of the occasion
instantly by allowing Brynhild to overhear an exchange between Lady
Cytherea Label and Palace:

> ''You mahst settle, Mr. Palace. You're just in taim. You know
> everything. Can a chimpanzee be crossed in love?''
> ''It's the only way you *could* cross a chimpanzee,'' said Mr.
> Palace, right on the spur of the moment and wondering what on earth
> he meant.
> It was accepted as suggestively brilliant. [Pp. 104–5]

In this setting Bunter, Brynhild sees, is "cast for the rôle of The Stranger," the "newly arrived, the last social mouthful," who "does not assimilate from the outset and gradually . . . becomes inassimilable." Since she thinks of herself as "cast for the rôle of a Quiet Lovely," she is sympathetically drawn to the young writer. As they converse, she finds the note of Wellsian outsiderism winning: " 'I had no idea,' he said, 'what these places were like and how many there seemed to be. I've lived in England all my life and I've never suspected what lay behind the gates and the palings and the notices about Tresspassing. It's amazing' " (p. 109). Before long he is speaking to her in the garden of the estate with some intensity about his career and his ideas, anticipating attitudes that were to become familiar on the British literary scene decades later: "This place is a wonder because it is rare. And yet we could make all our island a garden, an estate like this and as mellow as this. . . . We don't. That makes me Angry. . . . I am an Angry Man. . . . Almost professionally. You don't know my books? No? But that is what they say of me—the Angry Man. The world angers me. . . . I get angry and shout. I don't write books, I shout them." In a moment, without knowing that Brynhild is Mrs. Rowland Palace, he says, "I can't tell you how I envy at times the coolness, the empty, self-satisfied self-possession of that damned façade, Palace." Brynhild identifies herself to Bunter and gracefully disposes of most of his embarrassment. The remark serves only to bring them closer together and to prompt further private reflection on Brynhild's part about her relation to both men.

Wells has thus begun his extensive development in this chapter of a theatrical echo of his theme of shows and appearances. On the one hand there is the Wildely witty, but empty, dialogue of "that damned façade," Palace and his crossed chimpanzee, on the other, Brynhild's consciousness of Bunter's and her own less flamboyant roles, Stranger and Quiet Lovely. Bunter himself has come forward as the Angry Man. But this is only a beginning, for Wells soon moves past these intimations heartily into the dimension of the play within a play with Lord Valliant Chevrell's invitation to the entire company to play charades. This sequence is worth examining in some detail as an illustration of Wells's extraordinarily deliberate concentration on thematic considerations and on Brynhild's crucial relation to them.

The game is first introduced with appropriately erotic overtones: " 'Charades,' Valliant Chevrell would say, 'mix people nicely,' and there

is no doubt that charades as they played them under his direction mixed
them a good deal. There was a considerable amount of going off together
and going off apart, necessary whispering and conspiring close to the pink
receptive ear, a running about passages for needed properties, much
dressing up and undressing and helping to dress and undress.'' The actors,
moreover, have only partial knowledge of their endeavor: "Everybody
knew the one or two letters in which they acted, but only their host alone or
with some chosen confederate was supposed to know the 'Whole.' '' For
the first charade "Pluto" is the Whole, and Palace, along with Lady
Cytherea and others, is charged with the letter P. They decide upon the
Judgment of Paris, with Palace as the hero and Lady Cytherea as Venus.
Once again, as in the pageant that had begun the novel, Palace is richly, if
dubiously, costumed, once again purporting to be what he is and is not.
And once again the ludicrousness of this contrived appearance is laid on by
Wells:

> The three young ladies had undressed Mr. Palace very thoroughly.
> In place of a Phrygian cap they had put a red ribbon round his hair.
> He was wearing his bathing shorts under an arrangement of
> sheepskin rugs held together by brown luggage straps, and he carried
> a long alpenstock to which a crook-handled walking stick had been
> tied. A pair of plimsolls had been deprived of their uppers and con-
> verted into sandals with the aid of a tape measure which ran up his
> two shins and round his calves saying 23, 24, 25, 26, and 58, 59, 60
> respectively. He had been slightly rouged and his hair arranged for
> him and he carried himself as though he had recently been told—as
> indeed he had been told—that he was "aw'fly handsome." [P. 121]

On this occasion, the Apple of Discord is a large orange, "ripe to bursting
and not to be thrown about." One would never sense, in the ridicule of
Palace, or in Wells's whole skeptical comic handling of the charade
sequence, how passionately fond he was himself of such domestic
entertainments and games in his own home, Easton Glebe.[7] Brynhild
watches her husband with some distaste, and self-reproach for feeling it, as
his comportment recalls "all the worst excesses of all the pseudo-Russian
ballets she had ever seen." Palace's role as Paris, connoisseur of beauty
and sower of discord, even without his graceless exaggeration of it, is quite
an apt mythological counterpart of Palace's flirtatious behavior with Lady
Cytherea and others throughout the evening, none of it lost on his wife.
Following the Judgment of Paris, Bunter participates in the letter L
tableau, a Laocoön group which is done "with dignity and decorum."
Now it is Brynhild's turn. She is charged with representing the third letter,

U, by playing the part of Undine, the water nymph, and wishes to do more than merely mope under water for her lost soul and her lost knight. As a result of Palace's attentions to others, his own charade of philandering, she "felt far too much like the part to want to display herself in that fashion." Instead she decides to do it as a scene of exorcism with Undine's knight present. She seeks to reclaim Rowland by asking him to play her redemptive knight, but when, with Lord Valliant Chevrell at her elbow, she invites Palace to do so, he displays yet more of his objectionable behavior:

> He was saying something in an undertone to Florrie Caterham, who had to direct his attention to Brynhild. He looked up startled and grasped the situation. His expression became defensive.
> "You mustn't make me do all the acting, Bryn," he said, as if he addressed an unreasonable child. "No."
> For a moment Brynhild felt that she and Rowland held the stage and that every one was observing them.
> "This, my dear," said her guardian angel within her, is going to be a Scene—unless you hold tight. So hold tight." [Pp. 126–27]

Acting with magnificent restraint in this unscheduled drama—a kind of play within a play within a play—Brynhild shuns the obvious retaliatory move and deliberately avoids inviting Bunter, who like everyone else is watching the scene, to take the place of her husband and summons two other men instead. The exchange is an extraordinarily adroit piece of evocation on Wells's part. Here in the very midst of organizing appearances for dramatic illusion, for "show" in the theatrical sense, his characters uncover realities of feeling.

In addition, Wells is flirting with symbolic, mythological purport in an unobtrusive but suggestive way—a good deal less obtrusive, for example, than his deliberately self-conscious employment of the Delphic Sibyl in *The Bulpington of Blup*. Just as Paris emblematizes Palace's deportment at Valliant Chevrell's, and Laocoön, who denounced the Trojan Horse, represents, like the angry young writer Bunter, a figure warning against what threatens a civilization, so too Undine prefigures an important aspect of Brynhild's experience and its significance, one that in this case lies considerably ahead in the novel, so that the mythological implications have an anticipatory, prophetic force. The Undine legend is about a water nymph who could obtain a soul only by marrying a mortal and bearing a child. Brynhild's adventures, late in the novel, take something very like this form. Wells achieves a similar prophetic intimation with Bunter by having him return in another charade to play Pluto at the moment when Persephone takes leave of him on her annual trip to the upper world. Bunter "waved off her farewell embraces, indicated irritably that she must not keep the car waiting, featured all the natural relief of a husband who is seeing off a too attentive spouse, and then with an expression of impish sadism, a god left free at last to do as he pleased, bent forward, glanced over his shoulder to be sure she had really gone and prodded his scepter into young Bates with the gusto of a long-deferred pleasure. . . . Then Pluto, clawing his face with a glare of incredible malignity, considered what he should do to the two lady damned" (pp. 129–30). Although we do not at this point know these things about Bunter, he does in fact have a wife of sorts whom he has eluded in Scotland and another in Wales, and he will eventually cuckold Palace by having an affair with Brynhild. Yet neither of these prophetic parallels is forced on our attention by Wells at this juncture, precisely because they are prophetic. The enrichment that they bring to the novel is retrospective. Not so, however, the intimation of ludicrousness in certain forms of show that arises from Palace's participation, from such props as the Orange of Discord, and from the extensive treatment of household items pressed into absurdly exalted service as costume and décor. Employing a light touch throughout the sequence, Wells is able to mock symbolism at the same time that he utilizes it.

With Brynhild still looking on, Palace contrives another dramatic performance outside the charade framework. She notices that Palace has been deserted by Lady Cytherea and her friends in favor of Bunter. Desperately seeking to regain attention, Palace finally manages to detach Lady Cytherea. We remember now, if not before, that hers is another name for Venus:

> He must have made a direct appeal, because when about midnight the next charade (Nero) was over . . . he and Lady Cytherea disappeared through a door in the corridor in the most concerted manner possible and reappeared ten minutes afterwards from the direction of the front entrance, with a cleared-up expression on their candid faces.
> The pair of them took the center of the stage.
> "It's the mahst wonderful moon!" cried Lady Cytherea.
> "It's magic out there," said Rowland.
> Evidently it had been magic out there and he wanted everyone to realize it. There was something proprietorial in his bearing, there was an assertion. Whatever had happened in the garden out there was

as nothing to him in comparison with the dramatic assertion of close association conveyed by this entry.

Brynhild stood with a glass of barley water in her hand, marvelling quietly at life.

It had become necessary to both these remarkable people to intimate that in moonlight anyhow they were of importance to each other. . . . They were playing this at Alfred Bunter, at the company generally, at Brynhild and at themselves, and why they were moved to play this small drama and make this show, Omniscience only knew. [Pp. 131–32]

Alone in her bedroom later that night, standing nude before her mirror, comparing herself to the false Aphrodite, Lady Cytherea, Brynhild reflects: " 'A secret beauty is nothing to him,' she said to the living Venus before her. *'The show's the thing . . . .'* " Thus her emotional and moral alienation from Palace is established by means of the same metaphors that have been at play throughout the evening. Wells has gone a long way toward releasing her for an affair with Bunter. As she reads the young writer for the first time that night in bed, she estimates his work with extraordinary critical sensitivity. It might be young Wells or young Lawrence that she is reading: "It was an extremely turgid story about hampered and defeated people. . . . They lived in London as well as in the country; *The Cramped Village*, it seemed, was not a place, but life. They paralyzed each other. Dreams tormented them from above and lusts and savage passions from below. . . . The style was rough and yet stimulating. . . . She knew quite well how prose becomes patchy if you worry it too much. How it works into raw places and holes. . . . He was plainly trying to get more into his narrative than his narrative prose could stand. 'It's a splutter,' she thought. . . . 'Like a cat with its head in a bag. . . . A man trying to say something more than *can* be said. . . . But he never fakes.' " Then the deeply contrastive word linked with her husband rises in her mind from her conversation with Bunter earlier in the day:

She mused along these lines for a while and then she uttered one word out loud—because she wanted to hear it.

"Façade!"

"Yes, Mr. Bunter," she reflected, "you can hit upon the just word at times. The precise word. . . . Among others. Among quite a lot of others." [P. 136]

And so, one of the novel's leitmotifs, first introduced by Palace himself, now newly applied to him with some abhorrence, returns. Like the word "show," or the word "debonair" with which Cloote annoints Palace later on, it serves to reinforce our awareness of the extraordinary thematic concentration and design of the novel. It also, of course, comports with Palace's very name, being the false face of the edifice of egotism that is his life. Brynhild's mood toward her husband softens before she sleeps as she wonders what he might be doing in his room: "In through those two doors there was perhaps a real Rowland now. Perhaps the Façade like a discarded garment was hanging over the back of a chair." Finally, as she shuts the light, tenderly but unyieldingly extending the metaphor, she whispers "Good-night, Façade."

Wells's extraordinary consciousness of theme and his extraordinary devotion to a personal framework of thinking and feeling in the charade sequence—his Jamesian gestures—continue, unabated, in the major action of the novel. In the chapter wryly called "Exploring the Laurel Grove," Cloote effectively takes charge of Palace's career and person by setting before his client the irresistible gloriously engineered future of his Predestined Career. As Cloote speaks of prestige, public appearances, photographs, non-events, the motive terms "show" and "appearance" reverberate through the conversation. When he proposes an occasional visit to "some little country grammar school" to say something "deep and moving to those boys which they will remember, which their mothers will remember" and Palace objects to seeming to wear his heart on his sleeve, Cloote's reply is magically apt: " 'You don't. And I don't want you to. But—Wear your heart *up* your sleeve. Give them a glimpse of it and then—Presto! It's gone, and you get that enigmatical Palace smile' " (p. 148). As they talk, Palace also entertains the possibility of "a rather frequent, recurrent appearance with Lady Cytherea, for example. . . . There would be nothing in it and yet everything would be implicitly there."

Before long the essential brotherhood of the two men forces itself upon Palace's attention:

> "We differ in our manners, we differ in our gifts," said Mr. Cloote, "but we think alike. We are going to be a great combination."
> (It seemed horribly true.) [P. 143]

But later, as he observes Cloote's uncouth behavior at table, Palace comforts himself with the illusion of a distinction, at once real and negligible: "Curiously enough this [crudity] gave no offence to Mr.

Palace. He liked it. It opened a gulf between them; it mitigated that disagreeable sense of intimacy, of kindred, of something unpleasantly like being searchingly mirrored and told immodestly about oneself. A man who eats as one eats oneself is a friend and brother. But a man who scoops and engulfs food is an instrument. Cloote was much more endurable, Mr. Palace was realizing, as an instrument'' (p. 151).

Palace deceives himself here, for beneath the appearance it is he who becomes Cloote's instrument and toy. We discover the process in this same chapter first as a piece of linguistic and psychic susceptibility on Palace's part. Cloote vouchsafes Palace a word:

> "I see you," Mr. Cloote raised his eyes to heaven and for a time spoke after the manner of one who sees visions. "I see you. . . . May I use a word—a key word, Mr. Palace? About you. A quality. The word—Debonair! . . ."
> He calmed Mr. Palace with an extended hand, deprecating any interruption while his vision continued. "Let me make myself perfectly clear. Debonair. You could easily be *very* debonair, Mr. Palace. I've always thought Il Re Galantuomo a most attractive title. Il Scrittore—No!—Lo Scrittore Galantuomo. A man just a little aloof—aloof in his soul and yet not too aloof. Smiling but never mingling, friendly, assured, kindly. Capable of immense seriousness, but carrying it easily, lightly. Capable of—adventures. And naturally he was to be seen *unposed*—in transit—in action—caught unawares. A man rather heedless of his public. No standing at attention to be photographed." [P. 145]

The word takes, giving to all the suppressed yearning of Palace's life a name. Later that evening we discover him in his exalted, translated state:

> It was a Florentine nobleman who towelled himself in Mr. Palace's bathroom.
> At dinner that night he was unusually debonair. Brynhild couldn't imagine what had got hold of him. [P. 156]

And later still, indeed through the remainder of the novel, the word "debonair" rings out again and again in connection with Palace's conceit of himself, as the very emblem of his almost Malvolian folly. It also becomes Wells's arch means of indicating, in the Envoy, that not all of Brynhild's children are Palace's: "She developed an increasing social confidence and dignity and brought a bright and various family of three sons and two daughters into the world. Two at least of these offspring were quite debonair" (p. 302).

But another, more important instance of Cloote's control over Palace's life and illusions, quite crucial for the action of the novel, also appears in this chapter. While Palace pretends to be above such considerations, Cloote announces an ominous unilateral program for eliminating all literary competitors, Bunter especially. " 'This,' he said, 'is a service I do you and nothing I ask you to do. In fact the word for you here is—pardon me—"keep out." But we have to be chary of the growth of other reputations. A false reputation, shot up in the night, fungoid, that might take the wind out of our sails. . . . We can't ignore it.' " In thus becoming the autonomous agent of Palace's secret wish, Cloote initiates the action that throws Bunter and Brynhild together as lovers and that opens up the deepest and darkest exploration of the theme of appearance and reality in the novel.

Cloote's subsequent malicious investigation of Bunter uncovers the sordid truth beneath the young writer's promising career. We learn of it not from Cloote, though we sense him relentlessly closing in on his quarry, but from Bunter's long and moving confession to Brynhild in the tenth chapter. Bunter, whose real name is David Lewis, had thought himself married to a girl he had lived with for a week in Scotland during the First World War. After a time he left her and took up a career as a house agent in Wales. Here he was prevailed upon by an overpowering woman named Freda to marry her, thus becoming guilty, he thought, of bigamy. Worse yet, Freda's brother, Gregory, a cocaine addict, having discovered the Scots wife in Bunter's past, proceeded to blackmail him. Finding life with both Freda and her brother intolerable, Bunter dreamed of getting away, publishing the novel he had been working on and beginning a new life as a writer under an assumed name. One night when he found himself alone with Freda's brother, who had returned dirty and disheveled from a trip, the dream realized itself. After giving Gregory a hot bath, discarding his tattered garments and dressing him from head to foot in old clothes of his own, and supplying him with food, plenty of whiskey, and some money, Bunter accompanied him across a patch of open country toward the local railroad station. On the way, singing drunkenly and taunting Bunter, Gregory fell down a hole and drowned. Bunter was ten yards behind but felt that he might somehow have pushed Gregory. Frightened, he seized the opportunity to make off to London, hoping that when the body was eventually discovered it would be identified as his, David Lewis's, because of the clothes, and that having thus killed off his old self, he could assume a new identity as Alfred Bunter, the novelist.

But for Cloote, the plan would have succeeded totally, for Freda, after first identifying the body as her brother, reverses herself and pretends it is

David Lewis. " 'From the indignant Deserted Wife her pose changed in a night into that of the Desperate Woman protecting her Lover,' " says Bunter. Even the insurance company, though it knows better, decides to pay up on Lewis's policy for the publicity value. " 'Under protest, they said. As an advertisement. Five hundred pounds.' " The lie compounds itself, threatening to prevail.

But there is Cloote. His campaign against Bunter produces book review after book review discrediting Bunter as a writer of extremely limited social experience, inquiring insistently about his origins and credentials. Responding to this pressure and fear of exposure, Bunter makes his halting, anguished confession to Brynhild. Eventually, as Cloote gains possession of all the facts, Bunter is compelled to act. Returning to Cardiff as David Lewis, he clears himself of suspicion of murder, makes restitution, then vanishes. Very late in the novel we learn that having grown a beard—no doubt resembling Lawrence more than ever—he has been able to "rematerialize" himself as Alfred Bunter, living quietly abroad and resuming his writing.

Thus the angry young writer who at the outset embodies for Brynhild all the integrity and reality that her husband lacks, emerges at the end as the figure most deeply implicated in appearances, the charade of David Lewis's death and Alfred Bunter's life constituting appearances of a decidedly forbidding and disturbing kind. Like the Brynhild of the *Volsunga Saga*, the Brynhild of Wells's novel has been awakened by her Sigurd-Bunter from the enchanted sleep that her Odin-Palace had thrown her into, only, in this case, to discover that her young redeemer is also an illusion. But not quite. For she is also Undine and manages to win her soul, shape her own life, as a result of the child that she has by her knight, Bunter. We see this movement begin when after hearing Bunter's story, meditating on it, she dwells not on his deception of others but on his honesty with herself, "his passionate effort" to be sincere. "It was that passionate effort appealed to her most; it was as though something in him was wanting to get born through her. In her, he had intimated, for the first time he had found a chance of self knowledge. It made her feel incubatory" (p. 247).

The paternal birth image is striking, as is Brynhild's apt incubatory participation in it. For Bunter, despite the deceptions of the past, is, like Brynhild, and through Brynhild, profoundly concerned with knowing and abiding by the truth of his own real nature. In his case, his novels, as well as his intimacy with Brynhild, are the expression of that truth.

Consequently, when Cloote's disclosures are about to destroy both his career and his opportunity to remain with Brynhild, when he has determined to return to Cardiff as David Lewis, he speaks of the return as a fiction: " 'I don't want to spend months, years perhaps of pretending and play-acting. All this is more than a calamity; it's devastation.' " Brynhild is immediately totally aware of the extraordinary inversion of categories, as Wells is of the radical modulation of primary thematic terms. Recognizing that the life that Bunter left behind him as David Lewis in Cardiff is really now the life of another man who did in a sense die when Gregory died, Brynhild expresses it for herself and for the novel: " 'You go back to reality,' reflected Brynhild. 'And you go back to falsehood. As if falsehood *was* reality' " (p. 265).

So it is that the Undine part of her prevails as Brynhild remains faithful to the newborn reality of Bunter's life and by means of it finds the basis of her own. She gives herself to him compassionately and consolingly as he faces the crisis of complete exposure by Cloote—the chapter is called "Mr. Alfred Bunter Goes to Pieces"—and afterward, alone, she amends her most fundamental ideas. In an access of self-knowledge, scrutinizing herself once again in a mirror at her dressing table, she says to herself, to her image in the glass, that she has always been simple because she has never done anything unexpected; that she never thought anything could surprise her or that she could surprise herself; but that now she can realize how life can be complicated and how other people are affected by it. Wells suggests that at this stage her confrontation with herself is not complete by employing a delicate extension of the mirror imagery: "She looked down at her hand mirror which was prone on the table as though hiding its reflections from her" (p. 272). It is to the less intimate dressing-table mirror that she addresses herself. Before long, however, the confrontation is completed and the Undine motif fulfilled, with flickers of the Brynhild-Odin-Sigurd story playing over it.

Carrying Bunter's child and reflecting on Palace's amusing willingness to play the role of father—Palace who is "extraordinarily married to her, about whom he would never know anything at all, about whom he didn't want to know anything at all"—she thinks that while thoroughly married herself, now "she was escaping—going away from all that had held her paralyzed for seven years—to something profoundly her own, profoundly secret in its essence and profoundly real. She had become real. Her priggishness had been reft from her. She was a cheat now—like everybody. She was a secret behind a façade. And altogether human. She had grown up at last . . ." (p. 297). Thus Bunter, her knight and her Sigurd, has dragged her down into humanity and made her real by making it necessary for her to be false. The reappearance of the façade image, now newly applied to Brynhild, makes the moral egalitarianism complete, throwing us back to the nightmarish brooding on universal deception and disguise of the early Nocturne chapter. But there is a difference, an exception. There is Brynhild's child, Undine's child, as there was Brynhild, the child of her own passionately, if conditionally, honest father: "Her thoughts flicked off at a tangent. The child? The child, though, was going to be different. Her child would never cheat like this, never humbug any one. Her child was going to be something better than had ever been before. In some way . . . this sort of thing wouldn't do for her child. That was what she had to see to . . . ."

Thus Wells, working almost totally within the frame of Brynhild's consciousness and allowing both the powers and limitations of her vision to enter in as yet another intricacy, brings the theme of appearances into its climactic phase. It is the maternal conceit of things that speaks through Brynhild at the last: the impulse to validate her own existence by giving birth to realities in the form of offspring. But here as Brynhild dreams of their difference from her, from her passive, feminine will, and of their legacy from their father(s), the Wellsian note, unobtrusively enough, creeps in:

> She felt, as she had never felt before, that she knew her own mind. And that instead of being the most aimless thing in the world, she now conceived her essential business plain before her.
> "Not one child but *children*, and the best I can get. . . .
> "What I was made for. . . .
> "A stormy little rebel to begin with who will batter at the façades. With trouble and stubbornness in those brown eyes of his. . . .
> "When all that is fairly under way, then surely at last I shall take an intelligent interest in—say—education. And politics. So that they don't kill or waste or starve my children or leave them alive with nothing sensible to do. . . .
> "If there *is* any sense in things at all." [P. 299]

As there had been something in Bunter that wanted to be born through Brynhild (p. 247), so there is something in Brynhild that wants to be born through her children. As readers of Wells, we are not surprised to find that it is partly a new world, where education and politics will not "kill or waste or starve my children or leave them alive with nothing sensible to do"—all that Wells really wanted from any future society. His grafting that hope, merely in passing, on to the pregnant Brynhild has an entire maternal, emotional propriety. We almost fail to find Wells in it at all.

But primarily what wants to be born in Brynhild through childbearing, what is already being born, is herself. This rebirth is connected with the vocation of motherhood, but it also has to do with the most fundamental forms of biological and sexual self-realization. She has had to surrender her vitality in order to gain it: "It was her love for that gracious slender body of hers that had helped her to consent not to use it. But now it did not seem to matter to her at all if that grace departed from her. Perhaps, said the Great God Pan in her, behind every lovely thing is the possibility of something lovelier. If things hadn't happened as they had happened, she would have kept that beautiful figure and it would have grown stale and fruitless upon her. From being a fresh young body it would have become a preserved body" (p. 300). Her ecstasy is Lawrentian, for the possibility of something lovelier behind every lovely thing is not only, in this case, her child, though it is partly that, but also herself quickened, herself carrying and nurturing her child. Studying her body in her mirror, Brynhild delights in the little blue veins that have appeared on her changed throat and bosom. She has the sense of living anew in generating life. Her "stormy little rebel" will need, in the future, to "batter at the façades," and in her own life now "Façade she had to be. Every self-conscious behaving thing must be a façade, must turn a face to the world and be aware of itself." But a new reality has emerged deep in her, beneath all shows, feminine, undeniable, sustaining:

> All the same these juices in her blood that had taken possession of her, and filled her with this deep irrational satisfaction, had a very imperious suggestion about them of being real. [P. 300]

At the next moment, in the very last words of the novel proper, before the Envoy, Wells has her pull back, so as to keep the thematic tension intricately poised even at the last; but it is almost too late, at least for Brynhild: "If indeed there was in human experience as yet any such thing as reality." For the skepticism belongs, by this time, more to Wells than to his heroine. The distance between them is measurable in a phrase from the Envoy that recalls some of the mystical fullness of Palace's emptiness: "Mrs. Brynhild Palace's new half-mystical self-devotion to the physical rebirth of our world." We dwell, however, not on Wells, but on Brynhild, the fully realized, fully represented, fully felt Yeatsian mother worshipping, with Lawrentian fervor, images that animate her reveries. That some of her hopes, some of her dissatisfactions, even some of her reservations may be Wells's doesn't matter, for not the least of her victories is her managing to wrest her new life away from her creator's.

Brynhild is, then, unmistakably a novel about The Show of Things, but it is also in the end a novel about the reality of the self, either as Brynhild finds it in compassion, perception, and procreation, or as Bunter does in his work. Moreover, it is about the ways in which the lovers help one another to discover that reality. Bunter speaks of this process of self-defining communion to Brynhild in words that account for his experience and, incidentally, the wholly other experience of Palace and Cloote: " 'And never have I wanted to be known by anyone as I want to be known by you. . . . If I can get you to know me I feel that I shall begin perhaps to know something about myself' " (pp. 244–45). Such a validation of the self by means of another's accurate knowledge of it is precisely what Palace has been avoiding all his life and precisely what Cloote is hired to keep from happening. Cloote's method is to substitute a totally illusory self and make that known. The irony of the novel's structure is that Cloote makes use of the truth about Bunter's life in order to promote the deceptions about Palace's, but that in doing so Cloote eventually assists Bunter to purge himself. In the world as it is, unredeemed by sense, revolution, or good will, Wells allows Palace and Cloote their Nobel Prize, Brynhild and Bunter their façades. But he has also made it clear that the latter two are fortunate enough to have that within which passeth show.

Even this extensive treatment of the degree to which *Brynhild* is organized around its thematic center does not exhaust the matter. There are innumerable other instances, such as the various roles that Cloote has Palace play, including those on an extensive tour of Europe where Palace must first be the attentive husband, but later travel alone as the wild, lecherous man of genius; Cloote's striking description of the pretenses connected with the orderly sensuality of the French; Bunter's dodges at the newspaper room of the British Museum as he seeks to discover news about Cardiff without being himself detected; Brynhild's hiding her pregnancy from Palace for a time, and her posing with Bunter in the midst of his impassioned confession to her. Thematic resonance is everywhere in the novel. Yet at no time does it become tiresome or oppressive. Indeed, at no time does it become noticeable as an imposition on the novelistic substance, the power of the narrative and the characters to concern us, move us, engage us, however much my analytic isolation of, and concentration on, the pattern of appearance might suggest otherwise.

In fact, Wells is able to achieve a more than Jamesian unity at the same time that he provides a more than Jamesian variety. Much of this is owing to style. James typically has all his figures adopt his own voice and idiom, thus bathing his novels, the late ones especially, in a unity of language and sensibility, as well as one of "subject," action, value, and symbol. Even Kate Croy, Charlotte Stant, Mrs. Brookenham, and Gilbert Osmond have Jamesian sensibilities. As a result, we become imprisoned without recourse in the intensive unitary dimension that gives us our characteristic sense of the James novel, of one mind suffusing, animating, but also delimiting others. In *Brynhild*, on the other hand, Wells creates real distinctions among his characters' voices. There is the methodical extravagance of Cloote's public relations schemes, the outrageous yet pathetic hauteur of Palace, the impassioned, eloquent groping of Bunter, the demure, touching exploration of Brynhild, and, over all, the riddling, sympathetic irony of the narrator's voice. And each of these styles marks its possessor's relative grasp of the real.

Yet that grasp is never a matter of ideology or even ideas. These matter far less than the emotion and intent with which characters talk to one another and the degree of response they awaken. At one point Bunter speaks with enormous distress and power about life as a form of fear, about war as a form of life "hurried up, intensified, underlined, made plain by exaggeration," and about the pressing need for rebirth. But nothing that he says, indeed almost nothing that he ever says, is there for its own sake as an idea. When he breaks off, suddenly, rejecting it all, Brynhild offers the book's general intimation about such discourse:

> "Why should I spend our last moments talking this rubbish," he said, and left his sentence incomplete.
> "It's not rubbish," said Brynhild. "Everything that is worth saying seems almost impossible to say." [P. 269]

The action of *Brynhild*, like that of a James novel, consists of conversations, or exists in conversations. The major incidents—the death of Bunter's brother-in-law, Gregory, the imminent exposure of Bunter's past by Cloote, Palace's tour of the Baltic nations—are all treated in dialogue as either rehearsals of antecedent action or anticipations of projected action. Even the lovemaking between Brynhild and Bunter is merely an extension, not really presented at all, of the long conversation which gives rise to it. Yet the book is very far from being a dialogue novel in the sense that Wells expounds in his autobiography or in the introduction to *Babes in the Darkling Wood*. Wells's object in *Brynhild* is not to have his characters debate with one another, presenting views which have an intrinsic intellectual interest, and then, from the clash of opposing views and the consequences of the action, to cull the surviving ideas. He is far more interested in allowing Bunter to express his agony by "philosophizing" and pontificating and in having Brynhild express her humanity and sympathy by feeling her way tenderly and patiently through Bunter's verbiage to the pain beneath. He is similarly much more interested in the revolting comedy of their intercourse, their mutual exploitation, than in anything Cloote and Palace say to each other. Wells does take a certain delight in parodying the public relations mentality in both men, but this is hardly the stuff of the novel of ideas.

It is comportment that he works with here primarily, not so much what his people formulate as what they are, what they evolve into, and what this in turn signifies for his theme. Oddly enough, by thus charging them with themselves and relieving them of all responsibility for his own general ideas and personal history, Wells was able to write one of the most vital and touching novels of his last period. It was what Henry James had been telling him all along.

CHAPTER IV

Apropos of Dolores

\)

The Bulpington of Blup was dedicated "to the critic of the typescript, Odette Keun, gratefully (bless her)." Madame Keun, a widely traveled European of some literary and intellectual attainment—she is the author of *My Adventures in Bolshevik Russia, A Foreigner Looks at the British Sudan, I Discover the English, Darkness from the North: An Essay in German History, A Foreigner Looks at the TVA,* and *I Think Aloud in America*—had been Wells's companion for a number of years. By 1934, however, when *Experiment in Autobiography* appeared, their relationship had cooled considerably, and Madame Keun greeted the new book with a series of three articles in *Time and Tide* which were very far indeed from loving.[1]

Her purpose in writing them was to lay bare Wells's soul and pronounce judgment on it. In the first installment she acknowledges the impoverished, benighted Victorian upbringing which filled him with pain, humiliation, and anger, but regrets his inability to transcend it. Certainly, she says, the rationalism that he learned at the feet of Thomas Henry Huxley did not help, for it "destroyed in him utterly all spiritual and mystical values." Cut off from a saving religious tradition and any recognition of extrapersonal value, he could invoke only his own likes and dislikes as criteria. Before long, bearing his childhood grudges and devoid of religious understanding, he became a victim of his "fundamental egotism." "From the beginning he was actuated to speak and write and clarify and attack by personal causes. Not one of them was ignoble—no; but not one of them was abstract. Not one of them put him in touch with the universal. Nor were they scientific or humanitarian. His motivation was first and foremost the revolt of a powerful and outraged ego." Having sounded the note of egotism Madame Keun never quite relinquishes it again. Wells's inability to forget the wounds that society inflicted on his youth, though society has "opulently repaired the damage" with fame and fortune, makes him "a pathological case." "He was never sane enough," says Madame Keun, "to forget—much less, to throw off—his personal bitternesses." Nor would his savage self-defensiveness, self-justification, and "unconscious personal mental dishonesty" ever allow him to possess any genuine self-knowledge.

This much is prologue. She now proceeds in her second installment to the metaphor through which she seeks to embody Wells's self-absorption, irresponsibility, and failure. Work, she says, is either vocation or game. A vocation "is a summons, issuing from without," from an impersonal divine or spiritual source, compelling its subject to march forward "to the outer and greater, the implacably abstract Purpose which has commanded him so irresistibly to forget, to deny, and utterly to lose himself." A game, on the other hand, is only a manipulation in which a player, relying solely on his own gifts and skill, seeks a goal or an advantage over his opponent. Wells, says Madame Keun, was all his life long but a player, seeking his own gratification. There is not, in his life, his work, or his significance, "the faintest trace of that mercilessly impersonal objective which is termed a vocation, and to which a response must be made in humility and selflessness." He sought incessantly only to demonstrate his own superiority over his adversaries, to impose his own order on the welter of contemporary confusion. He functioned like a champion glorying in his own powers. "There is no vocation here; there is the enormous pleasure of indulging in an activity for which his nature, his tastes, and his aptitudes fit him better than anyone else at that time."

Not realizing that Wells was merely a player at his own egotistical game, young people of her generation all over the world, says Madame Keun, looked to him during the early phase of his career as their redeemer and deliverer. But after a time, she goes on, the truth began to emerge. One proof of a player's skill is his ability to use a multitude of varied, even contradictory styles, and Wells took delight in demonstrating this capacity endlessly. Year after year, in book after book, he changed the remedies that he prescribed for the ills of civilization: a Wellsian deity in *God the Invisible King*, quietism in *The Undying Fire*, psychoanalysis in *The Secret Places of the Heart*, the Open Conspiracy in *The World of William Clissold*, education in *Joan and Peter*, Universal Brotherly Love in *Mr. Britling Sees It Through*, etc. The works of his full maturity, "instead of erecting a secure construction where humanity may find shelter, represent a labyrinth out of which it cannot thread its way." Instead of a "system" Wells offers only "a swamping cataract of rushing broken notions"; instead of "a strong, steady, focused searchlight," only "the swaying, flickering, impish flame-points of a thousand-candled chandelier." As the years passed, his followers came to understand that Wells was playing "with tremendous gusto an infinitely exhilarating game."

In her last installment Madame Keun maintains that Wells not only jumbled solutions but sought to destroy them. With the Fabians, the Labor Party, and the League of Nations he followed a pattern of initial ardent advocacy followed by repudiation and ridicule, leaving the continuation of the struggle to more serious, dedicated, and reliable men. Having settled on a game, "whatever the opening gambit, however wonderful the preliminary moves, invariably something, inside or outside him, surges up to provoke the desire to change; he jumps to his feet, spills the pawns, as likely as not fetches his partners a thundering crack on the head—and so off with a whirl to a new table again." Indeed, Madame Keun continues, there was an appalling personal ferocity in Wells's quarrels with both enemies and former friends. He revealed "a vulnerability to criticism that was like a disease . . . turned intellectual debate into a private quarrel, and to ridicule his adversaries . . . even pounced upon their bodily blemishes." Worse still—and here Madame Keun unwittingly prophesies her own fate—Wells developed the habit in his books of making use of "people near to him, in whose lives he participated, whose circumstances, characteristics and failings only a close intimacy enabled him to know." At this point, touchingly enough, her own personal grievance against Wells peeps through:

> That mysterious sixth sense which he possesses in abundance in all matters concerning himself, which makes him instantaneously detect the imponderables, the ebb and flow of emotions and judgments that affect him, vanished in his personal associations. When a really objective biography of Wells will be written, instead of the enormous reel of self-justification which he is still producing, where his very cunning art of feinting, his very subtle trick of inaccuracy in confession, have again succeeded in blinding his audience to the nature of his play, it will be discovered that he has wounded and injured often beyond cure.[2]

She discovered at last, she says, that Wells, the supposed lover of mankind who affirms that he is working to save it, is, in reality, "*cruel.*"

Madame Keun concedes that Wells "made an age," that "in some ways it is not an exaggeration to say that he was one of the creators of modern man." Indeed, one might properly call the twenty-five years between the nineties and the First World War the Age of Wells, for it was largely he who wove its "intellectual texture." But his work could not endure. He did not create a school, a following, a movement—"not even the core of a movement." His failure, in the end, was the result of his incorrigible self-absorption: "Because his motivation was so personal, his activity so egotistic, his methods so devious, his destructiveness so incessant, his manner so ruthless—*because he played*—he gave no consistent service to mankind." In her closing words, Madame Keun does not hesitate to charge Wells with having missed his chance, out of selfishness and insincerity, to save the world:

> If he has failed to save us, the fault is in him. It was not we who left him. It was he who lost us. He had the brain, he had the vision, he had the ability. He had, at one time, the heart and faith of multitudes with him. But that thing which makes the common man endure for an end; which makes the nobler man die for an end; that thing which is integrity of doctrine and selflessness of idealism; that ultimate genuineness which in the last analysis alone makes for permanent force and influence in life—in no form and in no measure has he ever had it at all.

As an objective assessment of Wells's work, Odette Keun's analysis offers but little interest. Her assumption that enduring fidelity to one's allegiances—Fabianism, the Labor Party, or the League of Nations— however inadequate or misguided they prove, is an exalted virtue, and that all defections are contemptible, will bear little looking into. Nor will her impatience with Wells's evolving sense of what might benefit society in a given period; her idea here would seem to be that the world is a simple mechanism with a simple problem which some single, simple remedy, held hard and fast enough, ought to provide for. Indeed, the whole insistence on turning to Wells as a deliverer who might have saved the world, and then turning from him in pain and disillusionment when he did not, is naive in the extreme. It testifies to Madame Keun's fundamental misunderstanding of both life and letters, of what reasonable expectations we may have of thinking and writing in relation to action and history. Another sign of her misconstruction of Wells's career is her total neglect of his fiction, her treatment of him solely as deliverer, never as artist.

But however negligible her articles are as an assessment of Wells, they do afford considerable interest of a personal kind. She speaks as an injured woman to an audience that in large measure was aware of her relationship to Wells. With remarkably little taste she undertakes to vindicate herself, and her break with him, in the public prints, although in the course of doing so she expresses dismay at Wells's own willingness to attack his enemies on a personal basis. There is also a good deal of egotistical spite and presumption in her criticism. The distinction that she is at pains to make between great men with selfless motives and great men with selfish ones is notoriously difficult; any distinguished career is susceptible of this sort of base interpretation. One does better to deal with the achievement in such cases and let the motives abide in peace. Surely Wells's dedication to the idea of the world state over the years warrants more respect as an endeavor than Madame Keun is able to summon. It is curious, too, that in the egotism of her own attack she quite forgets the mastery of egotistical motive that Wells had demonstrated in *Bulpington*, the novel that he had so generously dedicated to her.

In any case, the culmination of the personal exchange came four years later in *Apropos of Dolores* (1938), for Dolores is based on Madame Keun. When it came, however, because Wells had that within him which passed Odette Keun's understanding, the personal feeling had quite miraculously been transmuted into high comic art, into an experience, that is, for others. Thanks to Madame Keun and her ill-considered attack, Wells gave us by way of reply in *Apropos of Dolores* one of his most searching and amusing studies of the egotistic personality.

Apropos of Dolores begins with the obligatory disclaimer. All of its characters and events, Wells tells us in a prefatory note, are fictitious. Stephen Wilbeck, the first-person narrator, is no more H. G. Wells than Tristram Shandy is Laurence Sterne. No less, either, apparently, for Wells goes on to hedge. Invoking the aesthetic that he had defended against James, he says that we ought not to go too far in "these now customary disavowals":

> Every proper novel is judged by its reality and is designed to display life; it must present real life and real incidents and not life and incidents taken from other books; it should not, therefore, be anything but experience, observation, good hearsay and original thought, disarticulated and rearranged. You take bits from this person and bits from that, from a friend you have known for a lifetime or from someone you overheard upon a railway platform while waiting for a train or from some odd phrase or thing reported in a newspaper. That is the way fiction is made and there is no other way. If a character in a book should have the luck to seem like a real human being that is no excuse for imagining an "original" or suspecting a caricature. . . . Nothing in this book has happened to anyone; much in this book has happened to many people.[3]

In view of the clear-cut resemblance between Dolores and Odette Keun, and of that between Wilbeck and Wells, this may appear disingenuous, a mere concession to the legal exigencies. But it is, in fact, a faithful expression of Wells's perpetual sense of the relationship between fiction and life, especially his fiction and his life. And in addition to offering an implicit answer to Madame Keun's charge of personal ferocity—at least as regards the fiction—it expresses with remarkable accuracy the modification, disarticulation, and rearrangement of actual experience that created the art of *Apropos of Dolores*. As a novel *Dolores* is obviously inspired by its origins, yet not in the least confined to them.

Wells's portrait of Dolores is a consummate depiction of egotism incarnate in the female of the species. The egotists of both *Bulpington* and *Brynhild* had been men, and the treatment of them had taken more of a sinister than comic turn. Dolores's extravagances, though they come in the end to the same thing, are outrageously feminine and lend a vivacity to the book which sets it apart among the late novels.

But this is not to say that she is herself happy. One of the earliest things we learn about Dolores is her profession of melancholy; she maintains that her own birth was a wrong done to her, a tragedy. She is fond of the phrase, "I was sentenced to life." But having learned this from her husband of thirteen years, Stephen Wilbeck, before Dolores even appears, we immediately suspect it as a piece of self-dramatization. As things turn out, we are quite right to do so. It is not so much that she is unhappy in herself as it is that she is the cause of unhappiness in others, notably her husband.

The entire novel is cast as a journal kept by Wilbeck and the opening chapter is an exquisite account of Wilbeck's happiness in Dolores's absence, as he tours Brittany looking for a suitable place for her holiday from their home in Paris. There is even an attractive local girl at one of the cafés, through whose eyes Rennes seems to look at him "with inquiry and invitation," but his "adamantine virtue was proof against the friendliness of her face" (p. 11). Indeed, his loving appreciation of the serenity of provincial life in Rennes is haunted by recollections of Dolores, as is his memory of a cherished conversation on happiness with Foxfield, a writer whom Wilbeck's firm publishes. Both Wilbeck's experience of happiness and his optimistic speculations on whether life is happy are intermittently marred by the existence, the memory, the presence, the example of Dolores. The Boswellian contentment and appreciative gusto that Wilbeck tastes at Rennes on August 1, 1934, and his rewarding contemplation of the biological probabilities for human happiness in discussions with

Foxfield at Portumere through August 5, come to an end by August 9 at Torquéstol, for he is by this time awaiting the imminent arrival of his wife, the embodiment for him, on both a personal and, increasingly, a philosophical level, of tendencies and impulses that simply will not allow life to be happy.

As he waits for Dolores at Torquéstol in something very like dread, Wilbeck, who is a successful, urbane, and serious publisher, reverts in his journal to his past life with her. From this account we gain a vivid understanding of his apprehension. They had met on the Riviera thirteen years earlier, shortly after Wilbeck's divorce from his first wife. Into the enervating atmosphere of the Hotel Pension Malta et Syracuse—"There were, I remember," says Wilbeck, "three young women in languid pursuit of the arts and in active pursuit of excitement"—Dolores descended like a sunburst. Her first appearance in the dining room created a sensation. "She was dressed," writes Wilbeck, "with a kind of fashionableness that followed no known fashion, as though she belonged to the smart set of another world" (p. 63). Looking tragic and Eastern, she produced a lorgnette and surveyed "her fellow pensionnaires with an expression of mitigated disapproval." After a time, her lorgnette came to rest on Wilbeck, where it remained long enough to signal her decided interest in him, which in no time took the form of her wishing to have an affair with him.

After a good deal of collective conjecture, Dolores's antecedents were clarified. Despite her Turkish trousers and gilt slippers, Wilbeck discovered that Dolores was not, as one of the guests thought, "oriental from the beginning" but only "quite transitorily oriental." Her father was a Scotch wastrel and her mother an aristocratic Armenian. "The ménage was neither happy nor unhappy but incoherent; the parents would probably have quarrelled even more bitterly than they did, if they had had a firmer grasp on each other's ideas of what constitutes French." After a polyglot education in Monaco, she married a "perfectly genuine" Egyptian prince who died in a car race a year or so later and left her very poorly provided for. Wilbeck learned all this from Dolores herself in the first few days of her stay at the Hotel Pension Malta et Syracuse, for she made no secret of her desire to fascinate him, even if her method was characteristically egocentric:

> Dolores talked fluent English with a few Scotticisms and hardly a trace of French accent. She has in fact talked fluent English to me ever since, pausing only for eating, sleeping and interludes of

passion. She talked about herself copiously and picturesquely and when she said ever and again, "Tell me something of yourself" it meant that she went on talking, but about her impressions of me. Her faith in her own intuitions and observation has always been remarkable. Some few statements I got in edgeways and she at once turned them flat side round and made the most of them, and also she asked a few questions, concluding with "Yes? No?" to give an indication of the number of words permitted in the reply. [Pp. 67–68]

In spite of this flood of self, Dolores was careful to flatter Wilbeck to the uttermost. Having learned from him that after inheriting a stable and respectable publishing house from his father, he was planning to launch a new series called *Way of the World*, which would be devoted to Wellsian educational projects, she administered large doses of worshipful admiration: " 'To think of you, so quiet, so unobtrusive, with those firm hands of yours, moulding the thought of the world! It is *beautiful*.' " Wilbeck freely admits its effectiveness: "My opinion of her rose with her opinion of me." She used another tactic as well to certify her relationship with Wilbeck: total revelation of all that passed privately between them. She told everyone at the hotel, after only a few days, how much she loved Wilbeck and how wonderful his idea of organizing people's thoughts and ideas through the *Way of the World* series was, although it was then only in its initial planning stages. Determined to share something with her that she would not care to make public, Wilbeck took her to bed, only to overhear Dolores telling her companion the next day that he was " 'the *perfect* lover.' " Never having met a woman "who liked a chorus to her love-making," Wilbeck "stuck rather markedly to her side to minimize her opportunities for overflow," going so far as to profess a violent desire to be with her alone in order to keep her away from the others (p. 73).

In the end, despite his disinclination, his vision of life as "a wild scramble to entangle and get away, a fantastic arena of struggling people with lassoes, hooks, crooks, nets, adhesive ribbons, chains, handcuffs," she forced Wilbeck to marry her by declaring that she was with child. After he did, "a sort of annunciation in reverse occurred," and Dolores informed Wilbeck, who had returned to England on business, that she was seriously ill with a "growth," and that the child was lost. Summing it up, Wilbeck writes, "I married to become the father of a prospective child, which turned out to be a volatile form of cancer and ended in an occasional spasm" (p. 81). All that remains of the episode is an occasional sharp cry of anguish from Dolores—" 'My pain,' she would explain. 'Oh my pain!' ''—uttered at the most unexpected moments, and Wilbeck's recollection that in those eventful early days he was willing to take her word unsuspiciously.

Predictably enough, the marriage turned into an ordeal for Wilbeck. Dolores surrendered her pretense of adulation and viewed the publishing business, which came to claim more and more of Wilbeck's time with his increasing appreciation of his situation, as nothing but a rival; she has always, Wilbeck indicates, viewed music the same way, her impulse being "to rustle and talk it down." The apartment in Paris where she insisted they make their home, and which she furnished in "unadulterated, invincible Dolores," made Wilbeck feel like an alien, a paying guest. "There was not a table, not a horizontal surface anywhere, that did not carry its burthen of bibelots, little unworthy pots, boxes, images, carvings, witnessing that in every age Satan has found some artistry still for idle hands to do" (p. 86). In its Byzantine splendor, its incurable exhibitionism, says Wilbeck, "it was not furnished to live in; it was furnished for Dolores to show off to her friends, to explain to her friends, to triumph with over her friends." " 'You ought to mark the prices of everything in plain figures,' " he tells her on one occasion, but the blow merely glances.

Wilbeck's attempts to introduce Dolores to polite society in England proved disastrous. Her startling costumes, loud revelations of the most intimate details of her relations with Wilbeck, and generally scandalous sexual talk—she was told on one occasion by Lord Synagogue that a woman of her sort would have been stoned in Israel—defeated Wilbeck's attempt at "*de*-Dolorification." Instead of modifying her behavior in these decorous surroundings, she intensified it. "How was it," asks Wilbeck, "that I could have imagined that she, whose essential life it is to pose herself and brag, could possibly be assimilated to a sort of life which has subtilized posing and bragging out of sight?" (p. 89). Less and less able to bear her presence, Wilbeck arranged to be away from Paris and Dolores on business trips all over the world for weeks at a time. Fortunately for him, Dolores was persuaded by a rough Channel crossing on which she "suffered with outstanding distinction" to relinquish England, and Wilbeck was able to establish a rewarding social life there without her. His London apartment, however, was a constant thorn in her side, for she perpetually, and quite unjustly, suspected him of harboring women in it.

Having sketched Dolores and their thirteen years together with singular wit and pointedness—having, that is, begun what he quite frankly calls the case of *Stephen Wilbeck contra Dolores*—Wilbeck now turns in his journal to the ominous present at Torquéstol, where he awaits her in the carefully chosen hotel in which they are to have a holiday together. Her arrival is an extravaganza. Expecting her in the afternoon, Wilbeck goes for a walk before lunch only to discover on his return that she has come and that crowds of people at the hotel are expectantly, anxiously awaiting him at the entrance. "As usual," he writes with his customary smiling helplessness, "I was quite unprepared for my part. I walked as unconcernedly as possible. I should have advanced with a sort of trotting motion and asked, 'Is she here? Is she better?' " (p. 99). A decided mistake, for the maître d'hôtel, in a state of "hurried effusion," greets him with, " 'Madame was so disappointed not to find you awaiting her,' " and Marie, Dolores's maid and "rockbottom confidante," adds, " 'She is lying down now. She has had her pain.' " But before the reproach can take effect, Dolores herself appears in "the middle of the stage," flings herself upon Wilbeck with a clutching embrace from which he struggles to be free and announces magnificently that she forgives him. Then to the sound of applause, this "sight of passion in its full maturity" comes to a close.

The averted crisis, however, is merely Dolores's introduction to Torquéstol. By August 24, 1934, less than three weeks later, Wilbeck finds himself both angry and, in a ruffled and resentful way, amused. "I am disposed to laugh at things," he writes, "but it is laughter with a split lip" (p. 101). For by this time, Dolores has become involved in a number of rows. The first is with the Baroness, another guest at the hotel. It begins with Dolores's initial entry into the dining room, always, as we know from the Riviera thirteen years ago, a critical transaction with her. Wilbeck confirms it on this occasion by noting Dolores's profound conviction that to begin well in a hotel one must be arrogant, and a confusion about seating arrangements gives her a fine opportunity for arrogance. When the considerable fuss that she makes has subsided, the Baroness, who has watched it from her table with acute disapproval, inquires about Dolores's identity. The maître d'hôtel replies that Dolores is Madame Wilbeck, the great English éditeur's wife, who was previously a princess. Wilbeck is amazed, as ever, at the speed with which this information manages to reach hotel and shopkeepers when he never himself divulges it. "As a princess," he says candidly enough, "Dolores is, I admit, unconvincing" (p. 104). The Baroness's response, clearly overheard by Dolores, is a declaration of war: " '*Quelle* princesse!' exclaimed the Baroness with amusement and resumed her lunch." Before long, in an equally audible voice, Dolores refers to her antagonist as an old hag, takes note of her deafness and her ear trumpet, and hopes that *she* will never grow old like that, adding, " 'Her face is as white as a clown's. It's hardly human. . . . And that nose peeping out. Like—like a mongoose.' "

But this is only a prelude. The main encounter comes at dinner that evening, when, among the subdued sounds of polite dining, Dolores's male dog, Bayard, is discovered copulating in the *salle à manger* with the Baroness's Pomeranian temptress. " ' Dégoûtant!'' cries the old lady and administers a hearty thwack to Bayard. " 'Madame!' " screams Dolores, standing up, " 'will you please to refrain from hitting my dog.' " Wilbeck and the maître d'hôtel quickly separate the dogs and with Wilbeck tucking Bayard under his arm, the ladies resume their seats, the Baroness "with great dignity," and Dolores "with even greater dignity." But instead of allowing Wilbeck to remove Bayard, Dolores insists that he put the dog down so that it may finish its dinner. Wilbeck does so in a temper, and Bayard immediately reverts to "his supreme preoccupation." A great altercation arises immediately, with guests and staff intervening to try to separate the dogs, but Dolores and the Baroness contrive to remain at the center of things. Wilbeck's account is masterly:

> Happily the two principal ladies remained in their places. But they expressed themselves with such lucidity, length and vigour that for a time the actual proceedings of Bayard and his little friend were practically disregarded. . . .
> Both ladies found it necessary to assume an extremity of aristocratic poise, pride and authority. They were, we were given to understand, 'grandes dames' of a type rare since the revolutionary close of the eighteenth century. But their desire for an icy elevation was shot with a passionate impulse to sting and burn. . . . In each a fishwife struggled with a queen. [Pp. 108–9]

Finally, Wilbeck brings the mock-heroic turbulence to a close by smashing a glass to attract attention, ordering both dogs removed, and insisting that from this time forward no dogs whatever be allowed in the dining room. Everyone agrees, and the episode concludes. A truce of "mutual disdain" sets in between the two ladies. Dolores, however, is deeply annoyed at Wilbeck over his insistence, despite her express prohibition, on "bowing with profound respect to the Baroness whenever I encounter her.'' She decides within the next few days that the Baroness is a leper and that everyone must be warned of the danger. Only by threatening divorce does Wilbeck dissuade her from sounding the alarm. Forced to surrender her great idea, she is reduced to ''insinuating the idea of infection by having tables moved and getting nearer the window and by large and ostentatious purchases of antiseptics at the local chemist's'' (p. 116).

A more fundamental and enduring problem than the Baroness makes itself felt at Torquéstol also. Wilbeck's frequent and considerable absence from Dolores over the years has persuaded her, as she admits freely in conversation, that her husband is carrying on innumerable affairs with other women, for she is unable to imagine that his travels, as he repeatedly tells us, are merely an effort to seek shelter from her. Her jealousy, like her possessiveness, becomes monumental and obsessive. She accuses him to his business associates of carrying on with ''dactylos''—the French term for typists—and with one dactylo in particular, a Miss Camellia Bronte, who turns out to be an elderly spinster serving as Wilbeck's personal secretary in London. Her imagination is inflamed by her shabby Parisian circle of friends, comprised of ''remnants of the Monégasque and Egyptian days, later acquisitions in Paris, milliners, beauty specialists, decorators, odd semi-resident Americans, casual Russians. . . . Oh, brilliant women they were!'' says Wilbeck. ''Mostly they bragged to one another of their lovers, who seemed as a class reluctant to appear'' (p. 124). Eventually, Dolores entertains the possibility that Wilbeck is in pursuit of homosexual relationships on his travels; but she surrenders this for something more sensational still: the suspicion that Wilbeck is carrying on an incestuous affair with his sixteen-year-old daughter by his first marriage, Lettice.

Wilbeck has, in fact, become interested in his daughter, but only to save her from the dull surroundings of the home that her mother and stepfather have made for her in Southampton. He wants to send her to a good college, make it possible for her to travel abroad, and gain from her the companionship of a woman other than Dolores, filial but hardly incestuous. Dolores's first response, three years before Torquéstol, to Wilbeck's plans for Lettice is predictably venomous: '' 'And so now, when I have grown accustomed to the tragedy of my barren life, I am to have that other woman's daughter thrust into my face. . . . And while you are supposed to be away from me on that marvellous business of yours, you are prancing about after that silly drab you had to divorce and her brat—which may or may not be yours for all you know!' '' (p. 133).

For the first time, the idea of murder occurs to Wilbeck: " 'If ever there was a born murderee,' I said, 'Dolores is the woman.' " The idea occurs again when he first learns from a cousin of his, during an excruciating lunch at his club, that Dolores suspects him of incest with Lettice and has mentioned her suspicion to others. But only for a moment; it is not quite the civilized way out of his difficulties. Besides, he realizes that with Dolores's taste for the sensational she "would rather like me to murder her, provided the thing was done in a properly dramatic and public manner. At least she would like the idea of it until I actually began" (p. 140). Oddly enough, for a narrative with the lightness of touch of *Dolores*, these speculations turn out to be prophetic.

When Wilbeck presses to have Lettice spend some time with Dolores and him at their Paris apartment on the grounds that he will not allow anyone to separate him from his own daughter, it is Dolores who threatens divorce, and with such proceedings as would shake the world: " 'And very silly you will look among your dowdy English lady-friends, when I show you up. Your own daughter, your own, so far as you can tell, that is, as co-respondent! That will set all London talking if anything can. And she won't be the only co-respondent. No! All your friends are not as discreet as you are. I know things. And that secret flat of yours! Well, you meant it to be secret. . . . Have you never heard of private inquiry agents? I'll bring in that Camellia Bronte of yours. And others. That will put a pretty light on your *Way of the World* series and your New Humanity and all that. That will make tongues wag.' " This attack, in turn, is followed an hour later by an amorous one: " 'I love you. *See* how I love you. Why do you misunderstand me so? Why do you do everything you can to distress me? I would do anything for you—*anything*' " (p. 142).

Lettice, however, is not the only point of contention. Before coming to Torquéstol, Dolores has suddenly and irresponsibly dismissed from service a man and wife whom she and Wilbeck had wooed away from their own business, a charming provincial inn, by offering them the prospect of long-term, pleasant employment. Wilbeck is immensely distressed by this manifestation of the upper classes' power of "interference and injury" over the lower, but is helpless to rectify the situation. In addition, there is a maid at Torquéstol with adolescent acne, for whose job and well-being Wilbeck fears because of Dolores's mobid fear of infection. "Show Dolores a spot or a stain on a human face," he writes, "and syphilis leaps to her mind." The demand to the management for the maid's dismissal appears imminent.

The immediate cause of the first epic battle that Dolores and Wilbeck stage at Torquéstol is a young English boy, no more than sixteen, and his mother. When Wilbeck discovers that these two have begun to cut him and to exhibit signs of extreme embarrassment and shock when Dolores appears, he surmises, quite correctly, what has happened. Dolores has obviously had one of her customary quiet talks with the youth, the gambit of which is the question whether or not he is a virgin. These conversations are *de rigueur* with the women of her Parisian set:

> The sexual education of the adolescent male and the relative merits of the men of various nations as lovers are topics of inexhaustible interest to all those ladies in Dolores' brilliant rustling circle. . . . They go over this stuff again and again. They roll their imaginations over it. A lover ceases to be a lover; he is a technician, he is a violinist under the scrutiny of a connaiseuse. Affection flutters away from this awful stuff in infinite distress, rather like our scared English lady. The interest in the sexual apprenticeship of son or nephew is worked up to a feverish preoccupation. It is very important to save him, at any cost, from misdirected desires. There are aunts; there are dear friends ready to vindicate normality. There is a whole literature of the subject; deeply sentimental novels, very grave, very tender—for facetiousness would spoil everything. Don't for a moment call it pornography. It is literary conversation; it is sociology. [P. 152]

Wilbeck also surmises, again correctly, that when the boy, looking extremely uncomfortable, had got up and gone away, Dolores attempted to pursue the conversation with his mother, who also left, declaring indignantly, "I don't understand *what* you mean."

As an Englishman, Wilbeck is quite sympathetic to the feelings of mother and son. He reproaches Dolores with "always rushing sex to the front" in any conversation with a stranger, with her habit of bringing all her talk around to "sex and filth," with "perpetual lewdness"; and he designates it all as "a contagious disease of the mind" (p. 154). Gathering momentum, he says that he finds it unendurable, and that since she has joined him at Torquéstol he has been irritated and bored. That is as far as he gets, however, before Dolores unleashes her "defensive offensive." She begins by wondering how she can love so solemn, dull, and bourgeois a bookseller as her husband, who, finding her at the outset "one of the most brilliant women on the Riviera, accustomed to *gentlemen*, to men of title, to princes, to men of the world, to unquestioning gallantry," has wrought a "marvellous" change, rendering her almost as dull as he is.

Wilbeck's reiterated interjection, " 'I want to tell you,' " fails utterly to impede the flow of her talk. But when she reaches the point, " 'Still I'm not sufficiently banale. I suppose I am to look at you and catch your eye before I speak,' " he concludes that it is best for him to proceed with what he wants to tell her regardless of what she may be saying. What he wants to tell her, and does indeed say, is that he is determined, once and for all, to leave her. There is some question, though, about how much of it she hears, for as she becomes aware of the audience of management, maids, postcard sellers, and guests that has gathered, she shifts more and more into French for their benefit and increases her tempo and shrillness. Outmatched, Wilbeck attempts to withdraw under cover of numerous repetitions of the line " 'There is a limit,' " but spoils his effect by knocking over a table on his way. Dolores holds the field, reclining back on her chaise lounge. " 'Pouf!' she said for the benefit of the audience. '*Quel* maladroit! Mon amant! Mais c'est drôle!' " (p. 156).

At this point Wilbeck begins to intersperse his narrative with large speculations on Dolores's character and its implications. Having provided a vivid dramatic embodiment of her nature and behavior, of her comic, farcical outrageousness, he turns now to its significance for him and the world. It would be unlike Wilbeck, to say nothing of Wells, to do otherwise. At this juncture, then, one of the major purposes of *Apropos of Dolores* commences to reveal itself.

In the quiet of his journal Wilbeck admits that Dolores's scandalous sexual talk, although it has become as predictable and tiresome as most of the rest of her conversation, is by no means a pathological obsession. It is, rather, a device for startling and shocking. The desire to startle and shock, however, far from being negligible, offers a major clue to her personality. "It isn't a diseased imagination," writes Wilbeck, "that impels Dolores to indecency, it is something quite different and innate; it is a devouring insatiable egotism. She must have attention, she must focus attention, at any cost—and she found quite early in life that the most effective way for a young woman to hold the attention of the guests at a lunch party or dinner party was to be frankly improper." So strong is "this blank craving for notice" in her, according to Wilbeck, that she has no identity, direction, idiosyncrasies, or personal tint of her own apart from it. "She is a human being," he says, "stripped down to its bare egotism. She is assertion and avidity incarnate. She is the most completely, exclusively and harshly assembled individuality I have ever encountered" (p. 159). Because she is a paradoxical blend of the most intensely egotistic and the least unique and distinguishable elements of character, Wilbeck is disposed to universalize her as "common humanity unmitigated"; the egotism that exists in mitigated, qualified form in everyone else lodges in her in a state of chemical purity.

When he asks himself why Dolores—or anyone—wants attention so badly, Wilbeck finds that neither love, nor hate, nor affection is the motive. Instead of the common psychological explanations, he offers one that is almost philosophical in its breadth: "What she seems to be after when she embarks upon one of her crescendos of showing off is anything but affection; her nature is much more aggressive. It is to rouse a sense of inferiority and admiration in her hearers. It is to impose herself upon the absent and the present. It is to achieve a sense of triumphant existence. That is the climax of the orgasm."

If Dolores is the unadulterated incarnation of a universal human impulse, then Wilbeck agrees that it behooves him to examine himself for similar tendencies. In a passage which Wells makes notable for its self-reflexive candor, Wilbeck does so. Wilbeck begins with an utterly merciless dissection of the touching opening pages of the novel, where he had described his happiness at Rennes, away from Dolores, and then proceeds to an extraordinarily magnanimous evaluation of her egotism in relation to his own:

I have been reading over the opening chapters of this manuscript, the part about the high road, the sunshine and Rennes and all that, and I remark how pleasantly he [i.e., Wilbeck himself] chuckles over and tickles and caresses every human being he meets, as though he loved them. He observes their rather petty activities, how lovably petty they are, he weaves quaint belittling fancies round them, notes their human absurdities. He does not obtrude himself at all, but he remains from first to last in his private imagination floating over them like a kindly divinity. The sense of triumphant existence—at least of successful existence—is the end sought in both cases. He gets it more subtly and skilfully and successfully than Dolores, that is all the difference. He does not try to rend it out of these others; he steals away with it. And instead of screams, threats, dismissals and so on towards servants, he gets the upper hand of them by creating a sense of obligation. Is there really a passion for fair play in him? Or does he merely like the people about him to feel that he is fair and trustworthy? Does he care for them as people or minions? I ought to know but I don't. Let us put a query to that. In the scales of a real divinity sitting among the stars, I doubt whether even on the score of

ego-centredness the beam of the moral balance would kick against
Dolores. It would tilt but not kick. Her egotism is crude and bare; it
is more primitive; it lies naked—flayed—on the inflexible limitations
of her life, and there it screams with resentment, suspicion and envy.
  He has an integument. [Pp. 160–61]

It is one of the great moments in the novel. In a passage such as this, the
book is lifted from retaliation and indictment—even brilliantly comic
indictment—to that plane of extraordinary disinterestedness that high art
achieves unawares. The amusing attack on Odette Keun turns here into a
serious quest for the truth of things. And Wells achieves the transformation
not merely with sincerity, or compassion, or courage, but with the
enormous narrative skill and resourcefulness that allows him to make such
convincing analytical use of the earlier Rennes section of the novel.
Wilbeck's moral repudiation of the most beautiful writing the book offers
becomes a measure of the new ground on which the narrative, he, Wells,
and we must stand.

But having established this plane of large disinterestedness, Wilbeck
finds that in fairness to himself he must qualify his concessions to Dolores.
There is still a crucial distinction to be made. "There *is* something between
Dolores and me," he writes, "that is in my favour. Our difference is not
simply that I am more subtle and elaborate than she. In many matters she
can be much more intricate than I. But I am not wholly an ego, and she is.
There is a certain good in me that she has not, there is something in my
make-up going beyond my egotism, that I am justified in defending, even
ruthlessly, against her devastating attacks."

At this point Wilbeck interrupts his speculations with a touch of
narrative which gives them added point, and which prepares for a later
scene that will knit the concrete and discursive elements of the novel
together memorably. He tells how after a grim, silent, tense dinner
following their quarrel, which spreads its pall over all the hotel guests and
staff, Dolores sends him a note in which, with her characteristic querulous,
incriminating largesse, she forgives him for everything, reminds him of the
suffering that he has caused her—"Remember I am in pain and still very
ill"—and agrees to go through with their plans to pay a visit to Foxfield,
Wilbeck's admired "scientific hack writer," at Roscoff. She also invites
him to come to her room to say "Good night" to her, and Wilbeck
recognizes that this crisis, too, is to end in the usual amorous way.

But his speculations on Dolores do not end with this narrative interlude.
He returns, in his journal, to the distinction that he has been adumbrating

between Dolores and himself. She cannot, he says, forget herself, "and since all individuals are, as individuals, doomed to defeat, since the outer world manifestly overrules and outlives them, her life has been necessarily a bitter struggle against the admission of her essential finality" (p. 165). The normal mind, however, is more complicated, not so completely contained by its egotism, by the "drama of the triumph or frustration of the '*I.*' " A large part of its self-education consists in an adjustment between the desire for "unqualified and triumphant self-assertion" and "outer non-egoistic motives." Thus Wilbeck concedes that while he too is egotistical, there is "extra matter" present in his nature:

> A part of his [Wilbeck's] being is evidently reservation and discretion—a deference. There is a sort of councillor, primarily devoted to his egotism, no doubt, but nevertheless functioning as a sort of family solicitor in his make-up, who says continually, 'Do you think—?' and 'Must you go as far as that? Have you considered that there are others concerned in this?' Possibly this something that was only present as a germ in the infant, but which has been developed by the conditions of his upbringing. It was there to train and so it has been trained. It has grown into a mitigating mental habit system that is now his second nature. His self-assertion has become so qualified that he now has a positive satisfaction in considering others and subordinating that primordial impulse to triumph over them, to their approval and acquiescence. [Pp. 165–66]

Wilbeck's characterization of himself is certainly recognizable enough as the normal civilizing process, observed by Hobbes, Rousseau, Freud, everyone. What is striking is his insistence that Dolores stands outside it altogether. For a moment he considers that the difference between Dolores and himself may be traceable, in part at least, to her education in a Jesuit convent school where "effort was stimulated by incessant displays, lists and changes of precedence, prize-givings, public and private praising, public humiliations, confessions," and where she was trained to take pride simply in winning— "a poisonous training," says the enlightened Wilbeck, "for any child." But the difference in upbringing is only part of the explanation.

The ultimate explanation, Wilbeck concludes, is biological. Apart from upbringing, Dolores and he started out intrinsically different at birth. "We did not start merely as different individuals, we started as different sorts of individuals" (p. 166). Wilbeck maintains that it is not training alone that has diminished his egotism and given him his sense of responsibility about scientific truth, the truth of historical statement, the general welfare of the community, or the beauties and decencies of town and country, none of which Dolores shares. "I do not mean that I have had these interests from the beginning," he says, "but they grew, just as my moustache grew, as my mind opened. I believe that the sort of person to which I belong has these natural impersonal solicitudes, just as I believe that her sort has not."

Having come so far—and it is where the novel has been heading from the beginning—Wilbeck is now prepared to frame a general theory of man. But he proceeds somewhat apologetically. It is very late at night, he reminds us, and his mind, as he sits writing his journal, is growing diffuse. He has also drunk a good deal of brandy in preparation for his "Good night" to Dolores. And he is fully cognizant of the long tradition of nonsensical generalizing about humanity—"simplifying its movements to explain them more easily, and dividing it in the most haphazard and uncritical way"—that the intelligentsia of the world have perpetrated. He is utterly in agreement with Henry Ford that all written history is bunk, whether Herodotus's, Spengler's, Toynbee's, or Pareto's; he has always been appalled by such empty, invidious categories as "the Orient," "the West," "North" and "South," "Aryan" and "non-Aryan," by such amorphous terms as the "Cradle" or "Spirit" of Civilization, and by most ethnological and nationalistic classifications. Dolores's habit of generalizing about "France" and "England" and "America" and "Germany"—"Never will she speak to Germany again. Germany must stand in the corner, face to wall, and Britain must wear a dunce's cap"—has always dismayed him, especially since these remarks of hers, like all her observations, are always prefaced by "that intolerable French idiom, 'Je trouve—,' which still jars upon my English ear as the quintessence of unsolicited ill-bred judgment" (p. 112). Nonetheless despite this "drivel of hate and vain comparison," Wilbeck finds himself disposed—perhaps it is the brandy, perhaps he is half-asleep and dreaming—to formulate his own generalization. Oddly enough, it turns out to be vaster than any of those he has been denouncing.

Wilbeck finds all previous attempts at human classification unsatisfactory. Neither race, culture, religion, nationality, sex, nor such biopsychological attempts as *cerebrotonics, somatotonics,* and *viscerotonics*—" 'Cerebrotonic' makes me think somehow of Aldous Huxley with neuralgia, faint but pursuing the ideal"—are valid for him. Still, he has discovered, partly with his friend Foxfield's aid, that there are certain real human races, hereditary strains, that do not readily lose their identity. He frames the idea in his characteristically biological-historical terms:

"There are breeds, I find, adapted to a spacious and generalized modern life, new variations perhaps, other breeds essentially parasitic, others timidly docile, and again breeds bitterly ego-centred and malignantly resistant to adaptation. . . . These breeds traverse all recognized boundaries" (p. 173). Then, in a dazzling fusion of the representational particularities of the book and its heady theorizing, Wilbeck reveals his whole hand:

> To begin with I abolish the species *Homo sapiens.* I propose to replace that by a number of species and varieties, new and old. *Homo,* I declare, is a genus with an immense range of species, sub-species, hybrids and mutations. For to-night anyhow. I am going to collect my specimens like any other honest naturalist. First *Homo Doloresiform,* a widespread, familiar type, emphatic, impulsive and implacable. Particularly implacable. Then *Homo Wilbeckius,* probably a recent mutation, observant, inhibited and disingenuous. Many of those new cerebrotonics may belong to this species. Its chief distinction is that it is flexible. Other species there are but this will be enough to start with. Later no doubt dozens of other species, variants, stabilized hybrids, will become distinguishable. But for the moment let us take the two main sub-genera of *Homo, Homo regardant* and *Homo rampant,* the former traditional, legal and implacable and the latter open-minded and futuristic, making Doloresiform the type-species of the former group and Wilbeckius of the latter. [Pp. 174–75]

The Dolores type, *Homo Doloresiform,* emphatic, impulsive, and implacable, is not human, says Wilbeck, if we accept *Homo Wilbeckius* as the norm, but "a human-looking animal of a kind capable of interbreeding with human beings." Nonetheless, he maintains, her species has been a dominant force in human history, the very type of all the "objectionable brunet peoples in history, the peoples who insist, the peoples who resist, the 'inadaptables' of to-day who created our yesterdays." For there are Dolores nations, races, and peoples: "A Dolores people is a tenacious, self-righteous people with an exaggerated past and great claims. Its gods are always jealous gods and it takes after them. The patriotism of such a people is a sacred national egotism."[4] A Dolores people, Wilbeck adds, "never forgets a grievance. It lives on grievances." "Its idea of the future is not, as mine is, a magnificent progressive achievement continually opening out, forgiving everyone, comprehending everyone, but a judgment day, a day of bitter reckoning" (p. 176). Preeminently, such a people has set its face against Wilbeck's—and, of course, Wells's—

biological, social, moral, evolutionary vision of the world to come: "For evermore these nations shall sit at their game and lose and win and squabble. . . . The old world was truly theirs, they made it and they fit it, and they struggle unrelentingly against the advent of a new." And it is Dolores who presides over Wilbeck's vision of human benightedness, the incarnation of his, as she has been of the novel's, large understanding: "She expands after the fashion of dreams to become all the obdurate, grievance-cherishing, triumph-seeking people in the world. She becomes everything that stands in the way of a World Pax and a universal system of mutual service. I see her down the corridors of time, the unyielding guardian of her own ways, refusing to adapt, refusing to tolerate, confronting her enemies, pursuing her malice, unable to forget her old world, unable to learn a new one" (pp. 176–77).

Although Wilbeck is by now quite full of brandy and discovers, after looking back at his wild scrawl on the page, that he *has* been writing in his sleep, there is no mistaking Wells's fundamental seriousness here, or the momentousness of what he wishes to say. The drinking and the sleepiness are part of the comic verisimilitude of the scene: Wilbeck confiding to his journal truths that he could never hope to impose on Dolores face to face in marital combat. His drowsiness and inebriation are invoked to excuse some of the audacity of his reflections, but there is a quintessential audacity about them which Wells does not wish to excuse at all. Dolores's limitless unyielding egotism, with its senseless, rigid allegiances, is precisely what stands, for him, between the grief-stricken present and all hope for a rational future. Earlier in the novel, recounting a conversation with Foxfield, Wilbeck had called such a perverse failure to adjust feelings, impulses, instincts, and traditions to the realities that press upon us "the modern form of the dogmas of the Fall and Original Sin" (p. 43).

And Wells himself, when in his last years he submitted a thesis to London University in order to earn his Doctor of Science degree, made the same point from another, rather suggestive, angle. He argues there that the "integrality of the individual," our sense of our own "mental unity," of "being one single self"—the indispensable ground, of course, of all egotism—is "a biologically convenient delusion."[5] And he maintains that the knowledge that personality itself, and all personal drama, is an illusion will affect the evolution of civilization: "To realize that the drama is hallucinatory will be to escape from most of the foolish dogmatisms and ultimate 'explanations' of life, the priestcrafts, presumptuous teachings, fears, arbitrary intolerances, tyrannies and mental muddles that have embittered human relationships hitherto, but it will not secure anyone against phases of extravagance and incoherence. It will not release human beings from the necessity of 'conduct.' It will however lift them into a new atmosphere of self-knowledge, mutual understanding, tolerance and mellowed judgment which will mitigate profoundly the confused motivation of that long 'Martyrdom of Mankind' which is now drawing to an end."[6] In this extraordinary document, human cooperation is made to depend not only on a dissolution of selfishness, which is as far as *Apropos of Dolores* goes, but on the indisputable heart of the matter, the dissolution of self.

The egotism and self-delusion of Theodore Bulpington had been charged, for the most part, with responsibility for the failures of the past which culminated in World War I. The egotism of Rowland Palace had blighted personal and marital relations. In Dolores, on the other hand, Wells anatomizes an egotism which not only incorporates these misfortunes but also invalidates the whole human future. Wilbeck, endeavoring to keep her representativeness and significance as large as possible, denies that the problem is connected with the stresses and confusions of modern marriage, or with her sex. Even after finding that he must agree with a misogynous fisherman he meets that he has never seen a woman fishing alone, for there is obviously some strange unrest in women's temperament that bars them from so simple a form of contentment, he refuses to view Dolores's self-absorption as feminine. There are, he insists, Wilbeck women and Dolores men. The trait is truly elemental in the human composition and, as we gather from his conversations with Foxfield which range through all of animal creation, only there.

These momentous speculations of Wilbeck's are interrupted by the visit to Foxfield at Roscoff, although interrupted is not quite the right term. For once again, Wells is adept at mixing narrative and discursive elements so as to enhance both. Foxfield's is the most abstract and speculative voice in the novel; he is Wilbeck's mentor in things biological and Wells's portrait of a truly imaginative scientific thinker. Dolores is, of course, Dolores, the novel's most concrete embodiment of outrageous, impedimentary selfhood. Bringing them together for conversation is, on the face of it, a way of integrating the planes of thought and representation. But Wells's manner of bringing them together, the interaction and dialogue that he devises for the occasion, allows him to make the most of the opportunity for comedy as well.

Things begin badly at Roscoff, for knowing that Wilbeck occasionally pays Foxfield money, Dolores at first treats the scientist with considerable condescension. He, for his part, appears not to notice either this or the several "almost audible asides" that Dolores addresses to Wilbeck on Foxfield's personal appearance. Foxfield, in fact, ignores her altogether until the party finds itself among the salt-water tanks, where, having taken Dolores's measure, he suddenly addresses himself to her and begins "a lucid and detailed account of the love-life of the octopus" (p. 179). Catching her interest by pointing out that the octopus is paying Dolores the rare compliment of looking at her, he proceeds to speak of the grace of its unfolding undulating movements, its capacity for passion, floating as it does undistracted by gravitation, "like painted gods upon a ceiling." Warming to it as his own peculiar way of getting even with Dolores for her earlier patronage of him, Foxfield offers her a new view of an aquarium as "an arena of passion," rich with unprintable observations on life in "the salt salacious sea." Dolores, quite unaware that both her legs are being pulled, is entranced and comes winningly alive herself with witty observations on some nearby fig leaves. "It was one of her brilliant days," writes Wilbeck. "She came near to being happy—and I liked her" (p. 182). When they leave, Dolores, completely won over, reproaches Wilbeck with underpaying Foxfield. " 'If I were a rich woman,' " she says, ' "I would endow him. Like Rousseau. Like Catherine the Great and Voltaire.' "

So it is that biology unbends, becomes playful, and earns Dolores's—its villainess's—praise. So it is that Wells, the comic artist, proceeds on his serious way, smiling.

The narrative resumes at this point with an unlooked-for, catastrophic swiftness. Chapter 4, "Dolores at Torquéstol," ends with Wilbeck's discovery that Dolores has torn the photograph of his daughter, Lettice, into fragments and deposited them in his wastepaper basket. Its very last sentence expresses his resolve, as he inscribes it in his journal, to confront Dolores with what she has done. Chapter 5, "Threnody," begins with the revelation that Dolores is dead.

The shock is immense. We are not, however, to be deprived of the confrontation scene or of the curious explanation of how she came to her end, for Wilbeck now takes up his narrative from the very point where he left it at the end of Chapter 4. Confronted with the torn photograph, Dolores proceeds to revile her husband with a paranoid malevolence sufficient to justify her fate, whatever it turns out to be. She calls Lettice, whom Wilbeck has rarely seen, his mistress, says she hates him, and charges him with having dragged her down from her brilliant, promising beginnings—she might have done great things in the worlds of literature, art, fashion, politics—into dullness and waste. She characterizes him as illiterate, stupid, clumsy, evil, perverse, and coarsely sensual. Then, in an astonishing stroke, she declares that she is finished with being magnificently selfless: " 'That long dream of servitude is past. I cast it aside. I mean to take care of my own life—from this time forth. Dolores for Dolores. Clear-headed and resolute as I am by nature, and now *absolutely* selfish . . .' " (p. 195). What is more, she will go to London and clean out Wilbeck's "secret" flat, ridding it of its English servants and English mistresses.

As he listens to her fierce monologue, Wilbeck has one of those extraordinary perceptions that suggest the essential largeness, if not justice, of his mind. "It was plainly a premeditated piece she was repeating. . . . It was her version of our relationship. . . . It was her rationalization of all her moods and impulses. And as I marked its hard fantastic unreality, I found myself wondering how far on the other side of veracity my own version might lie. Not so far as this surely." This is not the first, and certainly not the last, occasion on which Wilbeck, mirroring himself in Dolores, considers the reliability and fairness of his own indictment. Like most such admissions in narration, it has the effect of both raising doubt and allaying it, although at this particular juncture it for the most part enhances Wilbeck's trustworthiness, at least in connection with the horror of their life together.

But a moment later, Dolores has moved outside the province of this sort of magnanimity and become totally appalling:

Yes. I will send the whole of that harem of yours spinning. All those women over there shall be dragged out of the shadows in which you hide them. If they are married women I shall write to their husbands. What if there *are* divorce cases! And as for this nasty daughter of yours—yes, nasty, nasty, dirty, filthy—off she goes out of your life! Or else publicity. . . . All London will talk of you. Obscure as you are I will drag you out of your obscurity. It will be a stinking case—trust me for that. . . .

Oh, I hate you. I *hate* you. Never yet have I moved you to passion, to real passion—never. . . . I doubt if I could forgive you now whatever you did. I am your Enemy. We are at war. I want to ruin you . . . I want to ruin you—and ruin you I will, expose and ruin you, whatever it costs me in the process. I want to hurt you—beyond all things I want to hurt you. . . .

Wait till I come back to England. Wait till I deal with that
incestuous degenerate of yours, that street drab, that filthy simpering
girl, as she deserves. Couldn't you see? Even in that photograph . . . .[Pp. 196–98]

But even in the flood of this hysterical abuse, Dolores notices that Wilbeck
is strangely still. Struck by this, she looks closely at him, and we can
conjecture what she sees: "She caught some new quality of menace in my
stillness, and suddenly I saw she was afraid. I cannot imagine what she
found in my face." We can imagine it, though, when we consider the
insane ferocity of Dolores's last words on poor Lettice; something
doubtless very like murderous hatred has found its way into and out of
Wilbeck's eyes. In any case, the pause is followed by the ultimate moment
of confrontation: "The abuse died on her lips and she stared at me. We
held each other's eyes. For a mute moment we saw each other bare." It is
the most terrible moment thus far in the novel. Dolores immediately
retreats from it by crying out, " 'My pain! My pain!' " and demanding, as
she has on numerous occasions, that Wilbeck gives her some Semondyle,
her pain medicine. He does. She drinks. The next morning she is dead.[7]

And now our confidence in our narrator, publisher, diarist, paragon of
evolution, is considerably shaken. Until now he has appeared temperate,
civilized, decent, responsible—especially in contrast to his ravaging
wife—and honest, as we have seen, to the point of casting gentlemanly
doubt on the ultimate fairness of his whole case against her. But now he
tells us, and tells himself as well in the journal, that he honestly does not
know whether or not he himself administered the overdose of Semondyle
that killed Dolores. "Once or twice before," he writes, with something
less than total plausibility, "I have had dreams so vivid and prosaic that I
have had the utmost difficulty in distinguishing them from actual mem-
ories. Once or twice facts have thrown a somersault in my memory. And I
am not sure whether at the moment when I should have put the two tabloids
into a glass of water, it did not occur to me to put in the whole tubeful" (p.
203). What is certain is that he resolves that no court of law would be
capable of "deciding such fine issues as this involves" and that "it is
something that it would be unwholesome to brood over very much even
within myself." He intends, he says, to dismiss it from his mind and is
remarkably successful in doing so. The official verdict is that Dolores took
an overdose of Semondyle when she was half asleep.

It makes us wonder, for murder is something to wonder about, even the
murder of a woman as impossible as Dolores. It is true that the novel's

comic momentum tempts us to share Wilbeck's impulse to dismiss all details about the mechanism of good riddance, and to enjoy, with him, the delicious sense of freedom which it has produced, no questions asked. But there are other considerations too. We remember, for example, his strange first marriage and its strange termination. As a soldier home on leave during the First World War he had met Alice, an obviously unsuitable young woman, married her and then gone off to fight. In his absence, Alice had had an affair with an unprepossessing young man named George Hoopler, who was, she said, "practically an intellectual." When Wilbeck returned Alice revealed the relationship to him, expecting rage, revenge, passion. Instead Wilbeck calmly withdrew, in part because he knew what she expected. His tone, as he looks back at the episode in his journal, is eerily unfeeling:

> I was not behaving quite as she expected; I was rather like an actor who had learnt a part out of another play. She had, I know, expected me to behave as though she was the only Alice in the world. So perhaps I should have behaved a year and a half before. And she would certainly have made it clear in the most effectual fashion that my loss was not irreparable, if only I would realize the essential goodness and purity of the Hoopler affair. But suddenly the world was full of Alices for me, one for every man and a few over. It is one of the things that a woman finds hardest to understand in life, that for a time she can be the only rapture in the world for a man, sole custodian and dispenser of delight for him, and then in the twinkling of an eye become just one individual packet of an overproduced standard commodity. [Pp. 55–56]

Very hard truths indeed. The cynicism of the passage has a personal cast that sets it apart from the workaday disillusionment of the postwar period. Wilbeck is revealing an attitude toward women here which, as we come to see, he does not altogether relinquish when, during the thirties, the conditions in which it arose have disappeared. In the years following his divorce from Alice, he had numerous affairs but soon found that "for anyone with an imagination, promiscuity speedily becomes the dullest game in the world." From the vantage point of 1934, he confesses that he has always "found business a much more sustaining interest than women" and that competing for them bored him (p. 59). His idea of love, then and now, he writes, blowing remarkably neither hot nor cold, "was a cheerful natural reciprocity of help and pleasuring and a certain mutual flattery and reassurance—with no thought or possibility of third parties intervening from either side of the picture. Love, if it was any good at all, was an honest alliance of two people well suited to each other, against the impertinence of third parties. With laughter in it.''

This unstable mixture of bitterness and childlike faith is hardly the best preparation for his life with Dolores. It is not surprising that he has twice chosen badly, or allowed himself to be chosen badly, and that neither match has come to any good. And just as there is an odd passivity about his involvement both times, so there is an odd passivity about his extrications. The first time, with Alice, he merely stands aside, the second, with Dolores, he cannot be sure whether he has acted or not. In a novel centered so firmly on questions of love, happiness, and fulfillment, a man with so spotty a record with women will bear watching. As it turns out, he fares no better in his remaining relationships, first with his daughter, then with an attractive stranger. This side of his nature remains suspect. The question for any reader of the novel, now that Wilbeck has become as much an object of scrutiny as Dolores, is how far to let this side affect the others.

One answer to that question is that we should let the suspect side affect the others very little, for on the less literal, personally dramatic plane of the novel Wilbeck's significance, and Dolores's, dictates an abatement of such moral considerations. Not as mythic figures, but as the even more inclusive *Homo Doloresiform* and *Homo Wilbeckius*, it is altogether fitting in the long evolutionary perspective of the novel for Dolores to die out and for Wilbeck, mysteriously, fortuitously, through no conscious, deliberate contrivance of his own, to survive. This biologically projected dimension of the book, hitherto present largely as speculation, enters into the stream of action with Dolores's death; and in this perspective, Wilbeck need say no more.

Nonetheless, as a novelist meeting obligations of verisimilitude, Wells offers other answers too. In the days following Dolores's death, Wilbeck's grief and meditations redeem him, helping to restore all his former authority as narrator, no matter what, as protagonist, he may have done.

He touches us by confessing that the event has "bludgeoned" him. "I am going to miss her greatly," he writes. "I am going to miss her enormously" (p. 205). After "another enormous day" has passed, he sees to it that the stone cross over her grave will bear the simple words "Dolores, Pax," rejecting in his wry, understated way the implications of the local priest's wish to add "Resurgam." But there is the humanity of wishing rest for her perturbed spirit in this demurral, as well as the wit of wanting her to stay put. Similarly, with compassion rather than revenge, he arranges for Bayard, now getting on in years, to be buried at his mistress's feet, though the two feelings are, admittedly in this case, nicely poised.

Walking in the country surrounding Torquéstol to dispel his grief, Wilbeck meditates on a pony that he encounters, contrasting its direct, sensuous mode of apprehension with the complexities and confusions of human language and ideas. It is difficult to tell, he thinks, whether we human beings use our brains or whether they use us. Certain it is that our brains will not leave us alone, have taken to inventing things that often prove quite unmanageable. Then, in a moment, Wilbeck's own mind is filled with the key issues of the book, deriving from the example of Dolores and placed this time in a new biological, historical, moral perspective: "First the brain discovered individuality and concentrated itself about itself to produce the furious egotism of the Dolores stage of human progress . . . and then secondly came the realization of a possible collective mind, . . . and the brain began to launch these attacks against egotism which we call religion, science and philosophy. First the evolution of the conscious brain gathered *Homo* up into an individual egotism like a clenched fist, and then it (Nature or the Life Force or what you will) seemed to realize it had gone too far and turned upon itself. And so we have our moral conflict'' (p. 213). With this dynamic reflection, which succeeds in shifting attention away from Wilbeck the malefactor and back to Dolores the specimen evolutionary ego, we are once more intellectually as well as emotionally in tune with Wilbeck.

Consequently, we applaud his resolve to telegraph Lettice to join him and alleviate his terrible loneliness, and we enjoy to the full his adroit narration of his difficulties in patching together suitable funeral dress, minutes before the ceremony, in a town completely closed down out of respect for his bereavement. By the time he records his own elegaic feelings on Dolores at her graveside, we are content with their mingling of reservation, comedy, and regret; indeed, we are moved by it:

> Poor extravagant Dolores! Whose one outlet of living has been a torrent of self exposition. She was inside there *gagged*. I seemed to hear her: "Let me speak, Steenie, let me speak.'' I wished I could have let her speak. Maybe it would not have been so very outrageous. She was not always outrageous. Her mischiefs and meannesses went out of the picture. Her passion to hurt and injure became now merely silly. At times she had been delightfully absurd. Perhaps I had been unreasonably impatient with her. After all had any insult of hers really hurt me? How endearingly ridiculous she had been at Roscoff. . . . I began to think of her best moments and

to forget all the rest. Tenderness followed pity. To my utmost amazement, I wept. I wept simply and genuinely for that intolerable woman! And because she was silent! [P. 220]

Three weeks intervene between the funeral and Wilbeck's next journal entry, and the events between give us further reason to sympathize with him. He resumes after the interval by asking himself if the opposition between the Wilbeck type, capable of thinking and, at times, acting with complete self-forgetfulness, and the Dolores type, decidedly capable of neither, has anything to do with moral or religious standards. The question arises because he has been visiting a good many churches, shrines, and convents in Brittany with Lettice and reading St. Paul, whom his father had always regarded as the cardinal exponent of the unjustifiable distinction between the worldly and the spiritual, between the flesh and the spirit. In his father's eyes, this assumption constituted "the mental Fall of Man" (p. 226). Wilbeck has always liked St. Paul—"There was something con-scientiously evasive about him that I find very congenial. An exploring mind must not fix itself into over definite phrases"—and it is not surprising that he finds corroboration for his own distinction between ego-centered and non-ego-centered types in Paul's Epistles: "His Old Adam and New Adam," says Wilbeck, "are, I am convinced, my *Homo regardant* and *Homo rampant*, overlapping one another" (p. 228). But the differences, as Wilbeck is aware, are profound. Paul believed, "with obstinate assur-ance," that "by some magic of conversion one could be changed into the other. And that one was *good* and the other *bad*." Wilbeck purports to believe no such thing. "Nothing short of Semondyle, I am convinced, could have released Dolores from her absolute concentration upon her ego, and nothing whatever justifies any belief that I am higher or better in any way than she was. We were profoundly different; that is all." He is curiously insistent about the moral neutrality of the difference, profound as the difference is.

That insistence belies our experience of Dolores, our experience of Wilbeck's experience of Dolores, our sense of the whole novel; yet on the novel's impersonal scientific, speculative plane, or at least in Wilbeck's aspiration to that plane, it has a certain validity. Moreover, it is yet another sign of his unwillingness to bear egocentric grudges. Interestingly enough, he knows something of how, in judging, not to judge: "She belonged by nature to a world that is manifestly working out its own destruction by excesses of acquisition, assertion and malice, and I, to the best of my knowledge and belief, belong to a new, less acutely concentrated world that may or may not be able to emerge—wriggle out rather than emerge—from the ruins and survive.'' All is process. A kind of dread of egotism keeps Wilbeck from saying outright what he clearly believes: that a ''world that is manifestly working out its own destruction by excesses of acquisition, assertion and malice'' is worse, despite its participation in an all-encompassing process, than the world which he sees struggling to emerge, and to which he feels he belongs. That dread, and his aspiration to biohistorical objectivity, are the stuff of which his dismissal of his probable guilt in connection with Dolores's death is made. We accept it, for the moment at least, as an attempt to be large-minded in the face of a number of intense small considerations.

Writing now at Nantes on September 25, 1934, Wilbeck enlists our sympathy further. His three weeks of touring with Lettice, who has to fill the great emptiness in his life with meaningful relationship and true companionship, have been a fiasco, a ''comedy of disillusionment,'' for Lettice is herself a great emptiness. As Wilbeck labors to convey to his daughter some sense of himself, his purposes, his world, and to point out to her the immense historical importance of all that they have been privileged to see on their travels, he finds that she is simply not listening. As *Homo Wilbeckius*, he is sensitive enough to consider that she may be reacting to overbearing pedantry, but concludes that he must reject this possibility: ''She was not protecting any living mental process against irrelevance. She is not so to speak seeing and thinking for herself and fending off distracting direction and pompous ill-directed instruction. She is just not seeing or thinking about external things at all. They are too much for her. This world, which is a feast to me, for her is the menace of a stupendous indigestion. She says 'No thank you' to all of it and reverts to something within'' (pp. 239–40).

There is indeed something within, and Wilbeck is shrewd enough to guess that it is a young man, back home in Southampton. Lettice and Wilbeck have been reliving the exasperating continental tour of Catherine Sloper and her father in Henry James's *Washington Square*. Wilbeck makes Lettice very happy by consenting to allow her to return home three days earlier than planned so that she may join a ''Certain Person,'' who works in a shipping office, at the start of his holidays. After listening to Lettice's account of him, Wilbeck decides that he ''seems to be commonplace and average to the point of distinction.'' There is a notable intensity of distaste, of disinheritance, almost, in Wilbeck's reflections on the young lovers, one of whom, after all, is his daughter:

There are no signs of poetry or art or adventure or interest of any sort nor even of any great sensuousness in their relationship. Their chief excitement seems to be in just seeing each other, in expecting to see each other, in seeing each other unexpectedly (that is wonderful), in hearing about each other from other people. But maybe there Lettice exercises reserve and, hidden from me, wonderful and beautiful anticipations pursue each other through her inturned mind. Yet in that case, wouldn't these art galleries we walk through, or the occasional splashes of music we encounter, have something to say to her to which she would betray some kind of response? I cannot understand this real deadness of interest—in anything. Alice was not like this anyhow. She had a bright eye for the shopwindows and hoardings of life and got what she could of what she saw advertised.

I find that every shred of my personal interest in Lettice has disappeared. [P. 244]

The intellectual snobbishness of these remarks, Wilbeck's utter contempt for the ordinary life of man, and woman too, pursuing its primal, timeless ends, is perhaps understandable in a devotee of the brave new world likely to supplant all that is pedestrian and commonplace in our own. But something more seems to lie back of the disappearance of every shred of Wilbeck's interest in his daughter—something, we may conjecture, more personal. It is not merely that she lacks the distinction to be the truly suitable offspring of *Homo Wilbeckius*. It is also that Wilbeck has turned to his daughter in his loneliness seeking love, only to discover that she has found it elsewhere. Instead of admiring the cultivated, speculative gentleman who is her father, Lettice cannot take her mind off the clown that she has left back in Southampton. This disappointment underlies the ridicule of Wilbeck's observations, and even Alice, who had earlier been treated as something of a clown herself, is invoked to serve it. Lettice is the latest of those failures in love, beginning with Alice and proceeding through the promiscuous period and Dolores, that Wilbeck has been tracing for us, consciously and unconsciously, in his journal. *Apropos of Dolores* has been about love, we realize, as much as it has been about anything. Once again we have the sense that in addition to speculating about life and about the life to come, Wilbeck has also been living. Because Wells allows us to learn as much from the latter as the former, and because, in fact, the relationship between the two is profoundly reciprocal, *Dolores* is one of his most notable achievements among the late novels, a book whose thought and feeling come in the end very close to being one.

And now the problem of love, which has been implicit throughout, comes to its final resting place in the novel. Wilbeck has for some time been intimating in his journal entries that he has fallen "violently" in love and is eager to give the details. But first he must say something about the Bunningtons, a British widow traveling with two teen-age daughters and a son in his twenties. They are worth meeting for their own sakes—the mother is one of the comic delights of the novel—and because they lead Wilbeck to one of his most important reflections, an outburst which prepares for his final revelation about love. He first encounters the Bunningtons at an inn outside Quiberon by coming to their rescue when the son, "who used that sort of home-made non-idiomatic French with a restricted vocabulary which only another Englishman can possibly understand," experiences difficulty in ordering their meal. They meet again at Questombec, and Lettice, at least, is delighted, for, says Wilbeck, "she was manifestly getting almost more bored with me than I was with her" (p. 249). At lunch, while the young people are busy talking, Wilbeck notices that Mrs. Bunnington abstains from the conversation and instead sits regarding him "with a marked and peculiar fixity," struggling to make him meet her eye. Moved by enormous widowly interest in him, she begins the following conversation:

"You know, you are one of those people who feel things intensely."
"And how did you divine *that*?" I asked.
"I can see it. And sometimes it would be well for you to remember that nothing is as bad as it seems."
"As a general rule?" I said, trying to seem intelligently interested.
"Nothing is good or bad but thinking makes it so."
"Now that's familiar. Who said that?"
"My husband."
"Your *husband*! I didn't imagine—"
"Mr. Bunnington was a Mind Healer," she said. "He began as an Osteopath but afterwards he became a Mind Healer—with Physical Exercises. . . . Let not your heart be troubled," she said, almost in a whisper of encouragement to me. "Neither let it be afraid."
"Was that another of your husband's—inspirations?"
"Yes. He had many. But does it mean nothing to you?"
"Much," I said between mouthfuls. [P. 250]

The exchange with the laughable Mrs. Bunnington, however, does not, for Wilbeck, remain simply funny. As she presses her inquiry embarrassingly into the "shadow of a great loss" that she intuits in him, he finds her impossible to repulse. She enlarges lovingly on her husband's remarkable therapeutic career and her own Psychic Gifts, on their blessed life together, healing for many those ills which though not *altogether*, are yet *principally*, in the mind. Wilbeck's attention wanders. He feels, he says, "like a menagerie animal that is being poked at with a stick it does not want to notice." When, after urging him to bare his heart to her, she follows Wilbeck out to the terrace with every intention of pursuing their conversation alone, he resolves, in desperation, to put an end to it by declaring that it is his unalterable habit to let his mind lie fallow after lunch, while he smokes a cigar—alone. This succeeds in forcing Mrs. Bunnington to join the young people on their sight-seeing trip to nearby Saint's Leap.

Left to himself, Wilbeck reveals that his mind, and heart, are far from fallow. He proceeds to unlock a flood of irritated reflection and feeling on such "quackery" as Mrs. Bunnington has treated him to. This sort of "exploitation of human infantilism" seems to be gaining ground on all the "critical and educational forces" that he serves. It exasperates him, he says, "just as Dolores's trite rantings about personified races and nations" did, with a sense of ineffectiveness. "Shall we never make headway against this nonsense? Does human nature insist on it?" he asks. After every step forward there is a step backward, for, in Wilbeck's vivid metaphor, "these dying dragons bleed a spreading and corrosive juice" (p. 254). The American Negro escapes from "the artless Evangelicalism of the camp meeting" only to fall victim to Father Divine; and "up and down the scale of culture, the Fathers Divines, the gurus and guidances, the mind-healers and psychic confessors seep poisonously through the world of thought."

In his wrath, Wilbeck moves swiftly to what he sees as the blind, dangerous, powerful false assmption beneath all this activity, "so flexible and persistent that maybe it will defeat us altogether." That tenacious false assumption is the belief in Perfection. Wilbeck maintains that biological science specifically rejects the delusions of "perfect form and perfect health," which are the "*ideals*" of immature minds; but such minds refuse to believe that life must be forever a "struggling maladjustment." They imagine that there must be "a perfect way somewhere, a fatuous shiny *rightness*, so that, once found, they will thereafter be able to go through life in a state of eupeptic invulnerability" (p. 255). Wilbeck will have none of this utopian daydreaming that Wells himself was often erroneously charged with. Wilbeck goes so far as to invert the usual contrast between religious pessimism and scientific optimism: "I suppose the doctrine of the Fall is the large scale version of this fantasy of a lost perfection." The matter is indeed important to Wilbeck, and he enlarges upon it with an ire that touches us nearly on the faddism of our own time. Speaking of those deluded minds in search of a fatuous easy perfection he writes:

And when the Bunningtons of their particular cultural class come along with patter about the fourth dimension, the secrets of Tibet, Will and Direction, and with their marvelous recipes for the perfect life, breathe down your backbone, digest *consciously*, waggle your abdomen this way and that, never touch meat, never touch *tinned* food, eat the *peel* of your fruit, sit vacuous for fifteen minutes every day, come and participate in my 'aura' (for the moderate fee of two guineas the time) they succumb. *Now* at last they have it. Now they too will be and feel perfectly healthy. If only they believe what guru tells them and say it over every day, 'Every day, in every way I get better and better'—they get better—and better. The great secret is theirs. They just drop out of the thin and wavering, suffering, thinking and fighting line that still might recondition this floundering world. [Pp. 255–56]

Having put himself in a thoroughly vile temper over these defectors from the "austere truth" that he is convinced he himself represents, Wilbeck falters in his hopes for the future. His sort, he reflects, constitute an "ineffective minority" and will for ages to come. He considers the haphazardness and passivity of his personal life, despite his impersonal dreams and plans. It is marked everywhere by casualness and accident; he has steered himself no more than a "cork in a cataract." In the disintegrated, anarchic life of the twentieth century, he and others like him have had "only the vaguest ideas of what we wanted in the nature of associates until they happened to us." Looking back, he considers that Alice had been "normally wrong" for him in a world where all sexual relationships were askew. Dolores, who seemed "a rare sort of discord," was perhaps not so rare; countless couples everywhere were now undoubtedly carrying on a similar struggle. He is led to a brooding, distressing, climactic generalization: "Fantastic paradox it was of human life that we were in perpetual flight from loneliness and perpetually seeking relief and escape from the connections that ensued" (p. 260).

It is the nadir of love in the novel, a moment when both personal loneliness and large reflection conjoin to corroborate discouragement and defeat for all human association. And it is this moment of despair, with the mind almost at the end of its tether, that Wells galvanizes with a vision of the most perfect love that the novel has yet entertained. Fittingly enough, it is a vision indeed, and no more than a vision.

Wilbeck looks up from his brooding to discover a tall, blonde, sunburnt young woman approaching him on the terrace. She has a broad forehead above her frank blue eyes and a pretty neck beneath her golden, decidedly not flaxen, hair. As she comes nearer, he notes that her skin has been lightly powdered by the sun with faint gold freckles. His response is unusually intense and characteristically passive. "And without doubt and instantly," he says, "I realized that nothing so lovely had ever come into my life" (p. 261).

But after exchanging a few words with Wilbeck about the whereabouts of the chauffeur, the old gentleman, and the nurse with whom she is traveling, the young woman locates them, settles her account in the restaurant, and drives off in a large grey Hispano Suiza with her party. Wilbeck, who has managed to learn nothing about her destination, is instantly "overwhelmed by a sense of irreparable loss." [8]

Regretting, and vigorously shedding, his passivity, Wilbeck starts out in vigorous pursuit of his "slim goddess," without revealing to poor Lettice what he is up to, and without really knowing where to look. There is no sign of her at La Baule or at Nantes, where, Wilbeck tells us in one of his reflexive observations, he wrote the St. Paul section of his journal in order to distract himself from his obsessive quest, and where, as well, he "wrote in such a strain of depreciation about Lettice" (p. 261). He does, however, catch sight of his goddess on the road from Ploermel to Dinard when the big Hispano Suiza passes him with her at the wheel. He chases it as best he can in his rather tired Voisin Fourteen, but soon loses it again. He tries St. Malo and Paramé, but again there is no trace. At last, back at St. Malo, with Lettice scheduled to depart for Southampton the next morning, "after a final prowl in search of a large grey car," Wilbeck gives up: "And thus in all probability ends the astonishing episode of that Lovely Young Woman all spotted with gold."

But his heart is full. He is astonished at his behavior, its contradiction of everything he thought himself to be. "Why," he asks himself, "did I become suddenly like a child chasing a sunbeam?" The impulse was sexual, to be sure, but a very sublimated form of sexuality. There is no detail in his desire; "it is like a desire for a bright glow." He recognizes that he had been reproaching Lettice a few pages ago in his journal for the very same sort of "featureless obsession." He wants only "to see more of that lovely thing and to be with that lovely thing." The feeling seems altogether divorced from "physical craving." It is "a passionate going out to a particular loveliness for its own sake."

But he pushes his analysis further, placing it in the context of his personal history. Here his motives are susceptible of more definition. The girl, he sees, appeared at a time in his life when, lonely and, on the whole, thwarted in love, he seized upon her as a symbol of "a lost world in which I might be and am not living." She came smiling, says Wilbeck, clothed in the afternoon sunlight, "just as I was deep in self-pity at my essential and apparently irremediable loneliness." He reinforces the point: "Just when I was most acutely aware of the frequent dullness and discordance of my everyday life she came. Just when I was full of the lucklessness of all my intimate encounters and particularly of the wasted years with Dolores." So powerful is the redemptive glimpse of her he has been vouchsafed that he concludes he has been in pursuit not of a real person but of a goddess indeed, come to renew his faith and wonder. "That goddess chose to cast her cestus about a very charming young woman, but it was the goddess who bewitched me. It was Aphrodite herself who saw fit to remind me that even in everyday sunlight, this universe has something profounder and intenser than its everyday events. I perceive I have had as much of a vision as any of the saints. But of a different divinity" (p. 270).

However, before allowing himself to be carried wholly away into Bulpingtonian reverie, Wilbeck declares that his sanity has returned and he does not want ever to see the girl again. For if he were to become acquainted with her, "within a few hours the goddess would have slipped away beyond recall and I should have been left talking, very much in love, no doubt, with a nice limited human being, at least a score of years my junior, very upstanding and with very definite and probably very different ideas of how life had to be lived." Had he won her, in no time they would have begun "that subtle and tortuous conflict of individualities to which all who belong to the new world are doomed." And if these grapes are not sour enough, there is the prospect of marriage and children: "For to that end it was that old Nature, who is the mother of everything, sent her daughter Aphrodite, to lure and intoxicate me." Handicapped by the care of children, his handsome young wife, already twenty years behind him, would fall further behind as his ideas and ambitions grew. "Mother Nature's short ends would have been well served; ten thousand threads of dearness would have been spun between us; but it would not have been what I was promised, nor what my heart leapt out to meet in the Place of Questombec. I should have felt as I saw her domesticated that I, and Nature, had tricked her, as she and Nature had tricked me, with something that blazed gloriously only to vanish" (p. 272). And with this, Wilbeck's presentiment rises to heartbreaking utterance: "Surely it must be one of the essential tragedies of the intricate life we lead to-day, to love a woman still and remember how once one loved her.''

So Wilbeck sits writing, with his feelings tormenting his ideas, and his ideas, his feelings. And at the very height of this painful self-scrutiny, he has awareness enough to recognize that he has been rationalizing; that wherever he goes and whatever he does, he will be seeking ''that girl, who is really not herself but the masquerade of an eternal and unattainable goddess . . . just round the corner, just down the glade, in the next room . . . .'' In this remarkable segment of writing, Wells reveals, as he will again at the conclusion of the novel, how skillfully and persuasively he can make the speculative intellect express surpassingly poignant yearning, and so disclose that region of pain and frustration which the intellectual share with the nonintellectual.

The last chapter of the novel is devoted to Wilbeck's effort to pull himself, his whole life, together at Paramé after the storm of recognitions he has passed through. It begins on October 1, 1934, with his admission that he is in ''great perplexity,'' but the physical scene bodes well. He finds the beach pleasant and soothing. ''I like,'' he writes, ''the distant clamour of semi-transparent pink limbed children and rather opaquer white nurses. I like the little striped tents. I like the reflections of people on the wet sand. It is rare one looks out on a scene with so little malice in it'' (p. 273).

His first attempts are halting. He broods on the vulnerability to emotional whirlwinds which his ''spasm of irrational love'' for the young goddess has revealed, and he is apprehensive about a recurrence, about many recurrences, in the future. Dolores's ''passionate jealousy'' and ''thorny clamour,'' for all the trouble they were, shielded him against ''such raids of prowling imaginative passion'' and allowed him to concentrate on his work. Nature's old insistence on marriage and children will, he foresees, work on him still, although modern life has made remarkable inroads against her rule: ''We find ourselves detaching her cravings and urgencies more and more definitely from the ends that justified their evolution. We want loveliness for itself, we want companionship for ourselves. We see beyond the bait of the trap, we nibble away most of the bait, and we refuse to be lured and cheated and to have our hearts frustrated for a mere biological purpose which we did not clearly foresee'' (p. 275). He himself, he finds, has no emotional desire for children at all, not only because of his disappointment in Lettice, but because he is persuaded that he belongs ''to a newer kind of human being which comes of age not at one-and-twenty but after forty and when the pairing time is over." The fully adult human being, the New Adam, *Homo rampant*, because he will be "less completely ego-centred," will emerge from a life "of vividly self-conscious individuality" into a broader, more impersonal life in which there may be no permanent marrying at all. Mother Nature, "who does not care to have evolution taken out of her hands," will, Wilbeck foresees, trouble us endlessly, but we will have to "trick her and assuage her as we can." Thus, in the name of the future, Wilbeck renounces for himself the idea of romantic love and of a single close companion; but his very words are tinted with the feelings that he wishes to deny: "There are no such things for me now, there are no such things. It was just Nature's playful superfluous teasing" (p. 278).

He turns next to his work, his hope of saving civilization by a series of publications, and makes his sad rejections here as well. The idea of salvaging civilization now strikes him as quite misguided: it "suggests a sort of rescue of old masters from a burning country house." The truth is, he says, that civilization as we know it is not worth salvaging. The only endeavor that he can accept is preparing for a civilization that would be altogether new: "Escaping from the ruins is quite a different business from bolstering them up." Getting ready for the new "post-human" era must now constitute the general shape of our lives. Wilbeck recognizes that in the meantime, as we evolve like amphibians from one way of life to another, we "find ourselves in a three-fold quandary between brain, egotism and heart," with our reason urging us to create the new world, our ancient, irrational instinct seeking power only, and our hearts desiring the happiness of play and restful entertainment. But Wilbeck's solution for this considerable dilemma, at least at this stage of his personal reconstruction period, is surprisingly offhand and facile: "Plainly the best recipe for a working compromise with life must be to obey our reason as far as we can, play our rôle that is to say, sublimate or restrain our deep-seated instinct for malicious mischief, and gratify what we can of our heart's desire, so far as and in such manner as, our consciences approve . . ." (p. 280). This comes to little more than telling us that the way to solve the problem is to solve the problem.

But now Wilbeck does much better. After only a little more groundless optimism about human nature and an unconvincing diagnosis of the heart of the problem—"Human life is at sixes and sevens to-day and in perpetual danger, simply because it is mentally ill-arranged"—he turns to a more heartfelt matter, for himself and, we must conjecture, for Wells too. That matter is writing and the meaning of writing, and Wilbeck's remarks on it are so strongly felt that they do more than anything he has yet said to validate the conceptual dream of the future that he has been offering us.

He says that the nature of human intimacy is changing. Creatures contact one another by touch, men by touch and by words, through which they "clothe and elaborate love." "Words," Wilbeck writes, "become the mechanism of a vast abundance of suggestion and enrichment. We smell each other's minds in conversation" (p. 283). We recede from elementary physical contacts and achieve wider, lovelier ones which transcend time. Art allows us to embody experience by disembodying it: "We love the mind that speaks to us in music, we find beauty in pictures, we respond to the wisdom or to the caress in a poem. We love the woman Leonardo loved and writers who were bodily dead centuries ago live on to stir us. Our contacts stretch out more and more beyond the here and the now."

Then Wilbeck reverts to his happiness in Rennes on that first day of the novel and he treats it this time not with the cynicism of his previous recollection, but with loving appreciation of the real nature of his experience there. It was an experience of human contact reaching through history, for on that occasion "the faint flavour of intimacy with those who had planned and built the old place was a part of my happiness." Similarly, says Wilbeck, when he publishes books or writes in the very journal we are reading, he does it "for an unseen intimate." He hopes that someone whom he will never meet to quarrel with, or disappoint, someone whose everyday inadequacy he will never experience, will read his journal. Then, in an extraordinary vision of literary communion, he writes, "Maybe human intimacy is escaping from the prison of the present and the visible, the prison of our current life, unlocking the door but still using the old cell for sleeping and eating. . . . A man who sits in a quiet room reading or writing, listening or thinking, may seem to be solitary and isolated. But in fact he is in contact with myriads of intimates. He has a thousand intimacies, each closer and a thousand times finer than those of a peasant with his wife or with his dearest boon companions . . . ." So Wilbeck, declaring the faith of all writers with characteristic eloquence, has invoked it as an earnest of that larger faith in mental and spiritual transmission, in the future itself, which has now, perforce, become the center of his life. From that insight comes the conviction, at once emotional and ideological, that he is not solitary and is not going to be solitary. And if there is something compensatory, or overcompensatory, about his declaration, then we are forced to recognize it as the taint that attends the formulation of all ideas as they become incarnate in persons.

And now Wilbeck, very much a person, declares his final faith. There is a strong undertow of Job, Plato, and Matthew Arnold in it, mingled with a more contemporary agnosticism; and the whole of it takes strangely little note of the destiny of the race, fixing instead on the eternal arduousness of life in the present:

> Our superficiality and incidentalness seem to be inescapable. There is no coherent plot for the personal life; there may be no coherent plot for the whole. That too, like the ego, may be a delusive simplification. And yet there is something real going on, something not ourselves that goes on, in spite of our interpretations and misconceptions. That ultimate reality behind the curtains may be fundamentally and irresolvably multiple and intricate and inexplicable, but it goes on. It may be altogether incomprehensible to our utmost faculties, but it is there. And in some partial and elusive way we are not simply borne along by that, but we belong. We do not *happen* to exist. It is, for inexplicable reasons, our business to exist. . . .
>
> There is no Heaven for us anywhere, at any time; nevertheless there are many bright reflections and much amusing incident upon the surface of being, and there are loveliness and truth in its substance.
>
> These are not mere words—because words can be defined by other words. But truth and loveliness are primary things. . . .
>
> And I think, I think, that the conscience within me is a primary thing. It speaks out of an impenetrable darkness but it is real . . . .
> [P. 285]

We have come a long way only to have Truth, Beauty, and Goodness reaffirmed; but then, they are always timely. Indeed, they are strangely moving in the context of Wilbeck's obligatory modernism: incoherence, delusive simplification, inexplicableness, impenetrable darkness.[9] As a person, a character in a fiction, Wilbeck has come to rest by incarnating feelings and ideas. In his desire for peace and purpose, he has woven a faith out of negation and longing. If it does not scan intellectually, the failure follows from the very first premise, which is that human intellect is too limited to grasp the whole scheme of either the personal life or the cosmos. Wilbeck recognizes this by asserting that "Stoical agnosticism is the only possible religion for sane adults." Wells recognizes it by creating Wilbeck and Wilbeck's faith.

Having allowed Wilbeck to reach the peace that passes any understanding at all, Wells now concludes the novel with two reprises. We
remember we began with Wilbeck's "Happy Interlude" at Rennes, where,
momentarily free of Dolores, he had experienced the mystery of serenity:
"It is hard to explain, though I myself comprehend perfectly, why Rennes
should have presented itself as a compendium of human contentment that
evening, or why it was there and then that I conceded final complete
recognition to the value of the Boswell in my composition. It came upon
me with overwhelming force that to live most of the hours of the waking
life Boswell fashion is the only sane and pleasant way of living" (p. 4).
Now, two months later, starting for Paris, Wilbeck makes a sudden detour
to Rennes, which, he says, beckons to him. It is as he remembered it. The
evening is agreeably warm, the place full of dim young couples and dusky
movement, and he is treated with the same "cheerful matter-of-fact
kindliness" which had won him the first time. He has dinner again at the
same café, with the same waiter and the same red-shaded lamp on his
table. The same young woman who had approached him before approaches
him again, but this time, says Wilbeck, "I did not keep aloof." He finds
her "as simple and gay and friendly as her face . . . completely
extrovert, amused with life and taking things as she found them." She
sorts entirely with his mood, and we have here, finally and effortlessly, the
one sexual consummation and affirmation of the novel. But it is celebrated
in terms that accord with Wilbeck's speculative reservations about marriage and companionship in the world of the future. "Maybe it will be
good to return to Rennes and that essential sensual innocence of the
seventeenth century ever and again. Maybe it might be better if men and
women never met except incidentally, and were not obliged by all sorts of
secondary considerations to pursue and enslave each other. How little they
would know about each other . . . and how brightly and lightly they
would love each other!" (p. 287). This celibate strain, so strong in
Wilbeck, so far from the hand-in-hand spiritual pilgrimages of a D. H.
Lawrence, or, for that matter, from the ever-present ménages in Wells's
own life, is as much emotional as ideological. It is Wells's way of
registering dramatically the impact on Wilbeck of the years with Dolores.
In it we hear a wound speaking as well as an idea, though Wilbeck freely
admits that all such ideas arise from the wounds of marriage.

His last retrospect, and the very last words of the novel, are reserved for
Dolores. He reverts to his "probable crime," the likelihood that he is
guilty of having killed her with the Semondyle, but finds that he feels no

sorrow or remorse whatever. Indeed, he says that if he did not do it then, he would certainly do it now quite deliberately. And his happiness is involved once again, as it had been at the outset of the novel in his then merely temporary separation from Dolores. "I am happy," he writes, reflecting on her death, "I am glad beyond measure to find myself free from her and to think that she is free from herself" (p. 289). The cruel compassion of this last remark is elaborated at some length: there was nothing left for Dolores but to go on and on from bad to worse, "getting harder and sharper and viler"; no one could help her, she was "damned"; she would have made "an incredibly awful old woman," perhaps been treated as a madwoman; Wilbeck is sorry for her, but sorry for her way of living, not her dying. And again he pays his tribute to the peace of death: "She has ceased from troubling, the fever of her appetites is appeased, her insatiable boasting perishes with her, she sleeps and now she will hurt and be hurt no more."

Finally he hands down his formal judgment, implicating himself surprisingly. "In the case of Stephen Wilbeck versus Dolores I condemn both parties, with a recommendation to mercy. Each had a wicked heart and if she was an uncontrollable scream, he was a deadly self-protective companion for her. If she was pseudo-oriental and addicted to every extremity of emotional exaggeration, he had a heart as cold as it was light" (pp. 289–90). Suddenly, despite Wilbeck's cumulative self-vindication, we recognize the truth of this, the complicity in all human relations. Despite his complicity, or because of it, Wilbeck has anticipated us. Some ninety pages earlier, turning over the leaves of his manuscript just after the death of Dolores, he had written the last reverberating word on *Apropos of Dolores*: "It is a picture of a relationship even if it is not the portrait of a person" (p. 208).

Perhaps not the last word, for the history of a relationship may well be the portrait of two persons. This, assuredly, *Dolores* is. Coming to it from Odette Keun's articles on Wells in *Time and Tide*, we might anticipate the spectacle of two egotists calling each other egotist. But that hardly proves to be the case, for one of them was an artist who could create an imaginary garden with real sticks and stones in it. Wells's Dolores, unlike Madame Keun's Wells, is not a bill of particulars but egotism incarnate, a delightful, engaging, revolting demonstration of the thing itself as it lives and breathes and screams. From this rich representation of her we discover, without, as it were, being told, how little, in the end, the ego can win for itself when it is so exclusively intent on getting its due, and how dim the prospect of a new world is with people like Dolores loose in the present one. Wells had offered this intuition earlier, notably in *Bulpington*, but never before with such mordant economy. Dolores is a successful fiction, hence full of substantial, enduring reality. Through Wells's art, she has been lifted forever from the plane of his life with her to a new timeless existence which bears on the life of all his readers, of all the living and the dead.

The portrait of Wilbeck is at least equally successful, and a good deal more intricate. Wells's Prefatory Note to the novel, for all of its apparent equivocation, turns out to be quite correct. Although Wilbeck originates in Wells's life, the novel fashions him as a quite separate entity. Wells, as far as we know, did not intentionally or inadvertently administer an overdose of Semondyle to the companion he could no longer bear, nor did he forswear sustained intimate relationships with women as a consequence of his years with Madame Keun. There is, in this connection, a considerable imaginative "disarticulation" and "rearrangement" of his experience at the close of the novel. Wilbeck's renunciation of the young goddess merely glimpsed there is an act of sheer fictive invention, since Wells, renouncing very little, had been carrying on a liaison with her prototype, Marie Budberg, for years when he composed *Apropos of Dolores*. Wilbeck's renunciation has everything to do with the logic of the novel and nothing, overtly at least, with the circumstances of Wells's life. There is congruence enough, to be sure, between the novel's depiction of Wilbeck's life with Dolores and the reality of Wells's life with Odette Keun—like D. H. Lawrence, Wells preferred to make novels out of experience that was in some sense his own—but the thinking which that life gives rise to is subtly altered. Just as Wells does not join Wilbeck in the paeans to celibacy, so too should he be exempted from the narrator's tendency to overreach himself intellectually. Those biological, historical, religious, moral, and prophetic speculations of Wilbeck's that we have traced at length are compelling and, at times, beautiful; but we always have the sense that they are ideas that a man, a character, in a carefully particularized, frequently painful situation, has been driven to entertain.

They are, that is to say, ideas that have been transformed into emotive, dramatic speech—the most successful transformation of this sort that the late novels can show. *Brynhild* had suppressed ideas almost altogether and fixed instead on personal relations. *The Bulpington of Blup* had assigned ideological positions to a wide range of speakers and exploited the possibilities of debate. But in *Apropos of Dolores,* Wilbeck's debate is with himself. The dialogue novel here becomes a vivid monodrama, a peculiarly Wellsian conceptual dramatic monologue in which Wilbeck's ideas are really a transmutation of the feelings which gave rise to them in the first place and to which they continue to testify. In this perspective, it matters not a whit whether there is a new world a-coming or not, only that Wilbeck's life has been so unfulfilled that he craves one. The vision of *Homo Wilbeckius vs. Homo Doloresiform* is his ultimate stick and stone. Thus *Apropos of Dolores* is able to absorb an astonishing amount of speculation and remain dramatically engaging. Foxfield is a great help here. By assuming the major share of vast biological-historical brooding in Chapter 2, "Whether Life Is Happy," he frees Wilbeck to be a character, as he frees Wells to be a novelist. Wilbeck's speculations always derive from or apply to his distressing personal experience; hence they help to illuminate that experience. If we contrast *Dolores* with a novel like Aldous Huxley's *After Many a Summer Dies the Swan* (1939), with its deadly weight of dramatically unassimilated proclamation, Wells's artistry is clearer still.

Wilbeck's journal is Wells's means of achieving this new level of integration. If the quarrel that we have with others is rhetoric and the quarrel with ourselves, literature, then the journal format of *Dolores* deserves much of the credit for Wells's audacious transition from the somewhat rhetorical dialogue novel, as we have it in *Bulpington,* and will have it again in even purer form in *Babes in the Darkling Wood,* to the essentially literary monologue novel in *Dolores.* Wilbeck's wavering, groping, compensatory speculations are all confided to his journal and expressed there with a shameless freedom that enhances their dramatic implications. We have, throughout, the sense of a protagonist trying manfully to be honest with himself, succeeding, failing, trying again. Wells's device of having Wilbeck review what he has written previously— as he does with his remarks on Rennes and those on St. Paul—only to find that he must, on further reflection, deny or modify what he has set down, constitutes a brilliant structure of second-guessing, an ingenious means of keeping both thoughts and feelings alive, and alive conjointly.

The journal injects a similar dynamic quality into the action of the novel as well. Like the epistolary novel from which it derives, *Dolores* is set in a kind of portentous present. Events have preceded each of Wilbeck's entries, but, more importantly, events will follow too. In contrast to the conventional first-person narrator, who speaks in the past tense from the vantage point of a completed experience, Wilbeck, like Clarissa, writes in an anguished present tense, struggling with the uncertainty of the future and the meaning of the past. We remember the anticipatory dread that attends the earlier sections of the journal as Wilbeck awaits Dolores at Torquéstol, a dread somehow curiously heightened by the intensity of his recollection of joy at Rennes; then, entry by entry, that apprehension justifies itself as Wilbeck records the agonies, regrets, resolves, and failures in his day-to-day encounters with his wife, all the while fashioning the biological system in which to imprison and confound her; and finally, we watch Wilbeck struggling in retrospect to be fair to his dead wife while vindicating his own part in their relationship and, at the same time, formulating terms on which to continue life without her.

This structure of anticipation, outcome, and retrospect is pervasive in the novel, and Wilbeck's ignorance of the future always ensures its being exploited to the full. We have the pattern in little at the climactic moment when Wilbeck discovers the torn photograph of Lettice and declares his intention of having the matter out with Dolores in her room. The next journal entry catches us up by announcing that Dolores is dead, then proceeds to retrace the steps leading to her death and, ultimately, Wilbeck's loneliness. We have the pattern again when Wilbeck writes with eager enthusiasm of the coming of Lettice, only to be brutally disappointed in the event. We have it finally in his wild anticipation of catching up with his goddess at the close; but here the pattern breaks. Instead of gaining what he desires and finding it turn to ashes, he fails to gain it at all and then renounces the desire altogether. At this point, at the very end of the novel, by departing from the sequence which the journal form has adroitly reinforced, Wilbeck opens up his life to new, uncharted, impersonal possibilities. He has begun a radically new life—or death.

For the pattern of anticipation is not merely a consequence of the journal form of the novel; it is also a consequence of the temperament of the man who writes the journal. The journal merely allows Wilbeck to reveal himself, despite his uncommon self-awareness, better than he knows. From it we can see that the most important structural element in *Apropos of Dolores* is actually the succession of women in Wilbeck's life; his anticipations and disappointments are always focused on them. Everything outside of women is manageable for him, hence neither awaited nor regretted with much intensity. But his sad little marriage to Alice, his profitless philandering afterwards, his Homeric struggle with Dolores, his painful disillusionment with Lettice, his quixotic quest of the goddess, and his final fleeting consummation with the girl at Rennes are quite another matter. They are potentially the very stuff of life to him; like any number of Wells's heroes, he is to be known by what he makes of women, and by what he allows them to make of him.

Dolores is a novel about the failure of love, and its narrator is a man who has resolved to live without it. His means of doing so is to dream of a new life where love will not be so much needed, where splendidly evolved, "fully adult" human beings will "not pair at all," will never meet "except incidentally." They will know nothing of the ways in which egotism ravages love, or of the terrible proximity of egotism and love in the human heart, or of the enslavement of lover by lover. They will also, of course, know nothing of love as poor *Homo sapiens* has always understood it—problematical, anguished, glorious. But then, so great is Wilbeck's failure, disillusionment, or, better, incapacity, that he knows nothing of it as well. He surrenders, in pain and coldness of heart, what he has never had.

And Wells lets him do it, just as Wells has let him dream all his dreams and chase all his ideas. *Apropos of Dolores* is two comedies, the comedy of Wilbeck's bitterness and the comedy of Wells's recognitions. The first is scintillating. Nowhere among these late novels, or the earlier ones, for that matter, is there wittier, more pointed writing. On these occasions, Wilbeck's style has the snap and gleam of first-rate high comedy:

I have a loyal rather than a meticulous memory. It will do almost anything to please me. [P. 67]

For me she was an adventure but for her I was an acquisition. It was only gradually I realized how thoroughly I was being embraced when I was being embraced. [P. 70]

She moved [when playing tennis] with an active angularity that was practically independent of the ball. [P. 92]

I remember hearing her tell Lady Garron, who I believe was some sort of county champion: "When tennis is properly played, you do not even *see* the ball."
"But then you do not often see it properly played," said Lady Garron. [P. 93]

But this is the comedy of disparagement and repudiation—a species of satire, in fact, which takes for its targets almost everything and everyone in Wilbeck's experience. It is the humor of a disgruntled utopian.

Elsewhere, however, Wilbeck reveals a taste for metaphor. When he indulges it, we sense Wells peering over his shoulder, mitigating, assuaging the bitterness:

> It would be as risky as rattling about with a poker in a dark cupboard to find an egg. [P. 241]

> There was a broad-faced mother in half-mourning, with a general air of good-humoured geniality, through which ever and again a calculating watchfulness would gleam unexpectedly, almost like a bad character peeping out of the window of a respectable-looking house. [P. 246]

> It dawned on me that I was behaving more like a lost dog than a human being and that poor Lettice was having as thin a time as a dog whose owner is trying to lose it. [P. 265]

> It becomes plain to me that for the past thirteen years Dolores has played the rôle—I can hardly think of a metaphor—of a zareba, let us say, a zareba of spiked sounds, against such raids of prowling imaginative passion. Her way of filling that rôle was occasionally ungracious, but now taking the whole situation together, it seems to me I may have been ungrateful in not recognizing how her exacting passions and her passionate jealousy, the distraction of her thorny clamour, shepherded me to my work and made any serious divagations impossible. [P. 274]

> I have told myself that I am helping to build an ark for the human mind, but that ark-building is a gigantic proposition and I doubt if I am even a foreman riveter on the immense hull such an ark needs to be. [P. 280]

> When a substance which has been loaded and opaque crystallizes and becomes clear and definite in its form, thrusting the alien stuff aside, it is because its particles have fallen into place one with another. Nothing new has come, nothing that was not already there, but only a better arrangement has been made. [P. 282]

> It was Foxfield who said to me once that conscious life was "the thinnest and flimsiest of pellicules, strained midway between the atoms and the stars." [P. 284]

This is the language of conciliation, which bespeaks, even more in its form than its substance, sufficient interest on Wells's part in the things of this imperfect world to warrant establishing significant, if not loving, relationships among them. Wilbeck scoffs and dreams, like Odette Keun in her *Time and Tide* pieces, of deliverance. Wells, Wilbeck's creator, finds this funny too; but his laughter is compassionate. It recognizes and accepts so much that it is almost not like laughter at all. It is more like the queer aching, smiling resignation out of which the art that makes novels—and life—comes.

CHAPTER V

Postlude:
The Novel at the End of Its Tether

IN HIS LAST THREE NOVELS, Wells wrote many a dazzling page, but he was never again able to rise to the sustained, delicately balanced integration that marks *Bulpington, Brynhild*, and *Dolores. The Holy Terror* (1939) is his most politically sophisticated fiction of the last period, tracing the career of a spoiled brat who becomes dictator of the entire world in the years following 1939 by means of his immensely artful employment of rhetoric and bluster. But for all of its shrewd insight into men and societies as political organisms, it is less a novel than a fantasy. It is concerned not with things as in themselves they really are, but with how they may be prophesied, and not with the behavior of persons, but of ideologies. It has the further disadvantage of foreseeing an event which never took place, even as a tendency. *You Can't Be Too Careful* (1941), Wells's very last novel, is by all odds the weakest of the whole group. Regressing to a Dickensianism quite incongruous in 1941, Wells indulges himself in a nasty, occasionally funny book-length tantrum against his hero, Albert Tewler, for having neither mind nor soul enough to become an H. G. Wells, though he is fortunate enough to be born into the same stultifying circumstances as his creator. The entire novel exists in order to lodge all responsibility for the failure of the millenium with Tewler, who can ill sustain such a charge, being a figure of the most limited interest to begin with. *Babes in the Darkling Wood* (1940), though, comes closer to what Wells had achieved at his best in the previous decade. Even its limitations illuminate by contrast matters that we have been considering, and it will afford us a useful concluding look—less imposing than one could hope, yet impressive still—at the whole of this remarkable last flowering of Wells's imaginative genius.

It is clear that Wells meant *Babes in the Darkling Wood* to be a big book, a kind of intellectual and artistic testament on the eve of the Second World War. In his introduction he speaks of it as "the most comprehensive and ambitious dialogue novel" that he ever attempted and also as a book carrying a "very great burden of fresh philosophical matter."[1] Yet, despite its scattered impressiveness on both these counts, a number of problems arise in connection with them.

There are indeed several commendable dialogues, but a new, quite irresistible interest in long monologue tends to rob even the key dialogues of their centrality. Both the young hero, Gemini Twain, and his guru-like mentor, Uncle Robert Kentlake, hold forth in unrelieved, uninterrupted solos about the book's major concerns; and although Wells takes pains to give these monologues an exploratory, speculative cast, they belong more to the realm of expostulation than reply. Even Wells's effort to undermine Gemini and Uncle Robert's authority by a number of dramatic gestures fails in the end to vitalize or enhance their talk sufficiently to make it an adequate substitute for the intellectual and dramatic play of true dialogue; instead of hearing the voice of a particular, fully projected temperament, or of the truth itself, or of the sort of fascinating mixture that Wells was often after, we come away confused or impatient with Wells's artlessness.

There is some question, too, about the freshness, and the magnitude, of the novel's "philosophical matter." Its consideration, both in dialogue and monologue, of such matters as theology, sexual liberation, biology, psychology, and world revolution has a most familiar ring for readers of Wells, even if the talk about sex is spiced with allusions to D. H. Lawrence and the psychology with behaviorism. Moreover, these considerations never come to a really satisfactory focus. The various familiar topics jostle one another without fusing into an imaginative unity, just as they were to do even more egregiously a few years later in that nonfictional waste-basket, *'42 to '44*. Given its moment of publication and the prefatory satisfaction of its author, the novel itself can only strike us, in its intellectual structure, as falling far short of such a summing up of the mind of Europe on the eve of holocaust as Wells seems to have intended.

The central theme of *Babes*, like that of most of Wells's novels, is the need for a renewal of civilization. The reappearance of this theme in 1940 is not in itself tiresome or unpromising, for as both *Bulpington* and *Dolores* demonstrate, it could be a miracle of rare device, alluring and invigorating. Its failure to be so here is curious, occurring as it does under the shadow of the greatest threat to civilization that the world had ever known. Puzzlingly, the idea of renewal is able to enlist the subordinate issues of religion, politics, sexual liberation, and love without managing to weld them into a novelistic whole. Most curious of all, Wells himself approaches it with marked self-consciousness and uncertainty of touch.

The theme is broached at the very beginning of the novel. Gemini Twain, a twenty-four-year-old Oxford graduate who writes criticism for London periodicals, and Stella Kentlake, the beautiful twenty-year-old girl with whom he is living in a Suffolk cottage during the spring of 1939, are discovered, in the course of a stroll in the countryside, brooding about the fate of civilization and their own duty to the future. They come upon the sculptor Kalikov contemplating a massive block of alabaster in his garden. As Kalikov's hand traces possible curves in the air for shaping his stone into art, moving carefully, mystically, "as if he caressed the invisible," the book's major symbol is born. For Gemini sees in Kalikov's alabaster, gestures, and vision a perfect equivalent of his, and Stella's, relation to the present and the inchoate future. Deprived of a nurturing religion, or politics, or a viable set of traditions and institutions, they must yet lend their hands to the carving out of the great unrevealed world implicit in the block, which, uncarved, represents the structure of reality. " 'Our sort of people and more of us and more,' " says Gemini to his adoring, approving beloved, " 'have been astray, getting into disputes that don't matter a damn, blundering away at negations. That isn't the job for us. *Our* job is to realise the shape in the block, to get the vision of it clearer and clearer in our heads and then to set about carving it out. . . . It's *the* consolidating idea. The unrevealed statue. The unrevealed new world. The right world' " (pp. 12–13).

But along with the symbol and the faith that it embodies, Wells includes a disquietingly jaundiced view of both. He does so in the person of a neighbor, Balch, who appears to have been invented solely as a repository of political, utopian bombast. Balch is so taken with the notion of Kalikov's alabaster and the unrevealed world that he drowns it in the impassioned, indiscriminate rhetoric that Gemini and Stella call "Balchery" and "Balchification":

> "Citizens of a state that hasn't arrived; advance agents of a government yet to be. All the roads and railways and mines and factories, all the arsenals, barracks, warships, all the aeroplanes and aerodromes, from end to end of the earth, are the property of our unrevealed government, are *ours*, but mark you, in the hands of

usurpers. *Our* heritage—not handed over to us. Every actual government in the world, either a usurpation or a trust. Its end is to hand over or get out. All the universities and schools, all the churches and religions, are just the germs of our One Great World Teaching. Squabbling with one another, keeping us in the dark and failing to unite and develop. Slash and hammer and we clear the alabaster, dig out the shape in it. . . . I can't help talking, because the more I think of this phrase of yours—great phrase it is—the Unrevealed World, I realise that it releases all that has been accumulating in me—for years. I feel as though at last I was being born again. After a sacrament of bubble and squeak. . . . Think of the new behaviour our great idea demands. Because we new people are the real kings, the rightful owners, and our bearing must be masterly. Masterly," he repeated, as though the timbered ceiling had contradicted him. "Just in so far as we hold to our relentless aim, just so far are we living rightly. Complaisant to all that is decent and creative in the world, but inflexible to whatever is treason to one universal citizenship. Then we must resist; then we must withstand, not seeking martyrdom but facing it calmly, daring to say 'I disbelieve in your encumbering, separating faiths, I disavow your irrational loyalties. . . .' So!" [Pp. 24–26]

Gemini and Stella find the onslaught intolerable and absurd. " 'He takes anything,' thought Gemini; 'it doesn't matter how fine and good it is, he swallows it down and he brings it up, and he turns it into this sort of spew.' " But the distinction between Balch and his young friends is harder for the reader to draw. Apart from Balch's reckless overstatement and demagoguery—the simple-minded, programmatic enthusiasm with which he appropriates Gemini's idea—the substance of what he says is largely indistinguishable from the substance of the young people's inspiration, or, for that matter, from the aspirations that Wells himself had been promulgating for thirty years. Yet Balch's formulation offends hero, heroine, and author on the plane of taste and style, much as a purist might be offended by hearing the *Goldberg Variations* performed on the piano rather than the harpsichord, or worse still, transcribed for full orchestra.

To sound the theme of renewal in its purity, Wells falls back on monologue with, however, some interesting variations and intrusions. After the young people have been routed from their cottage love nest by Gemini's father and Stella's Uncle Hubert and forced to separate, Gemini begins an unconscionably long letter to Stella from London, in which he reaffirms their ideological and personal faith. He reviews the articles that are to constitute their "religion" and their "way of life." First, they reject the view that "the present moral, religious, political and social system is an inevitable, irreplaceable growth, in which the best thing to do politically is to manoeuvre about with treaties, leagues, Acts of Parliament and so forth, muddling along, staving things off" (p. 116). Secondly, they believe most devoutly that "in this gross, confused, moving and dangerous mass of a world as it is, there is hidden the possibility of a human existence of so general a happiness, such liveliness of interest and such abundance as no living species has ever yet known." This means, Gemini continues, that they are revolutionaries in the "fullest meaning of the word," not content with the Communists' fixation on private property and the capitalist system as the only social evils. For Gemini and Stella, as Post-Communists, "the fundamental social crime . . . is *interception or appropriation* in *any* form," whether it be class privilege, or party rule, or official authority, or racial discrimination. Taking due notice of the alabaster symbol, Gemini elaborates these ideas at some length in terms that do not altogether escape Balchery, though they are more temperate, modulated, and complex. When he arrives at his third point, however, he finds that he cannot go on to his own satisfaction. It begins as an agreement that "we love each other exclusively," but gets no further. With this entry into the question of love, Wells brings more personal and dramatic elements to bear, and they succeed in transforming the letter from discourse to soliloquy.

The dramatic element is by no means free of ideological considerations, but it mingles with them in the pursuit of ends that are not exclusively ideological. Like the issue of political and social renewal, with which it is potentially allied, the question of love has both a personal and abstract aspect in the novel. Gemini is committed to reviewing a book, *The Expansion of Sex*, by the fictitious American behaviorist Cottenham C. Bower, which explores the relationship of sex to political life and treats sexual conduct "from the standpoint of the conditioned reflex." Bower is one of those biological-psychological sociologists dear to Wells and calls to mind such figures as John Watson and B. F. Skinner. Stella had rejected Bower for not giving love its due, but Gemini now finds himself more in agreement with the American's ideas than he had been at the cottage. Craving Stella's company, Gemini now formulates the notion that "human society was a vast and intricate family, knit together mainly by mitigated, extended and sublimated sexual feeling," rather than a "rational complex of enlightened self-interest held together by an implicit social contract." This allows him to reconcile Stella's and Bower's ideas, "leading him to a sociology and economics of feelings, rather than a sociology and economics of facts and figures'' (p. 124). But oddly enough, it does not lead him to the completion of his pledge of love to Stella in the letter. Even the doctrine of renewal expressed in points one and two now seems rather pompous to him. Reflecting on Stella's habit of insisting on clear consistency and of holding him to what he says, he abandons the letter and goes out for tea, for without realizing it he has been scribbling away for hours.

After dining, faced with a lonely evening in London, and missing Stella terribly, he impulsively telephones Mary Clarkson, the owner of the cottage. She invites him to her flat where Gemini, "reeking with self-pity," tells her at length of his love for Stella and his misery over his separation from her. All sympathy, Mary soothes, caresses, kisses, and goes to bed with him in short order, offering him, in her feline way, the only substantial comfort she commands. Afterwards, Mary, an "experimentalist in *moeurs*" by her own description, and worldly beyond her years, helps Gemini to face up to his actually having known from the outset that what happened was going to happen. Fearful of again falling "prey to these spasms of bored desire," he resolves to leave London and seek out something "strenuous and grimly serious" (p. 140).

But before doing so he finishes the long aria of his letter to Stella. In a section of the novel headed "Gemini's Thirdly," Stella reads his Firstly and Secondly with approval, for these do indeed reflect the essence of the ideological agreement she had reached with him in Suffolk; but the third section has been conditioned by the intervening infidelity with Mary Clarkson. What Gemini has to say here has been dramatically inflected by experience and represents an important effort on Wells's part to transmute ideas into dispositions, responses, subjectivities, drama, and so to provide felt intellection, the Wellsian equivalent of James's felt life.

Gemini's Thirdly turns out to be an analysis of love under the aspect of behaviorism. It is an impressive, long-winded, intricate digest of Gemini's now revered Cottenham C. Bower. In it Gemini rejects such conceptions as soul, spirit, mind, self, and substitutes for them the notion that individual human beings are really only neurosensitive apparatuses governed by reaction and event systems. There is, as a result, no constant, fixed identity, but only the John Smith of the moment, John Smith No. 618, who has been through a particular experience and comes to a focus momentarily around it as, say, the indignant employee or the jealous husband. Because our bodies form a common habitation for this "armoury of selves," because in a Jungian sense we have a conception of our own persona, and

because there are external social and moral pressures on us to adopt a
coherent identity, we do so, employing "conduct systems" and memory to
fashion a recognizable self. Bower, says Gemini, has chosen, in *The
Expansion of Sex*, to apply these general truths to one particular "bunch of
drives."

> When the primary sex drive accumulates power and becomes
> dominant in John Smith or Jane Smith, we say the poor dear is
> amorous, lascivious, "on heat," and these isomers—I beg your
> pardon, these alternative personalities—of John or Jane Smith drive
> on to relief, setting aside at last every antagonistic system. If that
> happens to such individuals only now and then, they may do their bit
> of promiscuity, not get found out, and stifle the memory, or, if they
> are religious, they may get rid of the sense of inconsistency by
> repenting and confessing, or else they may dispose of it by distorting
> their memory or inventing some special excuse for it. . . . If they
> are more frequently under the sway of urgent desire than that, they
> may become defiantly promiscuous, even propagandists of pro-
> miscuity. Our Mary Clarkson is a case in point. [P. 176]

When Stella, who has been punctuating her reading of Gemini's letter
with skeptical and sardonic asides, thus affording us a sense of resistance
rather than full-blown dialogue, comes upon this, she intuits and confirms
what we have been sensing all along—that Gemini's exposition, for all of
its intrinsic interest and brilliance, is an excruciatingly intellectual rationalization of his feelings of guilt: " 'Plainly,' said Stella, her intuitions
flashing like sparks from an incendiary bomb. 'Yes. But why bring her
[Mary Clarkson] in just here, I wonder? . . . Yes, I wonder . . . .' "

Thus Gemini's epistolary monologue, which had begun in points one
and two as a disquisition on the theme of social, political, and cultural
renewal, redirects itself, in point three, as a dramatic utterance of a
characteristically Wellsian kind. Rationalization or no, the ideas on
multiple selfhood are themselves to be taken seriously, as Wells himself
took them in "A Thesis on the Quality of Illusion in the Continuity of the
Individual Life in the Higher Metazoa, with Particular Reference to the
Species Homo Sapiens."[2] But they are simultaneously to be apprehended
as the kind of serious thinking that a young man in Gemini's uneasy,
somewhat confused situation might be drawn to. In a rather complex
novelistic way, Gemini's observations are there and not there, valid and
discredited, as our eye remains on him making them. It is only natural for
the reader, however, even though Stella's skepticism does not help him
here, to entertain a similar double vision with regard to the main question
of renewal.

To forestall this, Wells brings the monologuish wise man of the novel, Uncle Robert, into play, though not without some attendant ambiguity. Stella asks for her uncle's help in escaping the clutches of her mother, Lucy Kentlake, who, upon discovering her daughter's affair with Gemini and seeing to it that the lovers were separated, has resolved not to let Stella return to Cambridge. Uncle Robert immediately descends upon the Kentlake home, cows his sister-in-law with Olympian ridicule of her priggishness, and whisks Stella off to live with him at Cambridge, where he can personally take charge of the growth of her mind and spirit. The first fruits of this association are twenty pages of monologue delivered by "the omniscient, the assured" Uncle Robert to his niece. These are not the report of an actual conversation between Stella and him but a compendium of all his views on university education, views which Wells apparently considers important enough to warrant this summary procedure at the expense of verisimilitude, although he justifies it, curiously, in the name of his story: "Uncle Robert answered [Stella's] questions on various occasions as this or that occurred to him. . . . But for the purposes of our story it is convenient to gather all he said and conveyed to her as if it were one sustained discourse, framed in the particular talk that centralised these things in her memory" (pp. 195–96). Given Uncle Robert's character and his function in the story as a fountain and current of fresh ideas, the explanation is almost unnecessary; for, at one point, when Stella answers one of his questions he tells her, " 'I don't want you to answer, my dear Stella. I don't want unnecessary answers. I ask these questions for rhetorical effect. Obviously. I am perfectly well able to answer them myself. In fact I insist upon answering them myself.' "

Uncle Robert exists in the novel primarily as a lecturer, in whom we can measure the degree to which Wells has compromised the ideal of the dialogue novel which he thought he had here realized. Yet as a lecturer or spokesman, Uncle Robert possesses an odd intellectual and dramatic ambiguity. Although he comes closest to mouthing Wells's own views, he is treated with irony. In addition to describing him with such epithets as "omniscient," "assured," and "self-satisfied," Wells invariably glances at Uncle Robert's pretension of getting at the Platonic essence of things: "He lifted his nose somewhat and directed his mind to the Real Truth of the Matter." Indeed, this initial monologue of his is entitled "Uncle Robert Tells the Real Truth about University Education," and Wells's phrase, "the Real Truth," with its wry upper-case letters, precedes almost all Uncle Robert's pronouncements through the book. Moreover, these outward ironic signs are corroborated by Uncle Robert's own startling pretensions in speech: " 'I am a man, Stella, as you know, of immense and terrible perspicacity' " (p. 205). With these touches, Wells makes us wonder about the authority of his novel's wise man, and makes us wonder, too, about his purpose in making us wonder.

Uncle Robert's inaugural lecture to Stella might well have been written by Thomas Henry Huxley, had he lived on into the heyday of behaviorism and been capable of Wellsian vivacity. It repudiates classical, humanistic education as a pathetic, irresponsible anachronism and indicts Oxford and Cambridge for remaining committed to it. Uncle Robert is particularly lively and effective in his refusal to believe that any classical don ever commanded enough Latin or Greek really to think, speak, or write significantly in those languages. For Uncle Robert it has been a culture of quotation only, a genteel imposture sustained for hundreds of years, which, with the aid of the Anglican church, has resisted every seminal development in thought, art, and science during the nineteenth and twentieth centuries. Its struggles against Darwinian theory, modern philosophy, semantics, and psychology have altogether discredited it as a means of understanding modern life. Now, says Uncle Robert, with the coming of war and the disappearance of undergraduates, Cambridge is a " 'dying failure,' " but he looks tentatively forward to a rebirth: " 'A world where one never graduates. Where one goes on and learns and learns to the end. And how? World University? With every man and woman alive, a learner?' " Just as he shares Gemini and Stella's hope for a new world, so too has he, curiously enough, been reading Cottenham C. Bower; he is quite taken with the idea that the problems of psychotherapy do not derive from the breaking up of such an original unity as the soul, or psyche, or undivided self, for "so far from the mind being broken up, it has never yet been got together" (p. 215).

Other occasions bring other topics for Uncle Robert, but always there is his urgent guardianship of civilization, his dedication to new ideas, new ways, mixed strangely with an undermining vanity and excessive self-assurance. When Stella, fresh from a mystical dream, comes to him inquiring if there is a God, he delivers the Real Truth about God, which is that the word "God" has been much abused; of all the myriad understandings and definitions of that term in human history, Uncle Robert has never found one that he considers credible. For himself, he says, interpreting Stella's feeling and being remarkably Arnoldian about it, there is "a rightness about things, a direction like the magnetic field that turns the compass needle north," an "ultimate rightness" (p. 243). But whatever this is, it is not "God," because "all the Gods men have ever invented are and must be subject to it." Surprisingly enough, he counsels reticence. Stella, he says, ought not even to speculate about her dream, for no one "has the mental apparatus to do that yet." It is enough to know that there is "truth, there is righteousness and right conduct in us and our universe." She is not to try to make a will or a person of the presence in her dream, for it will not do to add her own little private mystery "to the endless doll shop of the Gods." When Uncle Robert assures her that having once been spiritually where she has been she will go there again, Stella asks if he has been there as well. His reply is startling in its presumption: " 'I *live* there,' said Uncle Robert calmly. And added, 'Practically.' "

Uncle Robert's main discursive contribution begins as a monologue and grows into one of the key dialogues in the novel, a conversation with Gemini that audaciously merges behavioristic psychology and Russian politics in the interest of the theme of renewal. Gemini's quest for "strenuous and grimly serious" experience following the encounter with Mary Clarkson has taken him to Poland, where he lives through the horrors of the Nazi invasion, thence to Finland, where he witnesses the Russian invasion, and finally to Sweden, where in a state of physical, mental, and spiritual paralysis, he is hospitalized and placed under the care of a Freudian analyst, Dr. Olaf Bjorkminder. His mother, Dione M'am Twain, learns of his whereabouts and arranges his removal to Britain, engaging Uncle Robert to cure her broken son. Though a woman of rare independence of mind, Mrs. Twain has fallen under the spell of Uncle Robert's "confident omniscience." Consequently, as a prelude to the therapy itself, both she and the reader are treated to a monologuish disquisition by Uncle Robert on the diametrical differences between psychoanalysis and his own procedure, psychosynthesis. Lifting his nose once again into the air, he reverts to what has now become an intellectual leitmotif of the narrative. Like everyone else, he says, the psychoanalysts believe that "there is a concrete continuous thing in a human being called the mind or the soul or the psyche or the self" and that "in mental disease this simple, originally unified something goes to pieces, as people say" (p. 304). But since Pavlov and Watson it has become clear, as Uncle Robert—as well as Cottenham C. Bower and Gemini and Wells—never tires of saying, that "the mind is not something that can be taken to pieces but something that is being put together." If this idea of synthesis is substituted for the opposed idea of Freudian analysis, says Uncle Robert, then every case of

mental disorder becomes "simpler, clearer and more controllable." The
proof of the efficacy of the procedure, moral as well as psychological,
resides in his treatment of Gemini, a sequence in which Wells tries to pull
together the several intellectual strands of the novel.

This too, since Gemini is initially rather comatose, visited intermittently
by delirium and nightmare, begins as a monologue for Uncle Robert.
Insinuating himself into Gemini's room, he pretends to be preparing a
lecture on Cottenham C. Bower. As Uncle Robert recites his compact
summary of the essential difference between the new psychology and the
old, Gemini, for the first time since he has fallen ill, is drawn out of
himself, "out of the darkness and despair in which he had been hidden so
long," and listens "with intelligent appreciation" (p. 313). The young
patient even suggests some amendments. After an hour of this, Uncle
Robert withdraws. When Gemini next becomes aware of him in the room,
Uncle Robert is whistling Brahms. He breaks off to read his account of the
new psychology of mental illness. It turns out to be an application of
Bower to pathological conditions: " 'Suppose you take the body, the
brain, the individual, or whatever you like to call him, and put him into
strange and unaccustomed circumstances so that he is only rarely and
weakly reminded of those previous groups of reaction-systems in which he
has hitherto lived, he may develop a complex network of new associations
and responses to rule him, while personality number one recedes into the
background more or less completely. . . . [Priests and lawyers] would
call that new man a case, a case of schizophrenia, or perhaps, in a milder
case, of mere absent-mindedness and wool-gathering, schizothymia—and
they would say that there had been a more or less complete splitting of that
primary unity. But the real truth of the matter is that there never was
anything to split. Something has been added. Schizophrenia is one of those
countless question-begging words that confuse human minds' " (p. 315).
Uncle Robert indicates that the therapy for such a patient is to " 'revive the
central interest of his habitual work, and then get him to ask what is the
intrusive trouble that is shoving it aside; why he forgets, why he doubts,
why he is better sometimes and sometimes worse, why his energy comes
and goes.' " Then, after outlining how this approach would be utilized
with a patient who was a painter, or a young priest, or a stockbroker, Uncle
Robert turns to the case in hand, Gemini's own. And here, what has
essentially been an expository monologue becomes the novel's most
remarkable dialogue.

Gemini begins it by speaking of his profound disillusionment with human life after his experiences in Poland and Finland. When Uncle Robert describes this as little more than a young man's discovery of the grim nature of reality, Gemini accuses him of knowing nothing at first hand of the horror and suffering that Gemini has lately witnessed in the war. Uncle Robert's reply establishes a more universal context of pain: " 'A man may get deeper into life in a quiet room in Wimpole Street than by running about during the worst of air raids. I will just tell you I know infinitely more about disillusionment than you do, infinitely more. And leave it at that.' " But he does not leave it at that, going on, instead, to challenge the suffering that Gemini has seen:

> "These horrors you make so much of, this sort of horror, does not as a matter of fact involve any exceptional pain and suffering for anyone but the spectator like yourself. None of those dead you saw ever knew that they were dead. None. They had no time. . . . You saw human beings and bits of human beings quivering, dying, dead, torn to pieces. The point is that that distressed you. It was *you* who got the pain. It was *your* memory which carried off this slow-healing scar. Which is still tormenting you. . . . It was natural and right and proper that you, as an unsophisticated, social animal, should feel pity, indignation and fury at the time. . . . But, get it clear in your mind that those were the emotions that worked you, and that when the crisis was over and you'd done your indignant bit in the melee, they had served their purpose. Get that clear." [Pp. 320–22]

When Gemini replies that this argument reduces an air raid almost to a pleasantry, Uncle Robert charges him with wallowing in a specious disillusionment founded on the most implausible naiveté: " 'Those air raids you saw were outrages and crimes, but they were not revelations of any unsuspected cruelty in the nature of things and that is what you are making them out to be. . . . The fact remains that what has bowled you over, Twain, is not any foul discovery about the world. No sort of black revelation. You knew it could stink, you knew it could pinch, you knew it could make ugly faces and alarming noises before you were two years old.' " Like every other sane human being, Uncle Robert continues, Gemini had established a normal system of disregard for all such unpleasant facts, without which it would be impossible to go on living. But in Poland and Finland, Gemini was caught up in a string of "nasty events" that was too much for these defenses. Tired, sick, and starved, he capitulated, for there was something in his make-up that wanted to. The real truth about Gemini's make-up, says Uncle Robert, is that while he has always appeared to be a lively, active young man in his prime, he actually has had a very strongly developed "countervailing disinclination" underneath which has made him, in matters of action, a natural-born shirker and deserter. All Gemini's mental trouble now is his willful acceptance of the idea that life is too much for him—a failure of character rather than psyche. So too with Gemini's impotence and his rejection of Stella since he has fallen ill. " 'You are afraid to make love,' " Uncle Robert tells him, " 'because at one and the same time you think you will not be able to do so and also you think that if you are able to do so your excuse of utter defeat will be taken from you.' " Uncle Robert even reconstructs imaginatively a scene with a prostitute in Sweden where, unmanned by shame, fear, guilt, and the sense of his universe smeared all over with ugliness, Gemini first experienced the impotence he had half-anticipated and then seized upon it as a corroboration of his utter defeat: " 'This,' you said to yourself, 'is what I have always suspected of life.' " To this personal analysis and indictment Gemini now entirely acquiesces.

The reader, apparently, is meant to acquiesce to it as well, although he is also given a sense of Uncle Robert's moral and psychic bullying of his patient. We may be surprised, too, by the quite un-Wellsian insistence on the cruelty of existence, the "stink" and "pinch" of the world, in Uncle Robert's remarks, and by his somewhat facile dismissal of the suffering of others, of the air raid victims. But, for the moment, these views strike us as perhaps therapeutically justified; the healer may proceed as he will in order to bring his patient back to health. Perhaps, we say to ourselves, Uncle Robert is functioning here, and everywhere, more as a character in a fiction than as a spokesman for Wells. Elsewhere his conceit of himself makes his pronouncements problematic; here his concern for Gemini's cure does the same.

In any case, the dialogue now proceeds to enlarge itself, moving from the individual case to the representative. Gemini maintains that what has happened to him has happened to many of his generation: their hopes for the future of the world have proved to be an utter delusion, fixed as they were on the example of Soviet Russia. The Russian revolution, for all of its shortcomings, had been proof that "something saner, more generous and juster than the outworn, self-deceiving selfishness of capitalism" could establish itself; but the Soviet invasion of Finland broke that faith. Uncle Robert, listening attentively, sums up Gemini's position like a latter-day Matthew Arnold: " 'And you were left—you and a lot of your generation

—in a state of neurasthenia—not between an old world dying and a new world unable to be born—but worse, between an old world dead and in decay and an abortion also decaying' " (p. 327).

But when Gemini consents to this statement of the case, Uncle Robert indicates that he will himself have no part of it. He has never, he says, thought of Russia in quite such violent terms; it was never his land of hope and glory, and now, even after Finland, he thinks rather well of it. At this point, the voice of the non-Marxist revolutionary, H. G. Wells, is clearly discernible in Uncle Robert's remarks on the pivotal ideological difficulty of twentieth-century radicalism. Uncle Robert says that the Russian revolution, almost the only good thing that came out of the First World War, did, after all, abolish what it called the Capitalist System, along with most profiteering and the great parasitic classes of landowners and rentiers; that even if the job was done clumsily, or only half-done, we in the West "have everything still to do." When Gemini points to the new tyranny under Stalin, Uncle Robert offers an elaborate defense of the Russian leader, ranking him morally above both Hitler and Chamberlain, citing the inescapable inellectual narrowness of his formative years, the ridicule he suffered at the hands of the brilliant and cultivated Trotsky, his fervent, simple-minded allegiance to Marxist dogma and to *his* Revolution, his profound self-distrust and his consequent distrust of everyone else; taking everything into account, says Uncle Robert, "on the whole, according to his lights, this friendless, rather clumsy man in the Kremlin may still be trying to do right" (p. 333). When Gemini replies that Stalin bombed civilians and trains of refugees in Finland, Uncle Robert answers that Stalin probably knew nothing of that, seeing in his mind only the imperialism of Germany and Western Europe and all the elements of reaction in Scandinavia and Finland plotting against his sacred proletariat, with Finland as the spearhead of the attack. What it proves, Uncle Robert continues, is that Russia is human and that Gemini and his crowd of young people began by over-believing in it and have ended now by using their sense of betrayal to absolve them from all further participation in the great effort to renew civilization. At this point the dialogue reaches its climax with Uncle Robert unleashing his therapeutic thunderbolt, at once vituperative and heartening, and Gemini all but collapsing under the blow:

"Which brings us back," [says Uncle Robert], "to what we were talking about the other day, the underlying timid evasiveness of the human mind, and particularly of the youthful human mind. All intelligent young people, deep down in their hearts, are scared by life. Naturally. Deep down in your hearts is the profoundest funk of any real World Revolution, which calls for just what you find so difficult; steadfast effort, self-subjugation, balance, cooperation with people different from yourself—people perhaps wounding to your self-love by the difference of their gifts and of their unusual phrasing. Far easier and more congenial to break up what those others do than to do something yourself. Your young communists are the bitterest enemies of Revolution. They have a crazy, subconscious fear of it and will do anything to cripple or prevent it. What is the easiest way out for them? Not to work with anyone who isn't exactly on the Party line. The little fastidious darlings! Far easier to wave a red flag and yell stale party slogans. Far easier for your silly young students, who have found study rather perplexing and heavy-going, to stop studying altogether and shout. . . .''

"Anyhow," said Gemini, "for me and most of us that moral background has collapsed. What is left for us?"

"Life begins every morning," said Uncle Robert. "Grow up a bit and start a new and sounder moral background."

"With our damaged and disillusioned minds."

"With your chastened minds."

"From the ground upward."

"From reality upward." [Pp. 333–34]

Uncle Robert is speaking, but surely we are justified in sensing, at this point, that Wells is speaking through him, rallying all men of good will, in the face of the Russian behavior that dismayed and demoralized so many, to reaffirm their mature, realistic faith in the unrevealed world to which Wells himself had for years dedicated his life. Uncle Robert's words are therapeutic in this larger sense. But Gemini, like many of his generation, cannot respond. He says that Uncle Robert asks too much of them. The vast effort of liberating themselves from the ideas of Christian England and the comfortable classes and lodging their faith in communism has come to nothing. " 'And now,' " Gemini goes on, " 'you ask us in effect to make a clean sweep in our minds, go back on ourselves, re-examine the words and phrases we use, ransack the facts for what you call the true operating causes, and begin all over again, correcting the mistakes and false starts of the past ten thousand years and reconditioning the world. When it is already dropping to pieces out of its accumulated rottenness. "Re-make the world." You really mean it. We—a rally of beaten, half-educated youngsters! How can one face up to so vast an undertaking?' "

For his reply, Uncle Robert appears to draw legitimately on his strange affinity with the Real Truth of things, and of life. He smiles his exasperating smile at the sunshine outside and asks, " 'What else is there to do?' " Recalcitrant, Gemini answers, " 'One can do nothing.' " To this, speaking with an almost mystical realism, Uncle Robert says, " 'Life won't let you. While you are alive.' " Gemini utters his final refusal: " 'I have offered my resignation. . . . Oh! I'm tired,' he said abruptly. 'I'm broken. *Damn* life!' " But the last word, spoken in a perspective of impersonal, unanswerable verity—for he has been accumulating authority all along—is Uncle Robert's: " 'Broken or not,' he said, standing up, 'you are still alive, Mr. Gemini Twain. Like it or not, you'll find out you have to do something about it. Every morning life begins. Tomorrow will come along and say "Well?" to you, just as though nothing had happened.' " Thus the guru speaks for life, hope, amelioration as these are sanctioned by a supervening necessity.

Yet having said so much in behalf of life, Uncle Robert—undone, Wells tells us, by "the blind ruthlessness that flows beneath events in this world"—suddenly dies, crushed by a lorry after missing a curb and stumbling in the road. In this totally unlooked-for event, as in his constant notation of Uncle Robert's intellectual arrogance, Wells implies a judgment of the mind itself, of the whole problem of wisdom incarnate in persons.

On his precipitate deathbed, Uncle Robert dwindles into incoherence and regret. When he learns that a lorry loaded with gas cylinders rather than a car struck him down, he sees the hand of God, who "didn't do things by halves," in his demise, startling us once again with his spiritual assumptions. He tries to formulate some appropriate last words, but is unable "to fix my mind." He thinks, but "then the stuff flows away into something else." For an hour he lies "regarding the Real Truth of Things above the bed with a look of disdainful penetration," but then turns his face from it: "The Real Truth of Things, it seemed, interested him no more. It bored him" (p. 339). He thinks briefly of Gemini, who is not present, though Stella is, and he urges his young patient on in absentia to a recovery which he foresees because of the recuperative power of youth, though he warns Gemini, somewhat cryptically, not to "do it again." After lying still for a time, "as though thought had ebbed away from him," he seeks again some last word, "some summarising epitaph." It appears that "some austerer element in his make-up was putting his *persona* on trial," and again Wells is hinting at a spiritual, almost a religious, measure and drama, a "private Last Judgment." The epitaph turns out to be a self-reproach. Uncle Robert condemns himself for not sufficiently considering the feelings of other people, for insulting and estranging them instead, and enjoying it. Some ambiguous fluctuations follow. What may have been "the ghost of a cough or the shadow of a chuckle" succeeds this reflection on his delight in ridicule, but so too does a tear that Stella thinks she sees running to the corner of his mouth. In "mumbled soliloquy" he pronounces himself indolent and arrogant, before his voice dies down to "a mere murmur, the formless shadow of speech." But shortly after, he "very clearly" expresses protest and puzzlement, as though before the Judgment Seat, about everything and nothing in particular: " 'How was *I* to know?' " Then, finally, "faintly articulate . . . speaking drowsily, like a drunken man half asleep," Uncle Robert utters his final wisdom—that like others who have failed, he too will be forgiven: " 'S all ri'. . . . Qui' all ri'. Ob—. Ob-vi-ous-ly.' "

Thus the most imposing and audacious voice in the novel dwindles into inaudibility and conventional solace. We seem to be witnessing the dissolution of mind itself in a universe that has become too formidable and dark for it. Uncle Robert's earlier presumption and Wells's recurrent ironic tone toward him now appear at one with an even larger presumption: that given the "blind ruthlessness that flows beneath events in this world," wisdom should be incarnate in persons at all, vulnerable as they are, like Gemini, or mortal, prideful, and muttering, like Uncle Robert. As a good Bowerian, Uncle Robert here presides not over the synthesizing of his yet unrealized self but over the utter disintegration of it in death. It is strange, too, that this should happen to the figure who, in his personal presence and speech, is the novel's most ardent and vibrant incarnation of selfhood. At this juncture, the despair that Wells was to express fully several years later in *Mind at the End of Its Tether* comes decidedly into view, somehow heightened by Uncle Robert's conviction of forgiveness.

Ambiguous as he is, however, Uncle Robert yet remains an inspiration for the young people. Despite Gemini's impotence and reluctance and the horrible example of sterile marriage in *Lady Chatterly's Lover*, Gemini allows Stella, who is still deeply and touchingly in love with him, to persuade him to marry her. Indeed, it is through her dialogue with Gemini after Uncle Robert's death—a kind of continuation of the original psychosynthetic conversation on a more loving level—that Stella wins Gemini back to health. Honeymooning in Mary Clarkson's cottage, which Stella has now bought, the two young people bring the novel full circle, for the marriage is speedily, impulsively consummated in these conducive surroundings and they go off the following morning to see what has become of Kalikov's massive lump of alabaster. On their way they learn from the vicar that Kalikov, who is a Bulgarian, has been interned as an enemy alien because his accent sounded German to the tribunal, and that Balch has become head of the British Ministry of Propaganda in Brazil, where he "gets the real English idea over" to the Brazilians by delivering talks on the Heroines of Jane Austen and the Nonsense Verse of Edward Lear. Convinced that "Old England, generally speaking, has gone nuts," Gemini delivers a diatribe on the confusion of the national will, which ends with his declaring his intention to join in the war, perhaps as an antiaircraft gunner on a trawler, in order to retain his privilege of criticizing his country. Fearful of this prospect, Stella switches the conversation to Uncle Robert.

She recalls his jeremiad on education the world over. Lifting her nose in the air to imitate him, she speaks of the pinheadedness of civilization; of mankind, underneath its apparent forms and securities, as a "horde of frightened fools, fanatics, and greedy, scheming, criminal men" (p. 363). And she recalls, too, Uncle Robert's lamenting that he himself had done so little to change it all. Her comment on this is revealing, for it begins the demarcation between Stella and the talkative men with whom she has so much to do in the novel: " 'While he said it, it sounded true, but I didn't *feel* that it was *really* true. I felt it was just *brilliantly* true. You know?' " Gemini's response is equally brilliant and, for Stella, equally dubious. " 'Maybe while all the rest of the world has gone mad,' " he says, " 'we two are going sane.' " " 'Can anyone keep sane,' " she replies, " 'when the world goes mad?' " When Gemini answers that he feels sane for the first time in a long while, she thinks to herself of "the last exorcism she had had to perform" in bed in order to make him so and of the thankless work of being a woman. The conversation turns briefly to sexuality and its possible influence on human aggression as well as on mental and imaginative activity. And then they are at Kalikov's garden, apprehensively anticipating their new encounter with the block of alabaster.

It does for them all that might be expected of a symbol. Remarkably, terrifyingly, and a little implausibly, it manages to turn over, undermined and pushed by things growing beneath it, just at the moment of its young devotees' visit. "It had been a symbol before; now it was a living obligation" (p. 369). In the excitement of the epiphany, and in the lingering glow of their lovemaking the night before, Gemini accedes to Stella's conviction that "sex *is* the quintessence of life" and declares his love for her, as she has been yearning for him to do. From this point on, again a little implausibly, if not confusedly, sexuality, in both Bowerian and Wellsian formulation, mingles with reflections on the future of civilization; it is not that there are no emotional, dramatic, psychic, even intellectual links between the two centers of concern, but only that the links are not convincingly forged, as though the connection between Wells's own sexual and speculative life is so close and so innate that he is incapable of deliberately delineating it in others for others.

In any case, Gemini seizes on the movement of the alabaster as a portent of extreme urgency. Either the right world is to be carved posthaste from the living block or everything that makes life worth living for Gemini and Stella faces extinction. Under the pressure of this need, Gemini begins to talk of the future, of a world where every human being might be "lovingly educated," where science might improve the "texture and quality of the human brain." He speaks of the struggle that will be necessary to bring it about, the role that sex, as a "vital drive," might play, and the need for dreams and courage.

Then, as this familiar program and familiar yearning are unfolding in the familiar grandiose terms, Stella asks a startling question: " 'How?' " What, exactly, are they, is she, to do to help bring about the new world? " 'Carve our alabaster. Gemini—what does that *mean*?' " she asks. It is a fair question, one that the reader has been longing to ask earlier of Gemini, of Uncle Robert, and of Wells himself when the mood of visionary renewal is on him. Gemini falters. " '*Am* I a gas-bag?' " he inquires. " 'As bad as Balch for example?' " Stella answers kindly that there is a lot of Balch in all of us, but she insists that Gemini prescribe a specific course of action for them. He is not ready to do so and marks time by noting the characteristic weakness of the "progressive liberal," who always assumes that these envisaged things will come of themselves, that progress is inevitable. Gemini goes so far as to pay tribute to "good old Belloc" who warned that it is very far indeed from inevitable. But Stella is adamant; she reiterates "How?" and Gemini is forced to declare that he cannot tell how at this moment. He will think out "a full and proper answer": " 'And then I will deliver a discourse to you—without the faintest flavour of Balch in it. I promise. There shall be no signs and symbols. No rhetorical evasions. I'll talk prose, dear Conscience' " (p. 380). It is a high and welcome promise. We determine, as we read it, to hold him to it. The scene concludes with a more fearsome promise still—the sound of guns out at sea, conditioning the pledge with the urgency implicit in the historical moment of the whole novel's action and composition. Stella shivers at the sound, not with the urgency of the male quest for millenial salvation, but, like Margaret

Broxted in *Bulpington*, with the sheer womanly dread of the death by war that is at hand for many, including, perhaps, Gemini himself.

Three days pass before Gemini puts his "discourse" together. Just before he delivers it, Stella, coming more and more to represent the book's highest capacity for knowing and bearing reality, casts a cold, skeptical eye on the whole idea of discourse itself. Like Uncle Robert and his brilliant rather than real truths, her talkative young husband with his large appetite for speculation and debate belongs to another order of things, another understanding from her own—belongs, in fact, to the very paternal tradition against which he has violently rebelled: "There was still, she thought, a resemblance between father and son, if only in their dialectical mannerisms. Argument was in their blood. The shape of the two minds was the same, even if the ideas had been turned inside out. How obstinate is inheritance!" Nonetheless, she settles down to listen, as critically, almost, as we.

What follows is disappointing, yet intriguingly, wastefully redeemable, had we but world enough and time. In the face of the book's intimations of the insufficiency of mind and speech, especially in the darkling wood of 1940, Wells allows it to end with what is largely a twenty-five page monologue by Gemini exhorting us as hopefully as ever to lend mind, body, and tongue to the building of a new world out of the ruins of the old.

Gemini foresees an Allied victory, the dissolution of the British Empire, and the establishment of numerous international commissions for disarmament, reparations, displaced populations, transportation, industry, trade, etc., which will inevitably and almost indiscernibly lead to a federated world Union. Neither the "hard-faced business man" nor the Masses, which have "dispersed and disappeared," will be essential to this development, but administrative experts and the "broad base of the human community [which] is middle-class" will. The age-old struggle between Right and Left, between power-seekers and rebels, will give way to the rule of the Center, those who, like the artist, the skilled artisan, and the man of science, "get their sense of mastery in doing something they can do particularly well and in having that mastery recognised" (p. 390).

Like Stephen Wilbeck in *Apropos of Dolores*, Gemini acknowledges humankind's powerful egotistical desire to feel masterful and to compel a recognition of its mastery over others as a means of verifying its own existence; but unlike Wilbeck, Gemini is confident that the Center has dispensed with the troublesome aggressive means of satisfying this impulse, as he himself has. The present war is, for Gemini, merely one of the more intense phases of the endless historical alternation between aggressive persecution and revolt; the war itself signals the awakening of a new world revolution. Unfortunately, he says, the World Federation that will be established by the armistice and the commissions will not last beyond 1980, for the rational forces, the leading spirits guiding it into existence, will have spent themselves by then and a reaction will set in. The only way to avoid this, Gemini goes on, is to implement the Right Thing to Do: " 'The real truth of the matter, as Uncle Robert would have said, is that in every eventuality, there is a Right Thing to Do' " (p. 395). Since there is, and since it must be discovered, Gemini continues, it is clear that " 'the organisation of knowledge and thought in the world is the central and saving business before Mankind.' " Gemini is wise enough to know that "in a thousand matters" there is as yet no Right Thing to Do because the necessary knowledge and wisdom has not been secured. The new world, the new planetary society will require a "new education on its own scale," a vast, ordered encyclopedia of fact and thought and a vast organization of researchers, teachers, interpreters, priests, confessors, counselors, and "prophets also to innovate and reanimate its idea." Far from dispensing with religion, it will need a rebirth of religious structures on this vaster scale to hold it all together, a World Church, a World Brain, and a World Will ensuring that the Religion of Knowledge remains in control of human affairs.

Here Gemini pauses to pay tribute to Uncle Robert, acknowledging his debt to him for having spent a lifetime attacking the "intellectual self-complacency" that stands in the way of this new dispensation. " 'He knew a fundamental thing about the human mind,' " says Gemini, " 'the hardest thing in the world to know, which is that it scarcely knows anything at all. . . . He felt that it scarcely exists as yet. He was trying to assemble it. He was trying to put it together, strand by strand' " (p. 399). This latest echo of the Bowerian leitmotif becomes part of Wells's ambiguous paean to the mind, at least to the idea of mind embodied in Uncle Robert's career. Gemini speaks of him as a "devastating intelligence" totally devoted to getting "at the reality of the human mind," a great teacher to whom Gemini and Stella are indebted for their very intellectual existence, and whose "life was a declaration of war at this pervading, this uncritical ignorance in which mankind is blundering towards irreparable disaster." Inspired by his recollection of this example, Gemini salutes the mind in unqualified terms which clash, ironically enough, with our memory of Uncle Robert on his deathbed, with Wells's habit of toying with him, and with Stella's quiet skepticism:

"Because, you see, Stella, the one and sole *reality* in human life is mental. It always has been; it always will be. Our selves are the mental assemblage of our activities. Theology and worship, religion, philosophy, science, imagination, propaganda and teaching, are the essentials upon which all purposive action, all cooperation and material achievement depend. Violence and the forcible prevention of violence are both merely the realisation of ideas. A bomb is a whole complex of thought embodied. Of all human fools the man who shirks thought, despises 'theory' and fancies himself a practical man, is surely the biggest. He's a detached bit of dementia. His actions are epileptic. To live is to think; to act consciously is merely thinking by action; there is no other living." [Pp. 400–401]

Thus, with fervor, Gemini places himself in the mainstream of philosophical idealism and vindicates the work of men like Uncle Robert and Uncle Wells. The primacy of mind now dictates the course of practical action that he has promised to propose. It is to be educative.

As soon as the war is over, Gemini says, he will seek "some sort of chair or lectureship in pedagogy or social psychology or what not"—the "what not" is revealing—and Stella "would make the perfect head of a women's college." His mine-sweeping and her nursing are the immediate job in hand, but their true work, demanding all the self-control and self-possession they can command, is to constitute of themselves and of all who are similarly disposed a "class-unconscious élite" devoted to gathering, ordering, and disseminating knowledge. " 'We have to find out all that there is to be known and what is afoot in those various movements for documentation, for bibliography, for indexing, for all that microphotographic recording one hears about distantly and dimly.' " They will undertake nothing less than "a preliminary study of the possible intellectual enlargement of the world." Since man is nothing but a "cerebrum," since "the only real mastery of life is knowledge and clear thought," and since "all the present leaders of men argue and write, and the quality of their thought determines human destiny" and "thought and expression remain the reality of history"—since all this is the real truth of the matter for Gemini, he is quite convinced that he has devised an indispensable yet practical and modest program—"no heroics," he assures Stella—for them to embark upon. Indeed, he is rather pleased with the feasibility of it all: " 'I think I've de-Balched our outlook pretty completely now' " (p. 404).

Stella is less certain, rather stunned by it all; but she graciously subscribes to it as, after all, the only course of action for such as they. In her fervent wifeliness she calls Gemini "dear husband" for the first time, seals her devotion with a kiss, and hears again the sound of the guns, now louder than ever.

For the reader, however, especially the reader who has seen some of Gemini's prophecies come to pass without materially improving the prospects for mankind, the discourse remains far from de-Balched. Gemini's faith in the possibility of a new order to be established through the "intellectual enlargement of the world" represents as wild and generalized a dream as anything served up earlier in the novel, including Balch's own more militant version. It is a choice only between chattering and whistling in the darkling wood. Gemini's belief in the primacy of mind, thought, and expression as the sole reality in human life and history is moving; but the irrationality, perversion, and malevolence that the mind has shown itself capable of through all of human history hardly warrants optimism, as the novelist himself has intimated.

In Gemini's final monologue, Wells, for the last time in his novels, has allowed himself to voice the dream of a new world nurturing a new life. It is his most touching statement of his utopianism, because as he makes it, or allows Gemini to make it, he knows that it is not true, is not feasible, even though he refrains from supplying the answering voice in dialogue. Like Uncle Robert's Real Truth of the Matter, it is a Platonic yearning whose prospects are dim, darkling. Only a babe in the woods could express it and believe it in 1940. Gemini can, Stella less, Wells hardly: for him Gemini's groundless hope is but an ironic expression of his own growing pessimism. We have here the beginning of the descent through *You Can't Be Too Careful* to *Mind at the End of Its Tether*.

Only in fiction could Wells achieve this emotional, intellectual duality. All his life long he had utilized the novel as an opportunity to say things—to create personages who say things—which he was not sure he believed, which could be said for the experiment of saying them and for the delight of having them clash with other trial utterances. But the form of *Babes in the Darkling Wood* marks the effective end of this achievement.

Here Wells forgoes too much artistry, too much drama, too much incarnation of problems in persons, and relies instead on monologues which are not so much dramatic, though they are occasionally that too, as conceptual. His contrast between Gemini's hope and Stella's sensitivity to the immediate emergency is a conflict of ideas, but the novel does not frame them within its own borders of interest or concern. Wells had used the novel in the past as a frame within which ideas could take on the added interest of personal life, could take on no less a thing than flesh and blood, and so become part of a more intricate human whole which was not merely intellectual, political, or social. This had been true of *Bulpington* and *Dolores; Brynhild* was so fully devoted to the personal life that such general ideas do not even leave a mark on it. Now, however, in *Babes* the frame is slipping from his grasp, the blood drains from his figures, and we are left with the intellectual, ideological consideration only, or with enough of it so that we question whether fiction is at all the appropriate form for Wells's purpose. To the extent that we can still identify the timbre of Gemini's character in his speeches, of Uncle Robert's in his, and of Stella's in hers, *Babes* is a novel still; but to the extent that all three personages are less interesting to us than what they say, it has become something else, something closer to the Dialogues of Plato than to the art of Fielding, Dickens, George Eliot, and Henry James, all of whom remain decidedly within the frame.

Here at last, to answer the nagging question of *Experiment in Autobiography*, Wells is no longer a novelist in the sense that he had managed, amazingly, to be one hitherto. Along with the bitter political fantasy and prophecy of *The Holy Terror* and the malicious intellectual despair of *You Can't Be Too Careful*, the proliferating monologues of *Babes in the Darkling Wood*, though they come closer to making art of their thought, nonetheless mark the end of the novel as the best form for Wells to give expression to his sense of life. He had got from it what he needed and given to us through it what he could.

Notes

NOTES TO THE INTRODUCTION

1. Bernard Bergonzi's summation may stand for the prevailing critical consensus: "Wells, at the beginning of his career, was a genuine imaginative artist, who wrote several books of considerable literary importance, before dissipating his talents in directions which now seem more or less irrelevant" (*The Early H. G. Wells* [Manchester: Manchester University Press, 1961], p. 22).

2. See W. Warren Wagar, *H. G. Wells and the World State* (New Haven: Yale University Press, 1961) for an astute reassessment of Wells's intellectual career. The question of Wells's fundamental pessimism, early as well as late in his career, is argued by Anthony West in "H. G. Wells," *Encounter* 7, no. 2 (1957): 52–69; by Bernard Bergonzi in *The Early H. G. Wells*; and by G. P. Wells in his introduction to *The Last Books of H. G. Wells* (London: H. G. Wells Society, 1968).

3. The extent of critical neglect of these works is unprecedented in the case of a major figure. David Lodge, for example, as late as 1971, was able to take Wells's whole career as his province in an intelligent and often penetrating essay without once mentioning any of the last novels: "Assessing H. G. Wells," *The Novelist at the Crossroads* (London: Routledge & Kegan Paul, 1971), pp. 205–20.

4. Contemplating Wells's literary, rather than his intellectual, career W. Warren Wagar, in "Art and Thought," *Virginia Quarterly Review* 45 (Autumn 1969): 693–97, offers a rare glimmer of possible reassessment: "I am more and more convinced that we have been underestimating the artistry of Wells's later books and overestimating the artistry of the earlier ones" (p. 696). But just over the page, this glimmer fades into the light of the common criticism: "I am tempted to agree with Bernard Bergonzi that Wells wrote little or nothing in his later years artistically comparable to his first scientific romances, such as 'The War of the Worlds' (1898) . . . ."

5. For an admirable survey of Wells's reflections on the novel prior to his involvement with James see Gordon N. Ray, "H. G. Wells Tries to Be a Novelist," *Edwardians and Late Victorians*, English Institute Essays 1959, ed. Richard Ellmann (New York: Columbia University Press, 1960), pp. 106–59.

NOTES TO CHAPTER I:
ART AND LIFE: ONCE MORE UNTO THE BREACH

1. *Henry James and H. G. Wells: A Record of Their Friendship, Their Debate on the Art of Fiction, and Their Quarrel*, ed. Leon Edel and Gordon N. Ray (Urbana: University of Illinois Press, 1958), p. 267.

2. *The Letters of Henry James*, ed. Percy Lubbock (New York: Charles Scribner's Sons, 1920), 2: 488. Only a portion of this letter of Wells's has survived.

3. "The Scope of the Novel," later serialized as "The Contemporary Novel" and included under that title in *An Englishman Looks at the World* (London: Cassell & Co., 1914). Parenthetical page citations in the text refer to *Henry James and H. G. Wells*, where it is reprinted.

4. For a similar celebration of the power of imaginative literature to illuminate experience where philosophical generalization may fail, see Stuart Hampshire, *Thought and Action* (London: Chatto & Windus, 1959).

5. This essay was published in two installments in the *Times Literary Supplement* (March 19 and April 2, 1914), pp. 133–34 and 137–58. It is reprinted in *Henry James and H. G. Wells*, to which all citations in the text refer.

6. "Of Art, of Literature, of Mr. Henry James" in *Boon, The Mind of the Race, The Wild Asses of the Devil, and The Last Trump* (New York: George H. Doran Co., 1915). All page references to this work in the text are to this edition.

7. *The Works of H. G. Wells*, Atlantic Edition (New York: Charles Scribner's Sons; London: Unwin, 1924–1927).

8. Virginia Woolf offered such criticism in "Modern Fiction," "Mr. Bennett and Mrs. Brown," and in her review of *Joan and Peter* in *Times Literary Supplement* (September 19, 1918). The same disparity between interest in the present and interest in the future is discernible in James's comment, in a letter of 1906, to Wells on Wells's book *The Future in America*: "I seemed to see, for myself, while I was there, absolutely *no* profit in scanning or attempting to sound the future—the present being so hugely fluid and the direction (beyond mere space and quantity and motion so incalculable—as to the *whole*;) and yet here you come and throw yourself *all* on the future, and leave out almost altogether the America of my old knowledge; leave out all sorts of things . . ." (*Henry James and H. G. Wells*, pp. 114–15). James's own study, *The American Scene* (1907), profoundly immersed in impressions of the America that he revisited in 1904–1905, certainly illustrates the difference at length.

9. *The Common Reader* (New York: Harcourt, Brace, 1925), p. 210.

10. "Digression about Novels," in *Experiment in Autobiography* (New York: Macmillian Co., 1934), pp. 410–24. Parenthetical page references in the text are to that edition. *Experiment in Autobiography* by H. G. Wells, copyright 1934 by Herbert George Wells. Copyright © renewed 1962 by George Philip Wells and Francis Richard Wells. Reprinted by permission of J. B. Lippincott Company.

11. See James's two essays on Balzac in *Notes on Novelists* (London: J. M. Dent, 1914).

12. Lewis, Huxley, Priestly, and Snow are also directly indebted to Wells for their whole conception of the novel as a form and as an opportunity to assess and

influence life. Lewis's inscription in the copy of *It Can't Happen Here* (1935) that he presented to Wells reads "with the gratitude of one who has learned from him all that he knows" (Mark Schorer, *Sinclair Lewis: An American Life* [New York: McGraw-Hill, 1961], p. 611). Oddly enough, Wells's *The Holy Terror* (1939) bears resemblances, in turn, to *It Can't Happen Here*.

For an indication of how uncannily close even D. H. Lawrence could come to Wells's views on the inconsequentiality of the art novel, the exhaustion of the vein of sensibility, the regrettable division between fiction and abstract thought, and the role of the novel in helping to determine the nature of the world which will succeed our own, see "Surgery for the Novel—or a Bomb," written in 1923 and collected in *Phoenix* (New York: Viking, 1936).

13. (New York: Alliance Book Corporation; London: Secker and Warburg, 1940), pp. ix–xiii.

14. (London: Secker and Warburg, 1941). I am using the American edition (New York: G. P. Putnam's Sons, 1942), in which the introduction runs from pp. xi–xvii.

15. For exhaustive treatment of these and other attacks on Wells's novels see Ingvald Raknem, *H. G. Wells and his Critics* (Oslo: Universitetsforlaget, 1962).

16. Preface to *The Scientific Romances of H. G. Wells* (London: Gollancz, 1933).

NOTES TO CHAPTER II: *The Bulpington of Blup*

1. *The Bulpington of Blup* (New York: The Macmillan Co., 1933), p. 5. All subsequent page references to this work apply to this, the first American edition, and will be cited parenthetically in the text.

2. Introduction to *Babes in the Darkling Wood*, p. xii.

3. For a cogent discussion of some of Wells's reservations, see Norman and Jeanne Mackenzie, *H. G. Wells: A Biography* (New York: Simon and Schuster, 1973), pp. 54–57.

4. Wells makes important use of the Undine motif several years later in *Brynhild*. See Chapter 3 of this study.

5. *Experiment in Autobiography*, p. 532.

6. Five years later, Wells satirized the academic form of aesthetic detachment in *The Camford Visitation* (London: Methuen & Co., 1937).

NOTES TO CHAPTER III: *Brynhild*

1. See Antonina Vallentin, *H. G. Wells: Prophet of Our Day* (New York: John Day Co., 1950), Lovat Dickson, *H. G. Wells: His Turbulent Life and Times* (New York: Atheneum, 1969), and Norman and Jeanne MacKenzie, *H. G. Wells* (New York: Simon and Schuster, 1973), where she can be identified as Marie, or Moura, Budberg, a former secretary and companion to Maxim Gorki.

2. *Brynhild, or the Show of Things* (New York: Charles Scribner's Sons, 1937), p. 302. All subsequent page references are to this edition and will be cited parenthetically in the text.

3. See, for example, James's treatment of journalists and publicity in *The Bostonians*, "The Death of the Lion," and "Flickerbridge."

4. For a perceptive account of Wells's earlier flirtations with Jamesian practice, which were less extensive, less sustained, and less heartfelt, see Richard Hauer Costa, "Edwardian Intimations of the Shape of Fiction to Come: Mr. Britling / Job Huss as Wellsian Central Intelligences," *English Literature in Transition, 1880–1920*, 18, no. 4 (1975): 229–42.

5. In the *Experiment in Autobiography* Wells writes: "From [James's] point of view there were not so much 'novels' as The Novel, and it was a very high and important achievement. . . . He saw us all as Masters or would-be Masters, little Masters and Great Masters, and he was plainly sorry that 'Cher Maître' was not an English expression" (p. 411).

6. See the Prefaces to Volumes 7 and 12 of the Atlantic Edition of Wells's works. Or this, from his introduction to *The Scientific Romances of H. G. Wells* (London: Victor Gollancz Ltd., 1933): "Work of this sort [*The Autocracy of Mr. Parham*] gets so stupidly reviewed nowadays that it has little chance of being properly read. People are simply warned that there are ideas in my books and advised not to read them, and so a fatal suspicion has wrapped about the later ones. 'Ware stimulants!' It is no good my saying that they are quite as easy to read as the earlier ones and much more timely. It becomes a bore doing imaginative books that do not touch imaginations, and at length one stops even planning them" (p. x).

7. See Dickson, *H. G. Wells*, p. 261. Wells himself treats such activities quite affectionately in the heavily autobiographical *Mr. Britling Sees It Through* (1916). One wonders if Wells's Orange of Discord, in the extreme comic artificiality of the Judgment of Paris charade, bears any resemblance to James's "plump and more or less juicy orange of a particular acquainted state" "squeeze[d] out to the utmost" in the indictment of Wells's artlessness in "The Younger Generation" quoted in Chapter 1.

NOTES TO CHAPTER IV: *Apropos of Dolores*

1. Odette Keun, "H. G. Wells—The Player," *Time and Tide*, 15 (October 13, 1934): 1249–51; (October 20, 1934), 1307–9; (October 27, 1934); 1346–48.

2. Several years later, Madame Keun made what I take to be another allusion in print to her life with Wells. This time it is a compulsorily veiled glimpse of the end of the affair:

Philip [who she later reveals is a "mixture of the two most fundamental and invincible elements of my brain: my Latin reality of spirit and my Huguenot conscience"] materialized some years ago during a crisis of my own—I badly wanted to tell you [the reader] about it and did so in my manuscript, but my publishers, frightened of the demented English libel laws which don't even allow one to claim the truth, bullied me into taking it out—when I was drowning in a bewilderment and an anguish of which nothing in my life, although it has been plentifully sprinkled with upheavals, disasters, failures, rivings, perils, political imprisonments and expulsions, physical suffering and mental despair, had given me the faintest foretaste. Philip materialized immediately, completely and immutably, took charge, kept me from a lunatic asylum, and has never abandoned me since (Odette Keun, *I Think Aloud in America* [New York: Longmans, Green & Co., 1939], pp. 203).

3. *Apropos of Dolores* (New York: Charles Scribner's Sons, 1938), pp. vii–viii. All subsequent page references are to this edition and will be cited parenthetically in the text.

4. The terms that Wilbeck employs in characterizing these brunet Dolores peoples come very close to an all but acknowledged anti-Semitism. Wells, of course, was no more patient with Jewish nationalism than with any other likely to impede the coming of a future world community. Interestingly enough, it is a view that Odette Keun continued to share with Wells years after their break: "I do not denounce the Hebrews," she writes, "for what is usually held against them: their commercialism—it was a defense-mechanism against the military, administrative, social and legal tyranny to which they were subjected in all foreign lands. . . . But I do denounce them for the invincible and pernicious passion with which they perpetrate the past and block the construction of the future" (*I Think Aloud in America*, p. 118).

5. "A Thesis on the Quality of Illusion in the Continuity of the Individual Life in the Higher Metazoa, with Particular Reference to the Species *Homo Sapiens*," in *'42 to '44* (London: Secker & Warburg, 1944), p. 169.

6. Ibid., pp. 193–94.

7. For another fictional portrait of Odette Keun that agrees in all essentials and in a number of particulars—the uncontrollable impatience with virginity in young Englishmen, the epic tantrums, the hallucinatory jealousy, and the eventual dramatic death—with Wells's Dolores, see Anthony West's fine novel, *Heritage* (New York: Random House, 1955), where Madame Keun appears as Lolotte, the Gravin von Essling-Sterlinghoven. *Heritage* also contains magnificent imaginative accounts of Anthony West's parents, H. G. Wells and Rebecca West, and of Marie Budberg, the model for Wells's Brynhild.

8. All the indications are that this lovely young woman is, like Brynhild, based on Marie Budberg, who had an aristocratic background and entered Wells's life as Odette Keun departed it.

9. For a suggestive examination of the relationship between the novel's intellectual structure and Oswald Spengler's speculations in *The Decline of the West* see William J. Scheick, "The Womb of Time: Spengler's Influence on Wells's *Apropos of Dolores*," *English Literature in Transition 1880–1920* 18, no. 4 (1975): 217–28.

NOTES TO CHAPTER V: POSTLUDE:
THE NOVEL AT THE END OF ITS TETHER

1. "Introduction: The Novel of Ideas," *Babes in the Darkling Wood* (New York: Alliance Book Corporation, 1940), pp. xii, xiii. All subsequent page references are to this edition and will be cited parenthetically in the text.

2. Included in *'42 to '44* (London: Secker and Warburg, 1944).

Index